ON THE CLOCK: PITTSBURGH STEELERS

ON THE CLOCK: PITTSBURGH STEELERS

Behind the Scenes with the Pittsburgh Steelers at the NFL Draft

JIM WEXELL

TRIUMPH
BOOKS

Library of Congress Cataloging-in-Publication Data available upon request.

This book is available in quantity at special discounts for your group or organization. For further information, contact:

Triumph Books LLC
814 North Franklin Street
Chicago, Illinois 60610
(312) 337-0747
www.triumphbooks.com

Printed in U.S.A.
ISBN: 978-1-63727-065-3
Design by Preston Pisellini
Editorial production by Alex Lubertozzi
Photos courtesy of AP Images unless otherwise indicated

To those who have my back when I lose

CONTENTS

FOREWORD

FOR ASPIRING FOOTBALL players, you either get drafted or you don't. And once drafted, the clock begins, and your career, however long or short, takes you to the final event: retirement.

Sure, Super Bowls, Pro Bowls, and Hall of Fame accolades are awesome, and for the rather small percentage of players who enjoy that part of their stay in the sun, those moments always shine brighter. Most of us regular guys, though, remember when it started and when it ended. Not many of us are heralded when we enter, nor blessed with a "graceful" exit from life in the National Football League.

When I became eligible to be drafted by the NFL back in 1980, there were some sobering statistics with which I came face to face: 1) The chances of making it in the NFL, at that time, were roughly 1 in 140,000; and 2) The average career length was approximately 3.2 years. So, in general terms, the odds were that I was never going to get there, and if I did, it wouldn't be for long.

So, when the coach of the four-time Super Bowl champion Steelers came to work me out in Manley Field House on the campus of Syracuse University, in the pre-spring of 1980,

I was overwhelmed. But I had no idea just how personal it would get.

Literally, Chuck Noll was working out with me. He was physically pass-rushing me and teaching me the "Art of the Punch," which was a recent development and change in the rules of the NFL. No longer would offensive linemen have to hold their hands against their chests in pass protection. No longer would they be "heavy bags on two feet" and subjected to head slaps from the pass-rushers. Using hands to "punch" the pass-rusher and keep him from grabbing you was a technique that Coach Noll was attempting to teach me, after going through a couple of run-blocking drills.

We began with the punching technique being explained, and then demonstrated. Then came the walk-through, and then the pace quickening. After a number of awkward one-on-one physical matchups with Coach Noll, I could sense his mounting frustration and heard the tinges of it in his voice as he upped the intensity of each rush. Here I am, working on punching techniques with a future Hall of Famer, the head coach of the Pittsburgh Steelers, who had just won their fourth Super Bowl of the 1970s, and I wasn't getting it.

Coach was first and foremost a teacher and then a football coach. He prized teaching the basic elements of football and communicating them thoroughly. And if it seemed the teaching wasn't getting through to whomever he was instructing, there would be a noticeable rise in the anxiety level of the player he was instructing. And that player happened to be me.

The agitation Coach was feeling at that moment, because I was holding back, was bubbling to the surface and I feared that this "ballistic" job interview was about to go south. Chuck side-eyed me after another semi-aborted and half-hearted pass-pro punch went to the chest of a living legend.

Can you feel the quandary I was in?

After a few more semi-scowls crossed the face of Coach Noll, I knew I was on borrowed time. At long last, Chuck lined up in a three-point stance across from me and growled, "Now let me feel you punch me!" I knew it was now or never.

In a mild to escalating state of panic, I lined up. Chuck rushed, and I threw an uppercut. I punched him. Boom! I mean, I let him have it. Unfortunately, I was a little errant with my punch. My right hand glanced off Chuck's shoulder and popped him in the mouth. I mean, his head snapped back like a Pez dispenser. I hit him right in the grille.

Chuck abruptly came to a halt, and I was cringing after I noticed I had drawn blood. Surely, this "interviewing" process was about to be over, and Chuck Noll, the Pittsburgh Steelers, and I were about to go our separate ways.

Slowly, Chuck turned toward me, and I saw that flare of the squinted eyebrows and the famous bulldog look that his players had come to know whenever they screwed up. With my heart beating a zillion times a minute, Chuck touched his swollen lip, looked at the trickle of blood on his fingertips, and a smile broke out on his face. Looking directly at me eye to eye, he nodded his head and said emphatically, "Now that's a punch!"

When I got back to my apartment, I called my parents and glumly told them, "We can take the Steelers off the draft board for me. No way they'll draft me."

Several weeks later, the NFL Draft rolled around. I spent most of the first day sitting by a phone that only rang when

Grandma called to see if I had been drafted. At 5:00 in the afternoon, the draft officially shut down for the day. I wasn't totally unprepared for a first-day snub. I had been told by my head coach, Frank Maloney, that pro scouts thought I would be a second-day pick or a free agent. But I've always been a glass-half-full guy, so I was a little dejected when I left the house.

About 30 minutes later, the phone rang, and my younger sister Joyce answered. Joy listened momentarily and then chatted up the caller. After several minutes of listening, my mother asked, "Who are you talking to?"

Joy frowned, gave her a thumbs-down gesture, covered the mouthpiece with her hand, and said simply, "Some guy from Pittsburgh named Chuck."

—Craig Wolfley

Craig Wolfley is a 12-year veteran of the NFL who played 10 years with the Pittsburgh Steelers. He was selected in 2000 as a member of the Steelers All-Century Team and chosen to be part of the Syracuse University 20th Century All-Star Team. Craig is also a member of the Steelers broadcast team and co-hosts In the Locker Room *on ESPN Radio in Pittsburgh.*

INTRODUCTION

ODD AS IT may sound, a book's introduction is a great place for leftover stories that are too cool to leave on the cutting-room floor.

This narrative being the history of the Pittsburgh Steelers' drafts, I couldn't find the right spot to tell this tale about their very first draft pick, William Shakespeare, and his meeting with Ernest Hemingway. First of all, Shakespeare never signed with the Steelers, so it's rather moot. Secondly, I had to cut 5,000 or so words in order to keep my quirky Epilogue on the great Bill Nunn intact. But I couldn't get this story about Shakespeare out of my head. It's the quick one I tell those close to me whenever they ask how the research is going.

It is brief: Shakespeare was working in Havana, Cuba, and knew a former Pittsburgh sportswriter there who had become friendly with Hemingway. The sportswriter asked Shakespeare if he wanted to meet Hemingway, and Shakespeare said sure. They went to Hemingway's local hangout where he was arguing with another patron. Shakespeare stood nearby waiting for the argument to end so that his sportswriter buddy could introduce them. Hemingway didn't wait for the introduction. He saw the stranger near his table, stood up, reached out his hand, and said, "Hi. Ernest Hemingway." Shakespeare in turn replied, "Glad to know you. I'm Bill Shakespeare." Thinking the guy was a wisenheimer, Hemingway punched Shakespeare in the face.

End of story.

Pretty cool, eh?

I stole it from Joe Starkey. He had stolen it from The Village Smithy, a *Pittsburgh Press* sports column in 1963. We all know Starkey, and let me tell you, his 2020 column in the *Post-Gazette* on the overall first pick in Steelers draft history was the best thing I had read among the reams of copy utilized to bring you this book. It really was an amazing column. And I stole the guts from it without hesitation.

That's what I want to tell you here, because the book that influenced this book most was *The Laws of Human Nature* by Robert Greene. In between his psychology and sociology and anthropology are historic examples of, say, Anton Chekhov's childhood. I noticed Greene's brilliant storytelling wasn't interrupted by quotes, dates, attribution, etc. I noticed it about the time I was rifling through Rob Ruck's *Rooney* and finding his research was matching what I was finding in newspaper articles from the 1930s. As I pondered the attribution, Greene's book told me to just tell the story, to trust the research and make it easier and more entertaining for the reader. So, like a modern-day Internet aggregator, I began stealing without conscience.

Oh, I list the plundered books in the back, and I've personally interviewed many of those quoted here for my four previous books during my 28 years on the Steelers beat. But you won't always find formal attribution because I didn't want to muck this up. So, I ask that you trust this research to be impeccable.

I focused primarily on the Hall of Famers drafted by the Steelers. Since we probably know more than necessary about the playing careers of, say, Joe Greene and Terry Bradshaw, I wanted to focus on the stories that got them drafted, how the team viewed them, how the drafts broke for them, and the reasons they were selected.

In Greene's case, the story of an angry teen in a racist time and town who, by himself, scared an opposing high school team off its bus is as important to me as why he threw a ball into the upper deck of a stadium in his second pro season. And Bradshaw learning to throw a javelin farther than anyone else his age had ever thrown one in this country was just as important to his future career as the 82-yard Hail Mary he threw at Louisiana Tech.

On and on it went. I had four months to write this thing and, really, had no time for precise attribution. I had stories to tell. I hope you enjoy them.

1

ALL THE WORLD'S A STAGE

IN **BILL SHAKESPEARE'S** lifetime, he played many parts. Halfback for the Pittsburgh Pirates was not one of them, even though he was their first draft pick. In 1935, the single-wing left halfback, better described as the tailback, had thrown the touchdown pass that completed Notre Dame's rally from 13–0 down to beat Ohio State 18–13 in college football's first "Game of the Century."

Three months later, in the first NFL Draft at the Ritz-Carlton in Philadelphia, Shakespeare was the third pick of the first round by the Pirates, who wouldn't be called the Steelers until 1940.

Imagine the creative headlines in Pittsburgh—had there been any.

No, the draft had quietly gone into effect in the NFL after Bert Bell of the Philadelphia Eagles led his four-team delegation of losers—those who had lost money in 1935, including Art Rooney and his Pirates—in a petition for a systematic drafting of college players, so that the rich teams—the Bears, Giants, and Packers—could stop buying the best players and the league could become better balanced.

That was the hope of Rooney, so he backed his close friend Bell's play, and the NFL passed the motion. Not that it helped the Pirates. The handsome, charismatic, tough, and talented Shakespeare was considered a sure-fire gate attraction, but he passed on the Pirates to sell power tools at twice the salary. He then served in a heroic role in the Battle of the Bulge in World War II.

Shakespeare came home and joined a rubber manufacturing company in Cincinnati, rose to the top, spawned another William Shakespeare, and died in 1974 without having played in the NFL.

Rooney tried his hand at the draft again in 1937. His Pirates passed on two-time All-American Sammy Baugh out of TCU for Mike Basrak, a center from Duquesne University. Duquesne at the time was a national power. The program rose up in the late 1920s under future Notre Dame coach Elmer Layden, and the 1936 Dukes of Clipper Smith were ranked 14th by the Associated Press at the end of the year.

Led by Basrak, the school's first first-team All-American, Duquesne beat Mississippi State in the Orange Bowl. So Basrak made a lot of sense for the Pirates, who loved putting local players on the field. It also made sense at the time to pass on Baugh, who had gained his nickname "Slingin' Sammy" not as a passer of footballs but as a third baseman at TCU. He signed to play baseball with the St. Louis Cardinals and was moved to shortstop in the farm system—behind Marty Marion.

So with his baseball future looking bleak, Baugh turned back to football and accepted Washington's offer of $8,000 for one season, well out of Rooney's range at the time. Basrak signed with the Steelers but broke his leg and was finished with football after only two seasons.

Baugh, picked next, set an NFL record for completions as a rookie and led the league in passing yardage. He also led the Redskins to the NFL championship over the Bears, and his 335 passing yards were the most in a postseason game by a rookie quarterback until 2012, when Russell Wilson broke the mark.

Baugh's bigger impact on Rooney occurred in the 1937 regular-season finale, when Rooney watched the Redskins— led by tailback Cliff Battles, end Wayne Millner (who had caught the Shakespeare heave to beat Ohio State), and quarterback Baugh—lambaste the powerful Giants 49–14.

Rooney came away from the game convinced that his Pirates needed a triple-threat tailback like Baugh, who could take the direct snap and run or pass, and also kick, so Rooney set his sights on the player he hoped would become Pittsburgh's first professional football star.

At the turn of the 20th century, Alpha White dealt with the death of his parents by leaving Iowa to explore the West. He marveled at the Rocky Mountains and went back to Iowa to get his girlfriend, Maude. They married and left for Colorado.

The couple bounced around the state before settling with their two sons, Sam and Byron, in Wellington, a small farming community about 20 miles south of the Wyoming border.

Byron, the younger son by four years, worked in the beet fields at the age of seven. He grew up adhering to his father's credo that he work hard, do his best, and be considerate of other people's feelings. Even though Alpha never graduated high school, he stressed academics and hoped his boys would attend college. Alpha also rented a room to an incoming coach and teacher at Wellington High, and that coach stoked the boys' interest in sports while stressing the importance of academics.

Sam was the first to take advantage of a scholarship the University of Colorado awarded to the No. 1 student in each of the state high schools. He went off to Boulder to play football and basketball and study pre-med. He later won a Rhodes scholarship to study in Oxford, England, which set the path for Byron, who was an even better football player than Sam, but, like his uncle back in Audubon, Iowa, was more interested in law than medicine.

Byron took that same path to Boulder and succeeded wildly on the football field. He picked up the nickname "Whizzer" from a Denver sportswriter after one particularly dazzling performance, but it was a nickname Byron never liked, and, of course, it stuck.

A knee injury curtailed Byron's sophomore season at Colorado, but his coach, who had played with Red Grange at Illinois, taught Byron the finer points of the punting game. Bunnie Oakes also taught White to catch punts on the run to gain momentum for his return—fumbling be damned. He

also told Byron to continue to punt through his knee injury by altering his leg motion. It diminished the height and distance of the kicks, but allowed Byron to control his punts with uncommon accuracy.

Newspaper accounts compared Byron to another great football player out of the Rockies, Earl "Dutch" Clark, a unanimous 1928 first-team All-American at Colorado College in Colorado Springs. Clark, in fact, was White's freshman basketball coach in Boulder and molded him into a starting guard for the runner-up Buffaloes in the first National Invitational Tournament in 1938.

White had sprung to national prominence his junior year against regional power Utah. He scored all 17 points in a 17–7 win, and his "famous stiff-arm" during a 95-yard run was covered by a nationally syndicated sports columnist, but it was the photo of the Utes strewn throughout the field in White's wake that captured the fascination of the great Grantland Rice. Of course, Rice loved the "Whizzer" moniker and gave it the full work-up.

White began his senior season at Colorado as a nationally known athlete, but he disliked the attention. White doggedly continued his humble campus life of waiting tables, rose to the top of the class in academics, and was student body president.

As for football, here's how a teammate described Byron White: "He wasn't exceptionally fast, but he had a tremendous change of pace and could hit you with his hip harder than anyone I know. He didn't have especially high knee action but he could really hit. He loved to hit. If he had a fault as a leader, it was that he didn't lead enough. He did his job and expected you to do yours."

White once told an official he had whistled a play (and White's knee) down too quickly. The official hit Colorado with a 15-yard penalty, and as the Buffaloes huddled, a teammate lamented having to play against 12 men—11 defenders plus the referee. The players looked up to see the official in the huddle, and he hit them with another 15-yard penalty. After the players stopped laughing, they realized they were backed up to the 3 and turned to White. He went on a three-touchdown rampage over the next three minutes.

The final game of White's senior season was played on Thanksgiving Day at Denver University. He ran 51 yards for a touchdown on the third play, returned a kickoff 55 yards, ran for a 19-yard touchdown, passed 27 yards for a third touchdown, added a 46-yard run, threw a 14-yard pass for a fourth touchdown, and finished with a 46-yard touchdown run. He ended the season as the national leader in rushing, points, and punt-return average. He was also named Phi Beta Kappa after finishing first in his class. He had only two B's (sociology, public speaking) and the rest A's.

The undefeated Buffaloes were invited to the 1938 Cotton Bowl, the first time a team from the Rockies had been invited to a bowl, but White—who would be traveling to San Francisco to enter the regional competition for a Rhodes scholarship—convinced his teammates to turn down the offer. The governor, among others, pleaded with White and the players, who eventually accepted the offer and traveled to Texas to practice while White competed for the Rhodes scholarship. And he won.

Byron arrived in Texas and led the Buffs to a touchdown three minutes into the game and also returned an interception

50 yards for a 14–0 lead. But powerful Rice rallied for a 28–14 win.

White played on the basketball team, which ultimately played two games at Madison Square Garden in the NIT, where the Buffs were walloped in the finals by Temple, 60–36.

The Art Rooney of the 1930s was often portrayed in the sports pages as a somewhat cartoonish character. His football team lost often and sometimes in bombastic fashion with oddball characters involved. Rooney also dressed humbly, and the term "rumpled" was often used, so a "lovable loser" stereotype was pinned on "the Prez of Rooney U." Even when he hit it big at the racetrack, Rooney was portrayed as either lucky, as in getting hot tips from New York Giants owner Tim Mara, or as someone who got his info out of the stables.

Out of a natural sense of humility, Rooney played along and rarely corrected such perspectives, but he really was a serious student of not only horses but life. Rooney studied the *Racing Form* late into the night, and in the morning loved his quietude. Rooney spent his early mornings at the race-track, where he tuned into the day the way some might with meditation. Rooney also took in daily mass either before or after his morning routine at the track.

Such a routine resulted in Rooney picking winners one day in 1937 to the tune of—by conservative estimates—$200,000. He hit several other big scores that summer as big city sports-writers reported on "Rooney's Ride" with their own cartoon-ish flair. Most of it was awful reading, but the money was very real. Rooney gave some to charity, bought a new house, and socked a bunch away. He also thought it a good time to find that star tailback so necessary to Johnny Blood's single-wing offense in 1938.

Rooney had the money—at least the financial stability he had sought throughout that first decade of pro football—to sign such a player for his beleaguered Pirates, as he and Blood prepared for the 1938 draft of college prospects.

The Steelers were slated to choose fourth, and Rooney had his eye on Duquesne's star playmaker, Boyd Brumbaugh. The halfback led the Dukes to a 7–0 win over national champion Pitt in 1936, and then beat Mississippi State in the 1937 Orange Bowl with a throw that traveled nearly 70 yards in the air. However, Brumbaugh was chosen a pick earlier in the draft. That's when Rooney instructed his coach, Blood, to draft Byron "Whizzer" White.

White was the consensus best player coming out of college, but he had told the Cleveland Rams, picking first, not to choose him. They didn't. Neither did the Philadelphia Eagles. The Brooklyn Dodgers chose Brumbaugh, and then Rooney took the gamble on White.

Coming out of his fourth of five seasons in the red (estimates of football losses in 1937 ranged from $21,000 to $25,000), Rooney was determined to turn football into the moneymaker that both horse racing and boxing had become for him. But he needed a playmaker to not only complement the diminishing skills of player-coach Blood, but to draw fans in a city that was more interested in a Pitt team that had won back-to-back national titles under Jock Sutherland in 1936 and 1937.

Blood didn't exactly draw the gates Rooney had expected when he was signed as player-coach in 1937. A legendary character himself, Blood was now in his second stint with Rooney. The first occurred after he had drunkenly whiffed on a punt for the Green Bay Packers. Curly Lambeau sold him to the Pirates in 1934, but took him back the next year by offering him $110 per game, and only if Blood would stop drinking on Tuesdays before a game. Blood told him he could stop drinking on Wednesdays at $100 per game, and a deal was struck.

Rooney brought Blood back in 1937, and after finishing 4–7 their plan for 1938 was to convince White to put Oxford on hold and sign with the Pirates, who had drafted another playmaker in the second round, Frank Filchok of Indiana, the top passer in the Big Ten. Rooney dreamed that Filchok and White could match Washington's Sammy Baugh and Cliff Battles as the league's top playmaking duo. So Rooney offered White $15,000, almost twice what Baugh, the highest-paid player in the league, was making. But White turned it down. So Rooney sent Blood to Boulder to change his mind.

The ploy worked, but not right away.

White had become intrigued by Blood. Even though White was somewhat cold and aloof, Blood was a gregarious extrovert, and the two hit it off.

"I couldn't wait to follow him and see what happened next," White said.

Rooney and Blood went to New York City to watch White play in the NIT at Madison Square Garden on St. Patrick's Day. They cornered him in the locker room and explained that the Rhodes scholarship could be delayed for three months.

White remained committed to Oxford, but did ask his brother to investigate any such deferment. When Sam White confirmed to his younger brother in July that he could indeed wait until January to report to school, Byron called Blood—who was vacationing with Rooney at Bert Bell's place in Atlantic City—and told him he would accept the Pirates' offer and report to St. Francis University in Loretto, Pennsylvania, on August 10, four days after training camp had started.

Stirred by the news, Rooney wanted to add to his team, and a few weeks later traded his 1939 first-round pick to the Bears for one of the top ends in the game, Eggs Manske. The fact that Rooney sold Manske back to the Bears halfway through the season provides a clue as to how the Pirates' season went.

Between the College All-Star Game and the haphazardly scheduled exhibition games, White was beat up before the season even began. He was released from a hospital in Detroit and scored the only touchdown in a 16–7 loss to Dutch Clark's Lions. Two days later, White gained 175 all-purpose yards in a loss to the powerful Giants in front of a disappointing home crowd of 17,340.

The next Pittsburgh "home" game was played in Buffalo. The baseball Pirates were leading the National League, and with preparations for an expected World Series, Forbes Field was ruled off-limits to football. The Pirates lost in Buffalo as reporters blamed White's teammates. But the pounding on his body came from more than poor blocking—it had been White's sixth game in two weeks.

Rooney's Pirates won the next two games on the road, but by the time they returned home, Pie Traynor's Pirates had been

Byron "Whizzer" White, at De Witt Clinton High School field in the Bronx after signing with the Pittsburgh Pirates in 1938. He played one season, in which he led the NFL in rushing, before leaving for England and a Rhodes Scholarship.

eliminated by Gabby Hartnett's "Homer in the Gloamin'" and there was little enthusiasm left for a 2–3 pro football team.

The Pirates fell to 2–4 and then 2–5, as reports of dissension over White's high salary began to circulate. White repeatedly denied it, and as the consummate team player blamed himself for the losses. He even told Rooney to stop paying him, that he didn't deserve the money, and to only pay him $50 per exhibition game like the rest of the players instead of the agreed-upon $200.

Rooney wouldn't hear of it, and, in spite of losses that eventually reached $35,000 by the end of the season, mailed White's game checks to his lawyer without White's knowledge. As for the alleged resentment of White, teammates denied the allegation for years.

"Byron was liked by the players," said fullback Izzy Weinstock, a former All-American at Pitt. "But he was a loner. He'd disappear after practice. He had academic goals in mind, and he was home hitting the books."

Any dissension was more likely due to the fading Blood repeatedly inserting himself into the lineup, and, of course, the poor play of the team. However, White still managed to lead the NFL in rushing.

✦ ✦ ✦

After beating the Giants for the first time in team history, the Pirates didn't win another game. Byron White rushed for 567 yards and remains the only rookie on a last-place team to lead the NFL in rushing. But he left for England and never played for the Pirates again.

Eggs Manske, of course, was back with the Bears and in 1940 played in the 73–0 championship game rout of Washington. The Bears were quarterbacked that day by Sid Luckman, the player the Bears directed Rooney to choose with the first-round pick he had dealt them in August 1938. George Halas explained to those who were surprised that he would draft Luckman over the more acclaimed Davey O'Brien that Luckman was three inches taller, and height would be necessary in his T formation.

That made Halas the first "draftnick," and for decades Luckman would rival Sammy Baugh, whom the Pirates had passed over in the 1937 draft, as the greatest NFL QB of all-time—at least until Johnny Unitas came along.

The Byron "Whizzer" White postscript turned out better than expected after White was forced to cut short his studies in England when Germany invaded Poland to begin World War II. White returned home and enrolled at Yale Law School. Rooney tried his best to convince him to return to the team, but ended up selling White's rights to the Lions for $5,000, and White once again led the NFL in rushing in 1940.

White played his final season in 1941 before enlisting in the Navy, where his quiet, thoughtful manner was suited for intelligence work. White saw duty in the Pacific and was awarded two Bronze Stars and a Presidential Unit Citation for bravery under separate Kamikaze attacks. White also renewed acquaintances with John F. Kennedy, whom he had met at one of Ambassador Joseph Kennedy's embassy parties in England. White was the intelligence officer who interviewed Lieutenant Kennedy after his PT boat was sunk in 1943. The relationship culminated in President Kennedy nominating White, 44, to serve as a justice on the U.S. Supreme Court in 1962.

White contemplated a presidential run in the 1970s—or at least his old friend Johnny Blood ran the PR for such a campaign. "He's a poor public speaker—make that an ordinary public speaker—but the people are sick of these glib SOBs," said Blood.

But White never ran and remained on the Supreme Court until 1993. "Not as liberal as many expected, yet not wholly conservative, either," Joe Marshall wrote of White's judicial reign in *PRO!* magazine. "He is a contented prisoner to books."

White didn't like to talk about football in his later years, but would often pontificate on the value of sports. In that way, he served football well. He was a believer in contact sports and the preparation for life that it gave young athletes.

As for Rooney, he thought the one costly season with White was beneficial because of the publicity. But there was a bigger picture. As famed *Washington Post* sportswriter Shirley Povich wrote, "Rooney was trying to bring some class to the league."

He did that. Repeatedly. In that regard, Byron "Whizzer" White is remembered as the foundational piece of the Steelers Way.

2

TRIPLE CROWN

THEY BECAME THE Steelers in 1940 but were the same ol' Pirates in the standings and financial ledger. In eight seasons, Art Rooney's team had won only 24 games and lost close to $100,000. He sometimes used his racehorses as payment. One player turned him down and simply took the loss. "Those plugs he had would've kept me broke," the player said.

Rooney sold the team, regretted it, bought a piece of his buddy Bert Bell's Eagles, went through a complicated franchise swap, and was running the Steelers with Bell the coach to start 1941.

Bell had tried to integrate the T formation, and his successors that season, such as Aldo "Buff" Donelli, kept parts of it in place. But the league ruled that Donelli, also the coach of Duquesne University, couldn't coach two teams simultaneously, and so up stepped Walt Kiesling to finish 1941.

The revolving coaches served as mere placeholders for an owner who really wanted Jock Sutherland as coach. He and Rooney met secretly to discuss a hiring, after Sutherland had abruptly left the powerful Pitt program, but word of the meeting leaked, and an angry Sutherland said he needed to get away from Pittsburgh. That's what made the Steelers' upset of Sutherland's Brooklyn Dodgers in 1941 so tasty. It was the Steelers' only win of the season and knocked Sutherland's Dodgers out of first place.

Still, Rooney wanted Sutherland to coach his team, almost as badly as he wanted better players. With the first pick that went with the Steelers' 1–9–1 record, Rooney entered the 1942 draft in search of talent.

If only he could find a draft magazine as resourceful as the *Daily Racing Form*.

✦ ✦ ✦

Like his mother, grandmother, and great grandmother, Bill Dudley was born on Christmas Eve. This Dudley entered the world in 1921 in Bluefield, Virginia. His father, J.S Dudley, was the first mayor of Bluefield and gave his son a football for Christmas at age 10.

A precocious child who devoured all things football, Dudley developed an affinity for Knute Rockne. He entered high school at the age of 12, and the 100-pounder asked the coach at Graham High if he could play quarterback because he had some ideas about running the offense. The coach, though, had some ideas about not playing a skinny 12-year-old and told Dudley he needed to wait a year.

By Dudley's junior season, a new coach arrived and installed Dudley at left halfback. And Dudley installed the Notre Dame box offense, to which he knew all the calls, the ballhandling, and the motions. And he could throw a bit. Everyone knew Dudley could run, and they would eventually learn, in the school's great upset of West Virginia power Princeton, that he could kick. His 35-yarder won his last high school game, and Dudley was mobbed as he left the field.

In search of a college, the 5′9″, 150-pound Dudley, a voracious Bible reader and straight-A student, wanted to play at Virginia (Poly)Tech or Washington & Lee, but both coaches thought him too small. University of Virginia coach Frank Murray was impressed that Dudley had never missed an extra-point in high school, so he gave him an academic scholarship.

Dudley was the fourth-string tailback on the UVA freshman team, but as a sophomore, with three backs hurt, he was running even with the only other back on the roster. The coach flipped a coin, Dudley won, got the start against Navy, and ripped off a 90-yard touchdown run on a reverse.

In 1940, as a junior, Dudley was the No. 2 rusher in the nation, and in 1941 he became UVA's first All-American. As the youngest college team captain in the nation, Dudley ran a "bastardized version" of the T formation and led the nation in scoring and all-purpose yardage. He won the Maxwell Trophy and finished fifth in the Heisman voting during the best season (8–1) Virginia ever had. Dudley's greatest performance came late in the season against North Carolina. He piled up 333 yards of total offense and either scored or threw for all 28 points. He averaged 42 yards per punt, and when he was taken out with a couple minutes remaining, the UVA crowd gave him a standing ovation.

Grantland Rice did, too. The great sportswriter was at the game and called Dudley college football's most valuable player. His four interceptions in the subsequent East-West Shrine Game didn't diminish that commentary.

Perhaps the great sportswriter was the Steelers' primary scout in those days. He had caught Rooney's attention regarding Byron White, and now Rooney was interested in Dudley. This time, though, Rooney didn't have to wait until the fourth pick of the draft. Rooney drafted Dudley with the first pick in 1942. Even though Dudley had already been sworn into the Army Air Force, he had been deferred until December and signed with the Steelers. But he wasn't an impressive figure at training camp.

"Art must be going nuts sending kids like that up here," said Walt Kiesling after the coach took a look at the 170-pounder.

But in Dudley's first game, he rushed for 95 yards, including a 55-yard gain in a loss to the Eagles. Kiesling went from calling Dudley a kid to saying he ran harder than White ever had.

In the second game, Dudley returned a kickoff for a touchdown, but the Steelers lost to the Redskins after a blocked field goal was returned for a touchdown. In two games, Dudley had scored two touchdowns, passed for a TD, and set up another with a run to the 1. But the Steelers were 0–2.

Redskins owner George Marshall, a friend of Rooney's, was impressed by Dudley, as well as the Steelers' offensive line, and continued to try to convince Rooney that selling the team would be a mistake, that Pittsburgh would one day become a madhouse for pro football, that Rooney just needed to remain patient. Rooney had always believed that, but Marshall's support helped him stay the course.

The Steelers then beat the Giants. And the Dodgers. And the Eagles. At 3–2, they hosted the Redskins in front of 37,764 fans at Forbes Field. The Steelers didn't score, and lost to the Redskins, but as one reporter wrote, it was "the day pro football came into its own in Pittsburgh."

The 1942 Steelers won their next four, lost to the Packers, finished second at 7–4, and turned a profit. Dudley, of course, was the catalyst in turning around a 1–9–1 team by leading the NFL in rushing with 696 yards. He was named Rookie of the Year and the All-NFL halfback.

After the season, before an all-star game against the Redskins, Dudley was one of 16 halfbacks asked to compete in a sprinting competition. He finished 15th, but in the game returned an interception 98 yards. That, more than anything, described him as a runner. But he was more than that. "He's the best defensive back in the league," said Giants Coach Steve Owen, the defensive aficionado of the day.

Dudley was also an effective kicker. He dubbed his style of standing next to the ball with left foot planted as he reared back and kicked with his right foot, the "pendulum kick."

After Dudley collected his hardware, he was off to fly B-29s in the Pacific.

✦ ✦ ✦

Jock Sutherland left his team, the Brooklyn Dodgers, for the war in 1941 and rose to the rank of lieutenant commander in the U.S. Navy. He was no doubt an effective leader. Having played for Pop Warner at Pitt, Sutherland won as a coach at Lafayette, Pitt, and even with the Dodgers. He was coveted by Art Rooney, and the two began talking again in 1945. In December, Sutherland signed a five-year contract to serve as vice president and coach of the Steelers for $27,500 per year, with a bonus of 25 percent of profits and the option to buy out co-owner Bert Bell. And there were profits to be had. Right away, Steelers season-ticket sales rose from 1,500 in 1945 to 22,000 in 1946.

Sutherland watched the Steelers finish the 1945 season with a dismal 24–0 loss to the Redskins, in which star halfback Bill Dudley was never a factor. Dudley had returned from the war to play four games for the 2–8 Steelers.

That didn't block the enthusiasm that had enveloped Pittsburgh over the new coach, who was described as a strict disciplinarian. Sutherland threw out whatever remnants of the T formation the Steelers were using and brought back his disciplined version of the single-wing.

Even though young players were coming out of college well-versed in the T formation, Sutherland had the left half-back he needed in Dudley. But of course, Sutherland would never admit he needed anyone, and it's possible he came into the 1946 training camp with a view of knocking Dudley down a peg or two. After all, Dudley really wasn't fast, threw side-arm, and kicked with that peculiar pendulum style. As former Cardinals quarterback Paul Christman described Dudley the athlete: "He ran like he was staggering, threw the ball like it was a loaf of bread, and kicked it clumsier than anything I've ever seen. All he could do was beat you."

Dudley was also known to preach to teammates. Even as a rookie, this sponge of a football student coached up teammates. He reported to training camp in 1946 on the right day, but because of a miscommunication he arrived late. Sutherland pounced on his "star," and Dudley did not forget, particularly after Dudley, struggling in a passing drill, was overheard telling a teammate that perhaps the offense and defense should wear different colored uniforms. Sutherland exploded like the precursor to Bobby Knight that he was.

That night, Dudley demanded a trade, but was talked out of it, so he put up with Sutherland's constant badgering throughout what turned into a "Triple Crown" season for the Steelers' last NFL rushing champ.

Sutherland couldn't stand Dudley's improvisational running because the coach demanded the runner take three steps before cutting. It had to be three. Dudley, like most explosive running backs, depended on his vision and instincts to determine when to cut, and it helped him lead the NFL again with 604 yards, over half the Steelers' total.

Dudley also led the NFL with 385 yards on punt returns (14.3 average) and a whopping 10 interceptions. He was hailed as the league's third Triple Crown winner after Sammy Baugh and Steve Van Buren. Dudley also had the longest kickoff return and reception (both 80 yards) that season and became the last winner of the Joseph F. Carr Memorial Trophy as league MVP.

He played the seventh game with cracked ribs but led the Steelers to a win over the Redskins as they improved to

4–2–1. Dudley scored the first touchdown of the game but hadn't cut at the precise moment, so Sutherland excoriated him at a team meeting.

The Steelers lost three of their next four and Dudley repeated his demand for a trade after the season. Not that Sutherland cared. He told Dudley he was a great player, "but I don't have to have great players." The fans sided with Sutherland, and Dudley was traded in the summer of 1948 to Detroit for Paul White, Bob Cifers, the rights to 1947 Heisman runner-up Bob Chappuis, and Detroit's first pick in the 1948 draft.

"That deal broke my heart," Art Rooney said. "He was the best player I ever saw."

Dudley wrote a polite and thoughtful letter to Sutherland in requesting the trade. It's available in the Steelers' archives. Dudley spoke of forgiveness and said that it was better for a man his size to move on from a team that often played him for 57 of the 60 minutes.

Also available in the Steelers' archives is the letter Sutherland wrote to his team after learning his Steelers would face Dudley and the Lions in the 1947 opener. The Sutherland letter reeks of pettiness with Sutherland telling the team it was the victim of media propaganda. Sutherland also told the Pittsburgh *Post-Gazette* the players were glad Dudley was gone because he was "too bossy," and that Dudley changed his mind after the trade talks heated up and "begged" the Steelers not to trade him.

Reached in Detroit for confirmation, Dudley denied that he had begged, said he was happy in Detroit, and in order to diminish the public squabbling refused further comment.

Moments before the 1947 opener, Dudley walked to midfield for the coin flip as the Lions' captain and shook hands with the Steelers' captain. A moment later, Dudley looked up and saw Sutherland with his hand outstretched. The two shook, and Dudley opened the scoring with a 30-yard touchdown catch.

The Steelers rallied to beat the Lions 17–10, on their way to an 8–4 record, the best in team history, and their first playoff berth. Johnny Clement, No. 0, had replaced Dudley and finished second to Van Buren in rushing.

Dudley played six more seasons, including time in Washington with his friend Sammy Baugh. In one game against the Steelers, Dudley returned a punt for a touchdown. Rooney admonished his oldest sons, teenagers Dan and Art Jr., for cheering on Dudley from the Steelers' sideline during the return.

In March 1948, Jock Sutherland was spotted in a suit and tie while walking along a country road in the swamps of Western Kentucky. His car had gotten stuck in the mud, and he was picked up by a milk-truck driver who noticed an incoherence about Sutherland and drove him to the sheriff's office. The sheriff then drove Sutherland across the Ohio River to a hospital in Illinois, where it was determined that Sutherland was experiencing some type of breakdown.

A few weeks later, he was brought home to Pittsburgh, where doctors at West Penn Hospital discovered an inoperable brain tumor. Sutherland died the next morning. The

Steelers lost their star player and their great coach within a calendar year. Art Rooney would find a few more great players but wouldn't find another great coach for 21 years.

In the 1948 draft, the Steelers, with the pick acquired from the Lions in the Bill Dudley deal, drafted quarterback Bobby Layne third overall. Layne had mastered the T formation in its first—and Layne's last—season at the University of Texas. The Steelers, though, would stick with Sutherland's single-wing offense into the early 1950s, and that didn't appeal to Layne, who had also been selected in the AAFC draft. So the Steelers traded Layne to the Bears, where he backed up the last quarterback the Steelers had traded to the Bears, Sid Luckman, before spending the bulk of his Hall of Fame career with the Detroit Lions, where he picked up three NFL championships.

The Steelers got Layne back 10 years later, but it took that long for the team to continue the promise of those 1946–1947 seasons. The drought was due not only to poor drafting but the inability to compete with the new league for players.

CREAM OF THE '40S CROP

In 1962, *Post-Gazette* sportswriter Jack Sell published the Steelers' all-time team. Bill Dudley was the only player named on both sides of the ball. The other members drafted in the 1940s included:

+ **CHARLEY MEHELICH** (Round 5, 1945), a defensive end out of Duquesne who impressed Sutherland with his "teeth-rattling" tackles. "When No. 55

hit you, you stayed hit," the great Steve Van Buren said of Mehelich.

+ **JERRY SHIPKEY** (Round 8, 1947), a fullback his first three seasons out of UCLA, made the Pro Bowl three times as a linebacker in the early 1950s.

+ **ELBIE NICKEL** (Round 17, 1947), classified as an end out of Cincinnati, blocked in Sutherland's single-wing before becoming a receiving threat as the offensive captain from 1949 to 1957.

+ **BILL MCPEAK** (Round 16, 1948), a linebacker drafted out of Pitt, became a three-time Pro Bowler and then an assistant coach for the Steelers before becoming head coach and general manager for the Redskins from 1960 to 1965.

+ **BILL WALSH** (Round 3, 1949), a Notre Dame center, started the great lineage of Steelers centers by playing in the 1950 and 1951 Pro Bowls.

+ **JOE GERI** (Round 4, 1949), a single-wing tailback out of Georgia, made the Pro Bowl in 1950 and 1951 before he was traded to the Cardinals.

+ **JIM FINKS** (Round 12, 1949), a Tulsa quarterback, became the first T formation QB for the Steelers, the last NFL team to install the offensive alignment in 1952.

3

WRECKING BALL

IF BYRON WHITE and Bill Dudley established the Steelers
Way for offense in the early days, Ernie Stautner did the
same for the defense throughout the 1950s and into the early
1960s. The Steelers didn't win a championship during that
time, but they were never beaten physically. Stautner taught
them that.

A marine who saw combat in the Okinawa and Borneo
campaigns right out of high school, Stautner returned to the
U.S. in 1946 with a plan hatched by a teammate of his El
Toro, California, Marines squad. The ex–Golden Domer told
Stautner to head for South Bend, enroll in Notre Dame, and
show Frank Leahy he deserved a scholarship. But Leahy told
the 200-pound Stautner he was too small and too slow to play
big-time college football.

So off Stautner went to Boston College in 1946 and started right away at defensive tackle, next to another Notre Dame castoff, Art Donovan. They were two of 14 Boston College players drafted by the NFL during Stautner's time there, but their best record was only 6–3 in 1946. The next year, Stautner, nicknamed "Horse," appeared on a smattering of All-America teams, and those honors would continue through his graduation in 1950.

Born in Bavaria, Germany, Stautner landed near Albany, New York, with his family at the age of three. They bought a farmhouse in nearby East Greenbrush where Ernie grew up a Mel Hein fan. So when the Steelers drafted Stautner in the second round in 1950, a contract squabble ensued, and he asked the Steelers to trade his rights to the Giants.

Stautner loved the Giants.

But Art Rooney gave his pal Tim Mara a heads-up that Stautner was coming, and at the tryout Giants coach Steve Owen told the 6'1", 220-pound Stautner the same thing Leahy had told him: too small, too slow.

Stautner hated the Giants.

In spite of his mobility, superb conditioning, aggressiveness, and desire to play wherever coaches needed him, Stautner had no other option but to return to the Steelers. He grumbled about the $1,000 they had tried to shave from the original agreement of $7,000. So Rooney called Tex Schramm, the bright, young executive with the Los Angeles Rams. The Steelers offered to trade Stautner for a massive tackle the Rams drafted in the third round out of Penn State named Don "Garbage Pail" Murray. Schramm found a photo of Stautner and Murray that looked like "Mutt and Jeff," and told the

Steelers no thank you. But Garbage Pail couldn't play and was cut two weeks later. "The only thing he did well was eat with his hands," Schramm said.

Stautner signed with the Steelers and told himself he had to be mean to make the team. The defensive tackle was in great shape, down to 213 pounds after he and his brother-in-law had chopped down part of a forest to build a drive-in theater back home in Saranac Lake, New York. They did it with one axe and one saw, and those who were eventually belted by the patented Stautner forearm and his signature headslap realized the forest never had a chance.

Stautner wanted to specialize at another position to solidify his spot, so the rookie told his line coach, Walt Kiesling, he could kick. Kiesling got the okay from coach John Michelosen, and Stautner prepared to kick off in the exhibition opener.

Stautner carefully teed up the ball, walked off his 10 steps, counted the players as he was coached to do, and began his approach to kick the ball. Just as he got there, the ball was blown off the tee, so Stautner repeated his careful process. This time he got to the ball—a moment after his right foot had dug into the ground. A divot flew farther than the ball. Stautner sprained his ankle and had to be helped off the field. He missed the next three exhibition games and never kicked again. Kiesling would joke about it throughout the remainder of their time together.

Stautner did start the opener against the team he wanted to beat more than any other, the Giants. The small defensive tackle went up against the Giants' 6′5″, 270-pound guard Tex Coulter, and on the first snap Stautner threw a forearm into Coulter's face.

"Is that how it's going to be, rookie?" a stunned Coulter said after the play.

"That's it," said Stautner.

On the next snap, Coulter knocked Stautner on his ass. Stautner looked up from the ground and thought the giant was going to kill him. But Coulter didn't. And a legend was allowed to grow and prosper.

✦ ✦ ✦

By 1951, the Steelers' press guide called Ernie Stautner "one of the finest line prospects in Steeler history." This was after only one season. In the 1952 press guide, it was affirmed: Stautner was "an all-time great." This meteoric rise begged the question of how the Steelers were able to find him in the draft. What did they know?

All they knew was that he was an All-American. They knew that because of Ray Byrne, head scout and sole member of their personnel department. Byrne was an undertaker by trade, but perhaps the first true draftnick. He subscribed to all the magazines, bought the out-of-town papers at the train station, and wrote to schools for their press releases. Byrne and Pat Livingston, who would become sports editor of the *Pittsburgh Press*, were brought in by Jock Sutherland to serve in varied roles—publicist, bookkeeper, draftsman, whatever was needed around the office. Livingston one day angered Sutherland, and as punishment was sent out on the road as the team's first paid scout.

Byrne ran his grandfather's East End funeral home and "dug up" Stautner from his magazine collection. The other future Hall of Famer who came to Pittsburgh with Stautner in 1950, Jack Butler, was signed out of St. Bonaventure after the draft by Butler's father's former teammate, Art Rooney.

So the Steelers found themselves with Hall of Fame defensive pillars on both the line and in the secondary, and in the person of 1951 sixth-round pick Dale Dodrill they had their future four-time Pro Bowl middle linebacker.

They also had a quarterback. Coach John Michelosen, keeper of the single-wing formation taught by his mentor, Sutherland, finally acquiesced to the chanting mobs by letting Jim Finks finish the 1951 season at quarterback. It was only for a half. And it was on the road. But Finks rallied the Steelers past the Redskins, and the organization knew the T formation's time had finally come. Michelosen retired, and Rooney brought Joe Bach back as coach in 1952 as the Steelers finally moved out of the offensive dark ages.

Not that much of it worked. The Steelers lost their first four games in 1952, but Stautner took great satisfaction in the team's strong finish, in particular the 63–7 pasting of the Giants. On the same day, Steve Owen was scheduled to announce a deal for his new book on the Umbrella defense. The Steelers felt they were the reason the deal fell through.

"He forgot to open his umbrella in Pittsburgh," cracked Stautner, who was noteworthy in the game for bloodying the face of his future boss, backup Giants QB Tom Landry. The Giants thought Stautner out of line for the forearm to Landry's face with the game long decided, so they repaid Stautner by cracking one of his ribs.

Such was football life in the early 1950s.

Also noteworthy in 1952 was the drafting of Jack Spinks in the 11th round and Willie Robinson in the 25th. They were the first African Americans to join the team since Ray Kemp left in 1934. Spinks made the team and played in 10 games, but mysteriously left after the season. Robinson returned the opening kickoff of the exhibition season—for a safety. He had come out, went back in, was tackled in the end zone, and then cut the next day.

The 1953 draft was marked by the second-round drafting of future Hall of Fame fullback John Henry Johnson. But he signed with the Canadian Football League and wouldn't play for the Steelers until they traded for him in 1960.

In the first round of the '53 draft, the Steelers took quarterback Ted Marchibroda with the fifth overall pick on a tip from Giants owner Wellington Mara. Marchibroda never did unseat Finks as quarterback, and Rooney figured the "tip" was payback for the blowout a month earlier.

At least the Giants didn't crack Rooney's ribs.

The '53 draft also marked the beginning of the end of the Byrne era in the personnel department. Linebacker Joe Schmidt had endured an injury-plagued senior season at Pitt, so his draft stock was at a low. But it wasn't too low to escape the eyes of new publicist Ed Kiely and his sidekick Livingston. They adored Schmidt and repeatedly said so to Walt Kiesling, the assistant coach in charge of drafting defensive players. But Kiesling had other ideas, as he often did, and in the sixth round drafted Tom "Black Cat" Barton, who didn't make the team. The Steelers were still eyeballing Schmidt in the seventh round, and the Lions, picking one spot ahead of them, chose an ineligible player. That was brought to the attention of the league by Byrne, and, on the re-pick, the Lions chose Schmidt, the local star who went on to play in 10 consecutive Pro Bowls for Detroit and make the Hall of Fame in 1973.

That faux pas put Byrne on the fast track back to the funeral home.

The Steelers drafted their second Heisman Trophy winner in 1954, and, unlike Doc Blanchard in 1946, the Steelers signed this one—Johnny Lattner. But after a Pro Bowl rookie season, the Notre Dame running back tore up his knee playing service ball and never returned.

✦ ✦ ✦

Rob Ruck, the Pitt professor and author of *Rooney*, came up with an interesting theory while researching the Steelers' cutting of ninth-round draft pick Johnny Unitas in 1955. Jim Finks wasn't showing any respect that camp to his coach, Walt Kiesling, who eventually told Finks during practice, "Get the hell out of here and don't come back." Finks said fine. He tried to quit, but since the practice during that exhibition road trip was in Portland, the Steelers wouldn't pay his fare back to Pittsburgh. Art Rooney intervened and brought Kiesling and Finks together for one final season.

Had the Steelers paid Finks's fare back home and allowed him to retire, Ruck believes, the future glory of the Pittsburgh Steelers would've come much sooner than the 1970s, thanks to the rookie in camp, Unitas.

By the time Finks did retire, it was too late to keep the future legend. Unitas got cut, played some local semipro ball, was rediscovered, and went on to lead the Baltimore Colts to back-to-back NFL championships in 1958 and 1959. He would soon thereafter join the growing group of Hall of Fame quarterbacks the Steelers had either passed over, traded, or cut.

Unitas was a local athlete known to another local prep athlete at the time, Dan Rooney. He saw Unitas play with a splinted middle finger on his throwing hand—courtesy of an accidental, self-inflicted gunshot wound—and the North Catholic senior never forgot the 50-yard touchdown throw made by Unitas, then a junior at St. Justin's, a small school atop Mt. Washington in the city.

In 1955, after young Rooney had kept an eye on Unitas's progress through the University of Louisville, he monitored Unitas in the draft. Rooney was helping Byrne manage the process at the time, but the team was getting Marchibroda back from his two-year service stint and also had a backup punter, Vic Eaton, as a reserve behind Finks, so they didn't really need a quarterback—at least on paper. But by the time the ninth round rolled around, Rooney told Byrne it was time to draft Johnny U.

"Kiesling thought we were nuts," Rooney wrote in his autobiography.

And, yes, it was Kiesling who never played Unitas before cutting him, in spite of the ruckus raised by Unitas's favorite camp catch partners, Dan's brothers Tim, John, and Pat. They begged Dan to talk to Kiesling about Unitas's talent, but Kiesling ignored the 23-year-old Rooney, so the younger Rooney boys beseeched their father to overrule Kiesling.

Art Rooney's response was unfortunate, but it established another pillar of the Steelers Way: "Let the coach coach."

✦ ✦ ✦

If the Steelers of the 1950s weren't cutting Johnny Unitas, they were drafting busts such as Gary Glick first overall or passing on future legends such as Jim Brown.

In fact, the drafting of Glick in 1956 was a pass on future Hall of Fame running back Lenny Moore out of Penn State. The Steelers that year had the No. 1 pick, courtesy of a bonus system in place since 1947. There were three teams eligible for the bonus pick in 1956, and Dan Rooney, standing next to commissioner Bert Bell as he marked the three slips of paper, saw which one was marked B-O-N-U-S.

"I wasn't about to let a gift like this pass us by," Rooney wrote. And so he chose the correct slip, and the Steelers were able to draft Walt Kiesling's guy, Glick, out of Colorado A&M.

Moore came out of Penn State as the school's all-time leader in rushing and all-purpose yardage. He was drafted ninth by the Colts, who would have Moore and Johnny Unitas in their starting backfield by the end of the season.

As for Glick, the rest of the Steelers front office gathered to watch Colorado A&M game film a few weeks later, and, in the words of Dan Rooney, "Our hearts sank." Art Rooney walked downstairs from the viewing to update an awaiting sportswriter.

"You didn't like what you saw, did you?" asked the sportswriter.

"How did you know? I haven't said anything yet," said Rooney.

"You don't have to say anything," the sportswriter said. "I can see it in your face."

At least Glick made the team, as a safety, and played three-plus seasons in Pittsburgh before finishing his career with three different teams over the next three seasons. Glick remains the only defensive back chosen first overall in an NFL Draft. Still, he was a massive disappointment. As one prominent Pittsburgh sportswriter put it, "Gary Stick the Bonus Pick."

The choice of Len Dawson over Brown in 1957 wasn't nearly as egregious an error, but considering the Steelers could've entered the 1957 season with Brown, Moore, and Unitas in their backfield, it might be viewed as exactly that.

Actually, the Cleveland Browns wanted Dawson in the 1957 draft. Otto Graham had just retired following a 5–7 season, and owner/coach Paul Brown wanted to replace him with either John Brodie of Stanford or Dawson of Purdue.

Dawson was a three-time Big Ten passing champ and grew up a Browns fan in nearby Alliance, Ohio. Paul Brown also knew Dawson's high school coach and, prior to the coin flip with the Steelers for the fifth pick, asked that coach to ask Dawson to announce before the flip that he was going to play in the CFL. Dawson refused.

"So Pittsburgh won the toss and selected me," Dawson said years later. "Poor old Paul Brown had to settle for the guy from Syracuse." Dawson, of course, became a Hall of Fame quarterback long after he had been traded by the Steelers.

Kiesling, the coach who drafted Dawson, resigned for health reasons soon thereafter, and the Steelers hired Buddy Parker, who had an aversion to rookies, particularly rookie QBs. Parker traded for San Francisco's Earl Morrall and Detroit's Jack Kemp, released Ted Marchibroda, and let

Dawson rot on the bench. The next year, Parker traded for his other QB in Detroit, Bobby Layne, and Dawson threw 17 passes in two seasons as Layne's backup before he was traded to the Browns.

Layne, of course, ushered in a new era in Pittsburgh as he and Ernie Stautner led their respective units on the field, and off it.

✦ ✦ ✦

Ernie Stautner never played in a playoff game for the Steelers, but he played in nine Pro Bowls. One of those Pro Bowls in particular may have been his greatest game.

"That man ain't human," future Hall of Fame guard Jim Parker said after Stautner was named Most Valuable Lineman in the 1957 Pro Bowl. "He's too strong to be human," Parker continued. "He keeps coming, coming, coming. Every time he comes back, he comes back harder."

Word had it that Stautner was in a particularly foul mood that day, and that it had something to do with the Baltimore Colts. "I see a blue horseshoe, I kill the man wearing it!"

Well, Stautner may not actually have gone all Wyatt Earp about it, but he did perform quite the number on Parker, the great Colts lineman. Stautner beat on Parker with forearms, shoulders, and headslaps throughout the first half, and in the second half used his moves to wreck the rest of the West offense. In blocking a West field-goal attempt, Stautner ran over the holder and knocked the kicker out.

"It was the greatest game I've ever seen a defensive lineman play," said East line coach Tom Landry.

It was a precursor to a 1958 season in which the Steelers would ascend to the NFL's No. 1 ranking in defense. The 1957 season had been a turning point for the Steelers. They finished 6–6 but turned the corner with the hiring of former Lions head coach Buddy Parker. Parker had gotten drunk before a speech in Detroit and abruptly resigned on August 12, 1957. Only a month earlier, Parker had wrangled QB Tobin Rote from the Packers in a trade, and Rote was able to lead the Lions to the NFL championship that year after their starting QB, Bobby Layne, broke his ankle.

Layne and Parker had brought the first titles to Detroit in 1952 and 1953, but four years later Parker was done, and sportswriters in Detroit thought Layne was on his way to the scrapheap as well.

Art Rooney welcomed Parker to Pittsburgh two weeks after he resigned in Detroit. Sportswriters in Pittsburgh didn't hail the move as much as they decried the lack of a team builder—a legitimate general manager—to use the draft the way the smart teams did. In Parker, the Steelers got a great coach but a horrible general manager, at least from a build-from-the-draft perspective. He immediately began throwing draft picks around like confetti at a victory parade. In his first five weeks, Parker traded 10 future draft picks (1958–1960) in nine different trades.

The Steelers narrowly lost their 1958 opener in San Francisco and were blown out the following Sunday in Cleveland. Parker thought he had a good team but felt it was missing a leader. So why wouldn't he take Bobby Layne in a trade? That's what Lions owner George Wilson wanted to know after Parker called him on another matter.

Parker leapt at the opportunity, and on October 7, 1958, he traded Earl Morrall, a second-round pick in 1959, and a fourth-round pick in 1960 for Layne. The Detroit media snickered at the trade, since they believed Layne to be over the hill at 31. But Layne's Lions teammates howled their disapproval, and Parker told Pittsburgh reporters he had just acquired the greatest leader in team sports.

✦ ✦ ✦

As a kid, Ernie Stautner played tackle football on a paved lot and one day was beaten up so badly by the older kids that his father forbade him from playing the game again. But Ernie got his fix. He sweet-talked his parents into sending him to the Catholic school in Albany instead of the non-football-playing school nearby. Ernie began playing again and explained away the inevitable bumps and bruises associated with play to "being bullied again, Papa."

Ernie played the con all the way through his junior year, when he was named all-conference. Friends called Papa to congratulate him on raising such a fine ballplayer, thus Papa softened and allowed Ernie to continue with football.

What Ernie learned during this time was how to hide pain and injuries. That's what he was trying to do in Cleveland before a game in 1958. The Steelers had whipped the Eagles in Bobby Layne's debut, and Stautner was excited that his 1–2 team finally had a quarterback. Layne, in fact, had moved into Stautner's downtown apartment.

After missing Layne's second week of practice with a shoulder injury, Stautner so badly wanted to play in Cleveland

that he bugged Buddy Parker into getting relief. A trainer arrived, running late, and in a rush spilled several vials from his bag. He picked the wrong one back up and shot Stautner not once but twice with Demerol, a strong opioid, instead of the novocaine Ernie expected. The doctor asked the first time if it felt better. Stautner said no, that he needed more. The doctor gave him more. Demerol. It added up to an estimated 1,200 milligrams, three to four times the normal dose and more than twice the lethal dose.

"He gave me enough to kill a horse," Stautner could joke later. "Fortunately, I'm not a horse."

Ernie woke up in a hospital and fell back asleep as he heard a priest delivering the last rites. Ernie made it out alive. The Steelers did not, losing to Cleveland and falling to 1–3. Then they lost to the Giants and came home to a meeting. In a bar. Called by Layne.

The charismatic team leader railed, and his team rallied with a 6–0–1 record down the stretch. They even beat the Bears for the first time in team history. The Steelers were considered by many to be the best team in the league, but it was too little, too late, as Johnny Unitas directed the Colts to a championship win over the Giants in "The Greatest Game Ever Played" at the end of 1958.

✦ ✦ ✦

In January 1959, the Steelers drafted seventh. But not until the eighth round. Hurricane Buddy had wiped out their first seven rounds. It was little wonder that by the end of the season opposing coaches were saying the Steelers had suddenly got old.

They finished 1959 with a 6–5–1 record, giving them back-to-back winning seasons for the first time in team history. But the veteran team that wasn't being replenished by the draft began sliding backward. In 1960 the Steelers finished 5–6–1, and in 1961 they were 6–8. Bobby Layne was 35 and the subject of boos, which set Ernie Stautner off. He aired his grievances with buddy Pat Livingston of the *Pittsburgh Press*:

+ "I'm not happy playing in Pittsburgh. I never have been happy here, and I wouldn't have been here in the first place if I had any choice about it."
+ "They booed Elroy Face. Elroy Face!"
+ "What's wrong with these people? Do they have an inferiority complex or something?"
+ "Pittsburgh owes nothing to me. I owe nothing to Pittsburgh. We're all even on that count."
+ Pittsburgh is a "graveyard for football players.... Ask Big Daddy or Johnny Sample."
+ "I've asked 30 guys who were at that game if they booed Bobby Layne. Luckily, I haven't found one yet."

The following Sunday at Forbes Field, Stautner walked out to midfield alone. He expected to be booed but was instead met by a slow-growing crescendo of cheers.

Stautner and the city were at peace again as the NFL's version of the Gashouse Gang revved up for a final hurrah in 1962. It would be Layne's final year, and the Steelers felt rejuvenated with some fresh offensive skill players. Fullback John Henry Johnson's legs still had life at 33, and receiver

Pittsburgh defensive lineman Ernie Stautner, watching from the sideline during a game in the 1950s, played all 14 seasons of his NFL career with the Steelers and was inducted into the Pro Football Hall of Fame in 1969.

Buddy Dial caught 93 passes for over 2,000 yards the two previous seasons.

The draft, of course, hadn't been much help. Parker had decimated the 1961 draft by trading a first-rounder to the

Browns for Dick Moegle, the famed Rice running back who was tackled by a guy off the Alabama bench in the 1954 Cotton Bowl. And to get Johnson, the Steelers gave up a couple of mid-round picks in 1961 and 1962. The Steelers did draft Myron Pottios in the second round and Dick Hoak in the seventh round in 1961.

More of the same occurred in 1962. Parker traded away rounds 2–6 for mediocre veterans and got a head start on wrecking the 1963 draft by trading the first-rounder for backup QB Ed Brown. The Steelers did outbid the AFL's Chargers for 1962 first-round pick Bob Ferguson, the fullback from the same backfield as Paul Warfield and Matt Snell at Ohio State. But Ferguson suffered a head injury and started only three games in two seasons. He became as much a symbol of the Steelers' draft futility as he was a punching bag for Parker. "If I'd have known how ugly that Bob Ferguson was, I wouldn't have drafted him," Parker said.

But the wily ol' ball coach did know veteran talent. He not only rejuvenated Johnson, who rushed for over 1,000 yards in 1962 and 1964, Parker traded veterans for defensive linemen Lou Michaels and Gene "Big Daddy" Lipscomb. They lined up next to Stautner and the underrated Joe Krupa to form an outstanding defensive line that helped revive the club in 1962. The Steelers were thin at linebacker, but once their health returned, the Steelers won six of their last seven games to finish 9–5 and build hope for 1963.

But Parker talked Layne into retiring, Lipscomb died of an apparent heroin overdose, and Stautner was winding down. The Steelers came close in '63. Because ties did not count in the NFL's version of winning percentage, the Steelers played the Giants with a chance to win the division title, but lost and finished 7–4–3, their last winning season until 1972.

Stautner's number was retired the following season, the only number retired by the team until Joe Greene's No. 75 was retired 50 years later. Stautner's No. 70 was raised at halftime of an October 25, 1964, game versus the Eagles at Pitt Stadium. An assistant coach with the Steelers at the time, Stautner spoke at halftime and apologized to the crowd of 38,393 for not winning a championship. Parker dropped Stautner from the coaching staff a year later, but Stautner ended up winning two rings as the defensive coordinator for Tom Landry and the Dallas Cowboys. Stautner was inducted into the Pro Football Hall of Fame in 1969, his first season of eligibility.

✦ ✦ ✦

Hail, hail wrecking ball.

Buddy Parker busted out of Detroit in a drunken, impulsive haze and came to Pittsburgh as the proverbial bull in a china shop. He brought in a leader of men at quarterback to point the way and then went about robbing the future for the present. He did much of it while drunk.

Surly and unmasked by alcohol after losses, Parker cut and traded players without hesitation. Oftentimes he would resign, but the resignations were never accepted, and Parker would live to drink and coach another day.

That pattern was curtailed in the aftermath of the 1964 draft. The Steelers finished 1963 with a 1–1–2 final month. Their quarterback, Ed Brown, was 35. Their leading running back, John Henry Johnson, was 34. Their halfback, Dick Hoak, averaged 3.1 yards per carry. Their only real threat on offense was wide receiver Buddy Dial.

It was presumed that the Steelers would find an offensive complement to Dial in the 1964 draft when they selected Pitt running back/wide receiver Paul Martha with the 10th pick. The next player chosen was Ohio State running back/wide receiver Paul Warfield by the Browns. Martha ended up in the defensive secondary, Warfield in Canton.

The Steelers didn't have a second-round pick in '64, but Parker wanted Clairton's Jim Kelly, a tight end from Notre Dame, so he traded the first-round pick of the 1965 draft to the Bears for Kelly and a fourth-round pick (Ben McGee). Kelly caught 10 passes in his only season with the Steelers. That first-round pick in 1965 for the Bears became Dick Butkus.

Parker wasn't done. Sixteen days later, he traded Dial to the Cowboys for the rights to the fourth pick of the just-concluded draft, offensive lineman Scott Appleton. But Appleton signed with the rival American Football League, and the deal became known as the Buddy Dial–for–Nothing trade.

So, to recap, in slightly more than two weeks the Steelers passed on Warfield, traded Butkus, and received bubkus for their record-setting receiver Dial, the only viable playmaker remaining on the team. That's when Art Rooney finally stepped in. He put into Parker's new contract that he was to receive approval for all future trades and cuts from either him or his 31-year-old son, Dan.

That worked.

Until it didn't.

Early in 1965, with Brown struggling at quarterback and Parker unenthused about third-year QB Bill Nelson, Parker sought a veteran QB—specifically Eagles backup King Hill. He asked Art about trading McGee or another quality young defensive lineman, Chuck Hinton, for Hill. Art cautioned against it, but told Parker that he could make the trade. Parker didn't—until an exhibition loss two weeks later forced him into taking action. Parker got drunk, called Dan Rooney and suggested a different trade, but one that still included McGee, the talented, young defensive lineman. Dan told Parker to call him back in the morning because Dan didn't believe in making trades in the middle of the night after a loss.

That's when Parker resigned. And this time, for the first time, it was accepted. The next morning, Parker told Dan that he didn't think he could handle the team any longer.

"I don't think so, either," said Dan Rooney, who had received his father's blessing on the matter.

It was the day the Steelers lost their winningest coach.

It was the day they lost their wrecking ball.

4

THE FOUNDATION

CHARLES GREENE WAS 12 years old when he sat down to watch Johnny Unitas lead the Baltimore Colts to a win in sudden death overtime over the New York Giants in "The Greatest Game Ever Played." That game motivated Charles, better known as Joe, a nickname given him by an aunt who said he would become the next Joe Louis.

Instead, he became the first Joe Greene.

But he wasn't "Mean Joe" quite yet. No, this child, raised by only his mother in the prairie town of Temple, in the middle of Texas, was rather timid. He picked cotton and pecans, and at age 13 began working construction. It helped make him stronger, but Joe didn't realize how much stronger until he was pushed to his limit by an older boy named Speedy Vance.

A bully three years older than Joe, Vance stole $5 off the top of the Greene family TV. The $5 was to pay for insurance so Joe could play freshman football at Dunbar High, an all-Black school in Temple, about 30 miles south of Waco. Joe had had enough and set out for Speedy's house, and when he got there he pummeled Speedy and took the money back.

Vance was just one of the kids who bullied Joe at the time, and that fight ended all of that. In fact, Joe and Speedy became buddies, which wasn't good for Joe. He now knew he was strong, but he was running with the wrong crowd.

Speedy was shot to death five years later, but in the interim he influenced Joe, and Joe was an angry teen and an angry football player. He was part of a team that was bussed to a white high school for the use of its field, but not the use of its locker room. Joe knew all about segregation in 1963 Texas, and it was making him mean. He had gotten himself kicked out of every game as a sophomore, and then out of nine games as a junior.

Not that it sullied his reputation, because the local newspapers didn't cover the Black high schools. Joe later joked that the reason he was ejected so often was because he intentionally ran over officials. But there was no joking that his demeanor, with the help of "friends" such as Speedy, had soured.

Joe was especially sour after a loss. As a junior linebacker at Dunbar, Joe was trying to get over a loss when he walked into a diner in his neighborhood, where the opposing team, Waco Carver, was eating before it left town. Joe took an ice cream cone from the quarterback and smeared it in his face. One of the quarterback's teammates threw a bottle at Joe that hit him in the chest and Joe chased him toward the team bus.

The driver closed the doors just before Joe got there, but Joe pried them open and stepped onto the bus, only to see the entire team had retreated out the back door.

Charles Greene intimidated an entire football team. He was probably the baddest badass in the state of Texas, and this nearly three years before anyone would call him "Mean Joe" Greene.

✦ ✦ ✦

Terry Bradshaw was born in Shreveport, but after the second grade his family moved to the Mississippi River town of Camanche, Iowa. He played a lot of baseball in Iowa and only threw the football around his backyard. He didn't get to play football until his family moved back to Shreveport for Terry's seventh grade, and he excitedly went out for the junior high team. The coach met with 200 boys, and they were promised a fair tryout, one that wouldn't depend on size, just that a boy "looked like a winner." And then the coach picked the team on the spot, every big guy there. Terry was not a big guy and went home dejected.

Eighth grade brought the promise of a new school and new coach, but Terry heard the same speech, and the same lies, and left crying again.

The coach did throw a bone to the boys, telling them they could attend practice and watch from the sideline. Terry passed on the offer the first day but couldn't stay away the second day, and when a loose ball bounded over to him on the sideline, he picked it up and began playing catch with another boy, a small boy who most certainly didn't deserve to be picked for the team and had trouble with Terry's uncommon fastball. Terry looked up at one point and saw the coach in the middle of the field, in the middle of the practice, watching him. So Terry began hamming it up, throwing on the run like a shortstop, throwing harder to the poor child on the other end. This went on for 10 minutes before the coach walked over, put his arm around Terry, and asked, "How did I miss you?" The coach told Terry to stop by his office and pick up a uniform.

Terry skipped home merrily to tell his father, and the next day reported for practice. Right away the coach put him in the lineup—at middle linebacker.

Hey, young Bradshaw thought, *it's not quarterback, but at least I'm on the team.*

Another coach noticed Terry's arm, though. He was the track coach at Woodlawn High and he needed someone to heave the javelin. He gave one to Bradshaw and told him to go behind the stadium and learn how to throw it.

There wasn't a coach to teach him, so Terry thought he would figure it out, but really didn't put much time into it. This became apparent at his first meet when Terry ran up for his first throw and nearly fell down. He threw 142 feet and finished last, almost 20 feet behind the next best—or worst—throw. Bradshaw felt embarrassed for himself, his coach, and his school, but at least the coach realized that Bradshaw needed coaching. And he got it.

Bradshaw the next year improved to 175'1" and qualified for the state meet. As a junior, he routinely threw 180 feet, which won most meets. He won the 1965 district meet by two inches with a throw of 200'2" on his final throw.

Bradshaw came back bigger, stronger, and more confident for his senior season in the spring of 1966, and in the first meet, the Shreveport City Meet, he threw 217 feet and was named Most Outstanding Field Man. In his next meet, Bradshaw shocked not only himself but the high school track world by throwing 240'2" for a new national record. He smashed the previous record of 232'11" set by a high schooler in Washington.

Terry broke the record several more times, got his photo in *Sports Illustrated*, and his personal best—and the national record—settled at 243'7". But at one point he slipped as he threw and felt something tear in his elbow. He didn't think it was serious and continued in the hope of winning the state meet. He gutted out the final portion of the season and his throw of 239'11" did give him the state championship. In its wake, Bradshaw was flooded with over 200 scholarship offers. But he would never throw the javelin again. Nothing, Bradshaw knew in his heart, could compare to football.

✦ ✦ ✦

Dan Rooney was the first true foundational piece that his father, the Chief, Art Rooney Sr., had installed in the late 1950s. Dan grew to become the de facto general manager by 1965 and stood up to Buddy Parker.

Dan's younger brother, Art Jr., also wanted a chance to work for the organization. He had played offensive tackle at St. Vincent College, from where he graduated in 1957. He went to New York to become an actor but ended up serving in the Marine reserves before returning to Pittsburgh and telling his

mother he wanted to work for the team. She—Katherine—
asked her husband to find a place for Art Jr., and the Chief
hired him to sell radio advertising and promote ticket sales
for games at Forbes Field.

The job didn't satisfy Art Jr., so he asked to get into scouting. Since Parker had ravaged the future by trading so many
draft picks, the Chief felt safe in hiring Art Jr. for the job.
At least that was the family joke. But five years later, Art Sr.
told a reporter that hiring Art Jr. was the smartest move he
ever made.

Art Jr., 29, was put in charge of the Steelers' scouting
department in 1965, just in time for Parker's last hurrah.
The ol' ball coach, who couldn't stand rookies, was one of
the driving forces behind the Steelers getting involved in
BLESTO, which, in 1963, actually started as LESTO, for Lions-
Eagles-Steelers Talent Organization. When the Bears joined,
it became the acronym we know today.

Parker was the man who guided eventual BLESTO chief
Jack Butler on scouting, and the organization was based in
the Steelers' offices at the Roosevelt Hotel. That's where Art
Jr. learned the scouting business from the bottom up. He
streamlined and organized the Steelers' draft processes, and
with the help of BLESTO's pool of 9–10 scouts, Art Jr. and
the part-time Steelers assistant coaches hit the road every fall.
Forever trying to please his father and outshine his brother,
Art Jr. became obsessed with turning the Steelers' scouting
department into a vital cog in the machinery. His credo to
scouts such as Art Lewis, Ken Stilley, Will Walls, and Fido
Murphy was this: "Let's get so many good players that the
coaches can't screw them up."

Of course, the past had already ravaged the future, and with only one pick in the first seven rounds in 1965, the Steelers grabbed future Pro Bowl wide receiver Roy Jefferson in the second round. In 1966, with the third overall pick, the machinery sputtered out West Virginia running back Dick Leftridge, and in 1967, without a first-round pick, the Steelers misfired again on running back Don Shy in the second round.

While Art Jr. was misfiring in his early work, so was Dan, who had hired Mike Nixon in an emergency in 1965. Dan's first choice after a full interviewing process was Bill Austin, who went 5–8–1 in 1966 and 4–9–1 in 1967. Dan wanted to fire Austin after the 1967 season, but his dad talked him out of it. However, both the Chief and Dan asked Art Jr. to make discreet inquiries into potential head-coaching candidates while on the road in 1968. The name most often given to Art Jr. was that of a young assistant to Baltimore Colts coach Don Shula, defensive secondary/linebackers coach Chuck Noll. The next most prominent name given to Art Jr. was an assistant with the Detroit Lions, Western Pennsylvania native Chuck Knox.

But it was Upton Bell, the Colts' head scout and son of the Chief's late friend Bert Bell, whose opinion carried the most sway. Bell and his brother, Bert Jr., recommended Noll in the strongest possible terms. Art Jr. knew he had no say in the hiring. He just wanted the next coach to be colorblind and committed to building through the draft.

✦ ✦ ✦

Dan Rooney was also determined to add diversity to a team that employed one of only two Black players in the league in the 1930s. But Ray Kemp lasted only one season, after which both he and Joe Lillard of the Chicago Cardinals mysteriously disappeared from their respective rosters. The NFL never mandated that Black players weren't allowed to play, but the league remained all White into the late 1940s until a player shortage caused by World War II and the birth of the rival All-America Football Conference forced owners to sign Black players.

The Cleveland Browns of the AAFC signed Black players Marion Motley and Bill Willis in 1946, and that turned a young Pittsburgh sportswriter named Bill Nunn into a Browns fan. He and his friends routinely made road trips to Cleveland to watch Paul Brown's new powerhouse.

Cleveland's old NFL team, the Rams, had moved to Los Angeles after winning the 1945 championship, and under local and financial pressure signed a Black player, former UCLA star running back Kenny Washington, in 1946.

It wasn't until 1949 that the NFL drafted its first Black player, but because George Taliaferro signed with the AAFC, Wally Triplett of Penn State became the first Black draftee to play in the NFL, with Detroit.

The leagues merged in 1950, but the Steelers under Jock Sutherland and John Michelosen remained all-White. When Joe Bach became coach in 1952, he announced that players would be judged by ability, not race, and many Black players ventured to camp at St. Bonaventure for a tryout. The racism of some of the players and coaches became evident to 17-year-old Art Rooney Jr., and the resentment against 11th-round draft pick Jack Spinks was clear. One defensive player shouted his feelings after Spinks ran him over on the practice field. Afterward, Art Sr. told Spinks to "punch him out" the next time it happened. Spinks made the team but lasted only one season.

In 1953, the Steelers drafted Lowell Perry of Michigan in the eighth round and Jack McClairen of Bethune-Cookman in the 26th round. Both served military hitches before resuming their football careers, but the Steelers stopped drafting Black players after Bach resigned in 1954.

Speculation about racism followed the list of Steelers coaches through the end of Bill Austin's tenure. Of course, this could be explained by the fact the Steelers drafted primarily out of magazines throughout much of that time, and magazines didn't cover the Black colleges.

That explanation never sat well with Nunn, the son of Bill Nunn Sr., managing editor of the *Courier*, one of the nation's most influential Black publications, located in Pittsburgh. Nunn Jr. became sports editor of the *Courier* in 1950, and his Black-college All-America team made him a kingmaker to young Black athletes everywhere.

Nunn Jr. grew up in Homewood and delivered the *Courier*. He had an impressive résumé as a natural leader in athletics, which began at Westinghouse High, where in 1943 Nunn was the basketball team's captain. He and teammate Chuck Cooper gave the 'House two Black starters. There was a third who was shunned by the coach because that would've meant more than half of Westinghouse's starting lineup was Black.

That didn't sit well with Nunn, either. He brought the players together and convinced them to back his demand that the third Black player start, or none of them would play. They agreed unanimously, and Nunn went to the coach, the coach went to the principal, the administration relented, and Paul Devon not only played but led the team in scoring as the 'House won its first City League championship in 24 years.

After high school, Nunn hoped to attend Long Island University, but his father wanted him to attend a Black college. Instead of giving in to his father's demand, Nunn worked at Union Switch and Signal. After a year, he figured there had to be a better way and agreed to attend all-Black West Virginia State with his old teammate Cooper.

The 6' Nunn was the point guard and team captain for a team that went 30–0 his senior season. West Virginia State was the only undefeated college team in the country and won the unofficial Black college championship, and of course the dynamic team never got to play all-White champion Kentucky.

Nunn also played a little football at West Virginia State, but basketball was his game. The opposite was true for basketball teammate Joe Gilliam, who doubled as the school's star quarterback before beginning a legendary coaching career at Tennessee State. It was the first of Nunn's close relationships with the all-Black colleges.

The New York Knicks of the Basketball Association of America wanted Nunn to tryout and become the first Black player in the league, but Nunn was warned by *Courier* sports editor Wendell Smith—who had closely covered Jackie Robinson's first season in Major League Baseball—that Nunn could expect similar hostilities in basketball.

Nunn thought the Harlem Globetrotters might be a better opportunity; they had offered him a two-year contract to barnstorm the country via bus. Nunn also received an offer from West Virginia State to become an assistant basketball coach. However, Nunn felt he could better serve the world at his father's paper. He also marveled at the new home his father built at the top of the Hill District and thought his life could become just as abundant, so he joined the *Courier* in 1948 to follow in his father's footsteps. And he would—for a while.

✦ ✦ ✦

Terry Bradshaw was relieved when the coach at Woodlawn High in Shreveport moved him from middle linebacker to quarterback at the start of his freshman season. Only problem was Bradshaw dislocated his right shoulder and missed all but the last two games.

As a sophomore in 1963, Bradshaw was the starting quarterback for the J-V team. He sat behind varsity starter Trey Prather, the all-state QB who eventually went to LSU in 1965. Prather is also remembered as a marine who was killed in Vietnam a week before his 21st birthday.

Prather led Woodlawn to the state semifinals in 1964, but in 1965 the job was all Bradshaw's. The senior QB was surrounded by a starting lineup that included only one returning starter, so Bradshaw knew he had his work cut out for him. He and his best buddy, backup QB and leading receiver Tommy Spinks, worked on pass routes all off-season in preparation for a season that ended in the state finals.

Bradshaw didn't care much for the coach's "messenger guard" system that allowed the coach to call the plays, but Woodlawn did finish 8–1–1 and won twice in the state playoffs before losing in the title game.

In the semifinals, Bradshaw passed for 176 yards and 2 touchdowns in what he felt was the best game of his high school career. It resulted in scholarship offers from LSU, Baylor, and nearby Louisiana Tech.

Bradshaw originally chose LSU, but that decision wasn't well received in Shreveport. In fact, his girlfriend broke up with him, and his backfield coach wouldn't talk to him. The latter approached Bradshaw on behalf of Tech and told Terry that LSU was nothing more than a football factory that would chew him up and spit him out. The always impressionable Bradshaw changed his mind when he realized he wasn't ready for such a big program, and, two weeks later, when he went to LSU for a high school all-star game, he told the LSU coach he wasn't coming. Bradshaw then passed out from heat prostration during the game.

✦ ✦ ✦

Joe Greene's college decision wasn't nearly as difficult. Because there wasn't newspaper coverage of the Black high schools in Texas in 1964, only the University of Houston had heard of Greene. He was invited for a visit on the same night as his senior prom, and he chose the prom. But someone in Greene's hometown, an alumnus of North Texas State College (now University of North Texas)—a school located about 170 miles north of Greene's home in Temple—contacted their coach Odus Mitchell about Greene. North Texas State had spawned AFL great and former Steelers draft pick Abner Haynes, who broke the state's college football color barrier in 1957.

Greene drove to Denton to meet Mitchell and accept a scholarship to play linebacker for the North Texas State Eagles in 1965. They weren't the Eagles for long. Led by Greene, now a sophomore defensive lineman, and a defensive back named Charles Beatty, the defense was the driving force behind an 8–2 record. The school colors were green and white, and, because the defense was playing so well, the wife of the school's sports information director nicknamed the unit "Mean Green." Of course, "Mean" Joe Greene was just a shout away, and a legend was born. (Forever asked if the nickname bothered him, Greene once told a sportswriter from Cleveland, "It used to, but I guess it supplied some identity." Greene paused, thought of one of the Browns' top players, and said, "Just so no one ever calls me Fair Hooker.")

Coach Mitchell retired after the 1966 season, replaced by Rod Rust, who would go on to NFL acclaim as a defensive coordinator. Rust didn't need to look at film to know he would have the best defensive lineman in the country for two years.

Greene met his future wife, Agnes, at North Texas State, but he didn't know he also met a future teammate with the Steelers in Beatty. Greene was always impressed with Beatty as a player and forever held that Beatty had been the truly meanest green defender.

✦ ✦ ✦

The *Courier* began picking a Black college All-America team in 1925, and Bill Nunn Jr. began helping with picks in 1948. Little did he know it would be the springboard that brought him to the Pittsburgh Steelers.

In 1952, Nunn became sports editor of the paper, and in 1953 Wellington Mara was holding that paper up to his scouts with the New York Giants while pointing to the name Rosey Brown from Morgan State College. It was during the 27th round that the Giants drafted Nunn's first Hall of Famer.

In 1962, Nunn began feeling more pressure with his selections because three leagues—the NFL, AFL, and CFL—were now trying to fill rosters, and even the Washington Redskins—in spite of the American Nazi Party parading outside the new stadium to "Keep the Redskins White!"—had selected a Black player.

There was still one painful bias remaining in Nunn's attempt at athletic fairness, and that was the quarterback position. Nunn's former college QB, Joe Gilliam, was asked to play safety by Curly Lambeau at Green Bay, so Gilliam instead went into coaching. Roy Curry quarterbacked Jackson State College to 1961 and 1962 Black college national championships with spots on both All-America teams. Nunn thought Curry was the best Black quarterback he had seen since Choo Choo Brackins, who spent a few minutes at QB for the Packers in 1955. One of the Rooneys overheard Nunn talking about Curry and drafted him in the 12th round in 1963. Curry was promised a chance, so he turned down the CFL, but Buddy Parker put him at wide receiver. Curry made the team but strained his hamstring, sat out the rest of the season, and didn't make the 1964 team.

Nunn, in late 1964, began putting together a "Night of Stars" at the Pittsburgh Hilton Hotel to honor his All-America team and the Black college national champ. Art Rooney Sr., Dan Rooney, and Parker were in attendance when someone spoke about the plight of Black quarterbacks. Nunn took notes and wrote it up for the *Courier* and considered the evening a smashing success. Art Sr. even promised Nunn, in print, that the Steelers would use "any brilliant quarterback we can recruit, regardless of color."

Perhaps Dan Rooney was looking for that brilliant quarterback late in 1967 when he opened the *Courier* to read Nunn's All-America team. Dan wondered why he didn't know any of the names and then wanted to know why Nunn Jr.—whose father used to loaf with Art Sr. in the Hill District—rarely showed up at Forbes Field or the Roosevelt Hotel to cover the club. Dan walked to the lobby where the reporters worked and asked one of Nunn's colleagues at the *Courier*. The response was that Nunn didn't have much respect for the Steelers, so Dan called Nunn and set up a meeting at the Roosevelt.

Nunn told the truth. He said he didn't feel welcome in the press box and complained that no one from the organization ever contacted him about his All-Americans. Nunn also didn't appreciate the attitudes of coaches Parker and Bill Austin, whom Nunn perceived as racist.

Parker's longtime personal valet was a Black man named Boots, who would shine the players' shoes when he wasn't fetching coffee or running errands for Parker. Nunn also didn't appreciate Austin skipping his banquet every year. Nunn, in fact, knew one of Austin's girlfriends. She told Nunn that Austin "can deal with [Blacks], but he has a tough time."

Dan nodded, and then surprised Nunn by offering him a job. When Nunn hesitated because of his newspaper duties, Rooney offered the job part-time. He wanted Nunn to take notes on players and send reports to the Steelers. Nunn agreed to meet with Art Jr., and the two hit it off. They were after the same traits in athletes, and the two became excited about the possibilities.

✦ ✦ ✦

Bill Nunn began working for the Steelers in 1968, while also continuing to pick the All-America team for the *Courier*. The hard part was simultaneously doing the paper and the team justice, so Nunn would leave one or two draft sleepers off his All-America team. Nunn was so secretive about one pass-rusher that he didn't even go down to see L.C. Greenwood his senior year. Nunn Jr. scouting a Black college player was akin to Art Rooney Sr. standing in a public line to bet a horse. Their reputations brought out the glommers, which brought down the value.

Art Rooney Jr. instead went to Arkansas AM&N to scout the 6'6", 215-pound Greenwood. Art Jr. also had a running back and another defensive lineman on his list, and asked the AM&N coaches about those players first. The coaches talked up the running back, ran film for Rooney, and then did the same for Clarence Washington, the defensive end who had been moved to defensive tackle. Rooney liked Washington, and pointed the coaches to the other defensive end.

"Oh, that's L.C. We knew you'd spot him. He's special," Rooney was told. Rooney countered that Greenwood was too tall for his weight. "That's what they all say," said one coach. "Wait till you see him practice."

Later that day, Rooney watched the skinny Greenwood hold his ground, get under blockers and rush the passer. He reported back to Nunn that everything he had said about Greenwood was true. The two men had their first sleeper of the 1969 draft.

✦ ✦ ✦

No one was sleeping on Joe Greene his senior season. Art Rooney Jr. heard the early buzz about Greene while scouting at a Black college. Art Jr. became a steady visitor to North Texas State, where coach Rod Rust gave him free run of the facilities.

Bill Nunn also went to Denton, Texas, to meet Greene, who wasn't home, so Nunn walked in and waited on Greene's couch. Greene at first thought Nunn was an intruder, but calmed down, and the two had a great talk.

North Texas State's "Mean Green" defense was having its way in allowing only 1.9 yards per carry that season. Another future first-round pick, Cedrick Hardman, had joined the line and took some of the double- and triple-teams away from Greene, and the team finished 8–2.

After the season, Greene's No. 75 was retired by the school, and Greene's hometown of Temple held Joe Greene Day. Rust said that it wasn't just "the Negro part of town" but the entire town that was proud of their new favorite son.

The scouting reports were coming in on Greene:

✦ Art Jr.: "Quick as a big cat. Forces opponents to double-team him. Use of hands okay, should be able to develop a fine use of hands and arms. Does a real good job of rushing passer. Puts out all the time.

Would give us the inside pass rush we've been looking for."

+ Jesse Thompson, BLESTO scout in the Southwest: "AGILE, MOBILE & HOSTILE AS HELL...definitely my kind of football player."

+ Carl DePasqua, Pitt coach who scouted Greene for the Steelers the previous spring: "Great skill. Best kid I saw on my tour. Has quickness, strength, and speed."

+ Norm Bulaich, future Baltimore Colts and former TCU running back, on Greene: "He was something else. We heard about this 6′4″, 240-pound linebacker who ran the 40 in 4.6 and had a 34-inch waist. He struck me a few times."

+ Chuck Noll, defensive assistant for the Colts who had scouted and interviewed Greene the previous spring: "There was no doubt in my mind that this guy loved to play football and wanted to play very badly."

At the Senior Bowl, Jon Kolb, the center from Oklahoma State, met his future teammate.

"I remember seeing Art Rooney Jr. down there with the other scouts," said Kolb. "They took us out to a dinner on a big aircraft carrier. There were all these F-14s on this deck, and then there was Joe Greene. He was as big as this airplane. Next thing I know, he was the No. 1 pick of the team I was on."

✦ ✦ ✦

In Terry Bradshaw's freshman season, Louisiana Tech went 1–9, but it was sophomore Phil Robertson playing quarterback in the complicated pro-style attack. The only game Tech won was the game in which Bradshaw played. He replaced an injured Robertson that day but returned to the bench the following week.

Tech's coach retired after the season, replaced by a coach who believed—as did most of the young, innovative coaches of the day—that three yards and a cloud of dust was preferable to the two bad things that could happen with a forward pass.

Bradshaw didn't like what he was hearing and thought his talents could be better served elsewhere. So he drove from Ruston, Louisiana, to Tallahassee, Florida, to meet with the Florida State coach. Once Bradshaw arrived, the guy who had seemed so excited on the phone told Bradshaw to turn around and go back to Tech.

Bradshaw figured the new coach at Tech had learned of his desire to transfer and called the FSU coach. Bradshaw's intuition was correct, as new Tech coach Maxie Lambright told Bradshaw that things were going to change at Tech, that there would be real competition for jobs. And Lambright stuck to his word. Tech finished 3–7 in 1967 as Bradshaw worked into the mix with Robertson and passed for 951 yards.

Bradshaw was confident he would start his junior year over Robertson, the senior who, according to Bradshaw in his 1973 autobiography *No Easy Game*, seemed more interested in duck hunting than football. Robertson kidded Bradshaw about the younger QB's enthusiasm and his love of throwing the deep ball. Robertson would shout, "Bradshaw, the Blonde Bomma!" in the locker room, and newspaper reporters picked up on it. That's when Bradshaw became known as "the Blonde Bomber."

Bradshaw's instincts about Robertson were correct, as the senior starter abruptly quit the team. Bradshaw took over as the starter in 1968, and Tech had plenty of young, aggressive players who had not inherited the losing attitude that had permeated Tech the last two years. Even though Tech was picked to finish last that season, the team was a confident underdog.

Tommy Spinks, Bradshaw's old buddy from high school, was entering his second year as a starting wide receiver at Tech, and Bradshaw, in his first college start, hit him for a touchdown on fourth-and-10 to break a late tie against Mississippi State in the 1968 opener.

A few weeks later, at 2–1, Bradshaw and Tech stalled after first-and-goal at the 7 and lost to Southwest Louisiana. Bradshaw had a dream the following week that he won a game on a long touchdown pass in the final seconds. He believed he had ESP regarding dreams, so on Saturday, while trailing Northwestern State 39–35, Bradshaw drove Tech to the 10-yard line with just under two minutes left. He remembered the dream—and threw an interception.

Tech did get the ball back with 13 seconds left. They were on their own 18, and Bradshaw told his receivers to just take off. He threw it "a mile down the field" to Ken Liberto, who "caught it on his fingertips and stumbled into the end zone" to complete an 82-yard Hail Mary, which, by Bradshaw's description, had to have traveled 80 yards in the air. Tech went undefeated the rest of the season as Bradshaw put up big stats in front of more scouts every week.

At 8–2, Tech went into its first bowl game, the Grantland Rice Bowl. Yes, the sportswriter who had "scouted" Byron White and Bill Dudley for the Steelers was now unveiling

Terry Bradshaw to the world—or at least to Murfreesboro, Tennessee.

Against Akron, in freezing, blustery 35 mph winds, Bradshaw set four bowl records in Tech's 33–13 win. He was the MVP of the game and ended the season as the nation's leader in passing and total yards. Tech led the nation in total offense, and Bradshaw considered that junior season the key to his football career.

As for Phil Robertson, he went on to fame as a reality TV star on the show *Duck Dynasty*, proving Bradshaw really did have a sixth sense when it came to predicting the future.

✦ ✦ ✦

It wasn't ESP, but a premonition that struck Marianne Noll as she watched her husband's team, the Colts, stomp a 41–7 mudhole into the Steelers in 1968. Marianne was at the Shula home watching the game with the wife of Colts coach Don Shula. Marianne's husband, Chuck, was a defensive coach under Shula, who had guided the Colts to an 11–1–2 record in 1967 and were looking at 3–0 early in 1968. The Steelers were on their way to their third loss in three games and had secretly been on the prowl for Bill Austin's replacement for 1969. There was no way Mrs. Noll would've known that, but she no doubt knew enough about football to see that the Steelers were on their way to something akin to their 2–11–1 final record that season.

Noll and the Colts were on their way to the Super Bowl to lose to Joe Namath and the Jets that season. Noll was a defensive assistant along with Bill Arnsparger, another all-time great. Arnsparger had the defensive line, Noll the linebackers and secondary, and together they coordinated the defense. It wasn't their fault the Colts scored only seven points in the Super Bowl against the Jets defense.

Immediately after the stunning loss to the 17.5-point-underdog Jets, Noll went to the hospital with safety Rick Volk, who had reentered the game after each of his two concussions. Noll rode in the ambulance that whisked Volk to the hospital. Once Volk was stabilized, an ashen Noll went to a place that was nearly as somber, the postgame party. It was one of Noll's worst days ever.

Fifteen days later, Noll would enjoy one of his best.

✦ ✦ ✦

The *Evening Bulletin* of Philadelphia on January 3, 1969, reported that Penn State coach Joe Paterno had pondered an offer of $70,000—double what Bill Austin had made—to coach the Pittsburgh Steelers, and that Paterno turned them down. "He has a fine freshman team coming up for next year," the reporter explained. "Lydell Mitchell is a breakaway runner of promise and Franco Harris may fill Ted Kwalick's shoes." Kwalick played tight end, but Harris went on to play fullback and block for Mitchell on the 11–0 Penn State team in 1969.

Dan Rooney denied making the offer to Paterno, but there was no denying Rooney's interest in the 42-year-old college coach, who was the first to interview for the Steelers' coaching position left vacant by the firing of Austin. Rooney turned his interest to Noll, and he and his father interviewed Noll at the Roosevelt Hotel. Art Rooney Jr. was perturbed he hadn't been invited. As head of the scouting department, Art Jr. was chaf-ing about the lack of diversity on the roster and barged into the meeting to ask Noll if he had a problem drafting Black players. Noll's answer satisfied Art Jr., but Jr. also resented the assumption that Noll and his assistant coaches would take over the draft process. Art Sr. saw that complaint coming, so he turned to Noll and said, "Chuck, our next coach will have his assistants involved in the draft as much as he sees fit. And the final say on the draft and on trades will belong to him and nobody else."

Art Jr. shrugged. At least his first concern had been addressed. All parties involved were happy with the 37-year-old Noll, who received a call from 36-year-old Dan Rooney, who told Noll he wanted him to be the next Steelers coach. "I want that, too," said Noll, who got on a plane and later that day, at the Roosevelt Hotel, held his first press conference. He was asked about coming to a city of losers. "Losing has nothing to do with geography," Noll said.

The introductions over, Noll turned his attention to the next day's draft. He had scouted Joe Greene personally and wanted to build a defense around him. But the buzz around Pittsburgh was all about Terry Hanratty, the local prep star who had quarterbacked Notre Dame to the 1966 national championship. Noll and Dan Rooney summoned Art Jr. to the draft room at the Roosevelt to go over the draft board. Art Jr. did the rereads of his top 11 players as Noll listened for mentions of playing speed, football intelligence, and those who played with leverage. Noll smiled when Art Jr. mentioned Greene, and both men agreed that if he was available at No. 4, he would be the Steelers' first-round pick. Noll left the room, and Dan turned to his younger brother and told him that was his finest hour.

✦ ✦ ✦

On the eighth floor of the Roosevelt Hotel on January 28, 1969, Dan Rooney, Art Rooney Jr., Ed Kiely, and Fran Fogarty joined Chuck Noll for his first draft as coach of the Pittsburgh Steelers. The media, for the final year, also had access to the draft room.

The Buffalo Bills were on the clock first, and soon after 8:00 AM they drafted O.J. Simpson, a player so good that BLESTO chief Jack Butler, after scouting him, asked for his autograph. The Steelers hadn't seriously contemplated Simpson. They had Greene at the top of their board and awaited picks by the Atlanta Falcons and Philadelphia Eagles.

The Steelers were talking to Greene over the phone as the Falcons drafted George Kunz, a two-way tackle from Notre Dame who had been near the top of the Steelers' board. Now Noll and Dan Rooney were talking to Greene when the Eagles, who revealed after the draft that they were high on Greene, took Leroy Keyes, the running back from Purdue. That's when Art Jr. looked across the table at Noll and said, "Greene." Noll replied, "Let's go for him," and nodded to Dan, who made their pick over the phone. It was a seamless and perfect start for Noll and his new team.

In the second round, the Steelers wanted a defensive end from Texas Southern, Ernie Calloway, but the Eagles took him two picks earlier, so the Steelers made their fan base happy by making Hanratty the third quarterback chosen. The Steelers later grabbed Warren Bankston, a running back from Tulane who later became a tight end for the Oakland Raiders.

The Steelers got a steal in the third round in Jon Kolb, a center from Oklahoma State who went on to play left tackle for the Steelers in four Super Bowl wins.

In the fourth round, the Steelers drafted Penn State running back Bob Campbell, who contributed as a rookie. In the seventh round, they drafted Greene's teammate at North Texas State, defensive back Charles Beatty, who went on to start 27 games for the Steelers. In the 10th round, the Steelers got the pass-rusher Bill Nunn had left off the *Courier* All-America team in the hope the Steelers could steal him late. The Dallas Cowboys, picking late in the ninth round, also wanted L.C. Greenwood, but passed because of a bad medical report. And so the Steelers drafted Greenwood with the fourth pick of the 10th round.

In the 11th round, they drafted Greenwood's linemate at Arkansas AM&N, Clarence Washington, who stuck with the team for two years. In the 12th, the Steelers drafted a linebacker out of San Diego State, Doug Fisher, who played in 10 games. And in the 15th round, they took a flier on a kid who once caught a last-second, game-winning, 82-yard touchdown pass for Louisiana Tech, Kenny Liberto.

✦ ✦ ✦

"If given a choice, I would've picked the Pittsburgh Steelers last. I didn't celebrate the day I got drafted," was how Joe Greene put it years later. The fans weren't much happier than he was. In an infamous *Pittsburgh Press* story the day after the draft, the double-deck headline read:

Fans' Reaction:
Who's Joe Greene?

The story relayed the results of a random street poll that only three of 20 interviewed had heard of Greene. "Joe Greene presses pants right over there," an interviewee from Cleveland joked. But the man added a nugget for Steelers fans: "You're lucky to get Chuck Noll. I know him personally, and he's a super guy."

Noll, of course, was a Cleveland native, and he was at least as important an addition to the Steelers as Greene. At the first day of preseason practice, Noll told the players who would go 1–13 that season, "The majority of you will not be with us very long. Keep your bags packed."

If Buddy Parker was the wrecking ball, Chuck Noll was the broom that swept clean. During one of his 1969 camp speeches at Bonaventure Hall, Noll told the players about his ultimate goal of winning the Super Bowl. Don Shy, a backup running back, laughed out loud. A few days later, Shy and Ken Kortas were traded for Saints leading rusher Don McCall and two draft picks.

The purge was underway. Over the next 14 months, Noll cut or traded 12 starters from the 1968 team. From that team, only five starters—punter Bobby Walden, center Ray Mansfield, right guard Bruce Van Dyke, defensive lineman Ben McGee, and outside linebacker Andy Russell—would play in a

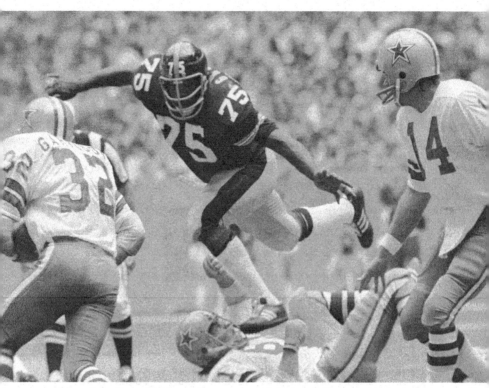

Steelers All-Pro defensive tackle "Mean" Joe Greene (75) flies at Cowboys running back Walt Garrison (32) during a game at Dallas in 1972. The drafting of Greene in 1969 was called by Steelers linebacker Andy Russell "the turning point in the history of the franchise."

Steelers playoff game. Walden, Mansfield, and Russell played in a Super Bowl, as did running back Rocky Bleier and left guard Sam Davis, rookie reserves on the 1968 squad.

Noll really didn't care whose feelings he hurt. Ask actor Ed O'Neill. He once scored four TDs in a game for Polk High but was cut by Noll in July. Noll didn't waste time in trading Bill Saul, selling Bob Wade, or cutting Clendon Thomas, backup tight end Richie Kotite, and poor Kenny Liberto. Black/White, drafted/undrafted—all Noll cared about was whether a man could play football.

"I'm convinced Noll is colorblind," said Bill Nunn, who quickly came around to Noll's savvy. Nunn, like Art Rooney Jr., attempted to get inside Noll's mind by asking questions about his view of Black athletes. "I'm prejudiced against bad athletes," Noll told the scouts. "I'm prejudiced against slow guys, dumb guys, bad actors. Get us people who can think on their feet, who are tough, strong, fast, people of good character, and I will teach them."

It was about this time that Greene ended his 23-day holdout and reported to camp. He was about to be taught some lessons by veteran leadership. Or so those veterans thought. On his first day, Noll directed the first-round pick to the Oklahoma Drill, where Ray Mansfield had been waiting, probably since Greene was drafted. Mansfield stepped up to face the rookie and winked at his teammates. But Mansfield was tossed out of the way with one arm by Greene, who quickly slammed the running back to the ground. The team grew quiet.

Bruce Van Dyke was next. Same thing. He was followed by Sam Davis. Same thing.

There was no more winking, or even talking. However, one young offensive tackle was overheard telling another, "We might as well pack our bags." Other linemen began moving back to the end of the line. Andy Russell called it the turning point in the history of the franchise. Joe Greene just wanted to know who was next.

✦ ✦ ✦

In the fall of 1969, Art Rooney Jr. flew to Shreveport, Louisiana, and from there drove to the Louisiana Tech campus near the Arkansas border. He stopped to see his good friend, Eddie Robinson, the coach of Grambling, and Robinson raved about Terry Bradshaw.

As a senior, Bradshaw's stats dipped a bit due to the blowouts and late-game reps given to the underclassman. Tech went 8–1, the only loss to Southern Miss on a late field goal.

At a December 10, meeting in Pittsburgh, Jack Butler and the BLESTO scouts made their final determination on the college seniors, and Bradshaw was No. 1. But Chuck Noll did have concerns. There was the story that Baylor and LSU had stopped recruiting Bradshaw because of his SAT scores. Noll directed Art Jr. to talk to a Tech alumnus who had worked with Noll under Sid Gillman. The source told Art Jr. not to believe the rumors, that Bradshaw was smart enough to run a pro offense. Noll was also concerned about the level of competition Bradshaw faced in the Gulf State Conference. Noll would seek clarity at the 1970 Senior Bowl.

✦ ✦ ✦

The Steelers won their first game under Chuck Noll—and then lost their next 13. "Miserable. Miserable. Miserable," was how Joe Greene described it. But Greene was causing just as much misery for opponents. He was ejected from his fourth game after knocking Fran Tarkenton out with a forearm shiver, while out of bounds, a full 1.5 seconds after the whistle. All-Pro Browns guard Gene Hickerson went up against Greene in mid-October and predicted greatness for the rookie. The next week the Redskins triple-teamed Greene, but he still sacked Sonny Jurgensen three times. Against the Bears, Dick Butkus was taking 10-yard runs at rookie center Jon Kolb and "giving him an ass-kicking," according to line coach Bob Fry. Kolb once fell to the ground and tripped Butkus, who chased Kolb to the sideline while threatening to kill him. Butkus was having so much fun he jumped on special teams and laid out L.C. Greenwood in front of the Steelers' bench. As Butkus stood over the rookie, Greene charged the field and grabbed Butkus by the shoulder pads with one hand, pulled his helmet in a threatening manner, and spit in his face. Butkus freed himself and trotted back to the middle of the field. As Andy Russell wrote, "There was a new baddest man in the NFL that day."

The following week, in the Cleveland rematch, Browns QB Bill Nelson threw an interception and ran to the sideline in stark terror as Greene pursued. Said Nelson's coach Blanton Collier about Greene: "He's the fastest 275-pounder I've ever seen. I don't know if he's faster than those other two rookies [Greenwood and Clarence Washington], but I can't remember if any team ever came up with three rookies like that in the same year."

The following week, Vikings coach Bud Grant called Greene "a 275-pound Alan Page." But Greene even put a chill into the great Vikings defensive tackle that day after Greene had been penalized for extracurricular "business" against a Vikings offensive lineman. As Greene was leaving the field, with benches on the same sideline, Page and Carl Eller mocked him. Greene went into the trainer's toolbox, grabbed a big pair of tape-cutting scissors, and spun toward the two while making slashing motions in their direction. Page and Eller both ran toward the stands. Greene surely wouldn't murder them in plain view of fans, would he?

Greene was voted the Associated Press Defensive Rookie of the Year with 31 of 46 votes. "I wouldn't want to play anywhere else, no matter what the record was," he said. "I'm a part of this team, and I want to grow with it. I've been very impressed with the coaching staff. They know what they're doing. They are building this team. They aren't trying to win it all in one year, but looking to the future."

✦ ✦ ✦

One of the most impressive athletes to enter the 1970 draft was busy finishing up school in Louisiana. He was a 6′3″, 203-pound cornerback/safety from Southern University in Baton Rouge, by way of Vidalia, Georgia, where Mel Blount was raised on a 2,700-acre dirt farm. He was one of 11 children and went barefoot around a home that had no plumbing or electricity. Mel attributed his 4.5 speed in the 40 to chasing rabbits for dinner. For his strength, Mel got up early every morning to stack tobacco for his father. On weekends, he and his brothers played what they called "country football."

The Blounts didn't have a TV, so Mel walked two miles to his friend's house to watch Lenny Moore, Ray Berry, and Night Train Lane play NFL football. Mel bragged to his friend that one day he would play in the NFL.

That day was coming. The Steelers secondary was being shredded, and by more than QBs. Chuck Noll wanted a whole new cast and was lopping defensive backs off his roster as quickly as possible. All he had left by draft day 1970 was the previous year's seventh-round pick, Chuck Beatty, undrafted rookie free agent Clancy Oliver, and journeyman acquisition Lee Calland. That was it. Thus, the interest in Blount.

Art Rooney Jr. had helped the Southern coaching staff with tickets to a 1969 Steelers exhibition game in Baton Rouge, so they returned the favor with inside info. But Bill Nunn had no choice but to include Blount on his *Courier* All-America team. Blount was a known commodity as the Southern team MVP his last two seasons while playing both cornerback and safety. Those were also the points of disagreement during the Steelers' draft prep for Noll's second draft.

"I thought Mel was a safety, long-legged and all," Nunn said in 2004. "Chuck thought he could play corner. We went back, and Chuck showed me film. And Chuck was right, naturally, because Mel's in the Hall of Fame. But I just felt that being as tall as he was, he'd have trouble. But the one thing I didn't take into consideration at the time was the bump and run. Mel could stymie you at the line of scrimmage."

✦ ✦ ✦

At the North-South Shrine Game in Miami, Terry Bradshaw was coached by the Florida State coach who three years earlier had sent him back to Tech. This time, the coach, Bill Peterson, played his own QB for three quarters, and Bradshaw—who had injured a hamstring while practicing on the uneven field surface—couldn't rally the squad in the fourth quarter. Bradshaw left the Shrine Game for Mobile, Alabama, and the Senior Bowl with "blood in my eye." He was driven to prove himself against the big-timers, but on the first day of practice, while running a 40-yard dash, he reinjured his hamstring. Bradshaw's coach, Don Shula, offered to send him home, but Bradshaw refused and at the end of the week played the entire game. He was named MVP of the Senior Bowl, even though he broke three ribs late in the game.

This toughness impressed Chuck Noll, who was still worried about Bradshaw's intelligence. BLESTO scout Dick Haley persuaded Bradshaw to take an IQ test, and the results said he was NFL-ready. Noll was satisfied, but the coin flip the day before the Senior Bowl game would determine whether the Steelers had the rights to Bradshaw. They and the Chicago Bears had finished 1–13 in 1969. The Pittsburgh *Post-Gazette* installed the Bears as three-point favorites in the flip as Noll and Dan Rooney arrived at the ballroom of the majestic Fairmont Hotel for the toss. Noll sat at the edge of the stage while Rooney went on stage with commissioner Pete Rozelle and the representative from the Bears, Ed McCaskey, the son-in-law of George Halas.

Art Rooney Sr. always preached to never call a coin flip first, to let the other person feel the pressure and make a mistake, so Dan looked at McCaskey and told him to call it. McCaskey called heads and the silver dollar hit the floor tails. A Chicago reporter shouted that McCaskey was a bum, while Rooney shrugged his shoulders about whom the Steelers would draft. Rozelle gave the coin to Rooney, who gave it to Noll that night at dinner with their wives. Rooney told Noll it was the beginning of good things to come.

✦ ✦ ✦

The draft comparisons of Terry Bradshaw to other top quarterbacks were coming in from national sportswriters:

"Built along the lines of Roman Gabriel."

"A clean-cut Joe Namath."

"A Namath with knees."

BLESTO director and former Steelers defensive back Jack
Butler called Bradshaw "Bobby Layne with an arm."

One Steelers scout wrote, "You could charge admission
to watch him warm-up."

Bradshaw's immense physical attributes were obvious,
but of course there were negatives. He was expected to have
trouble reading defenses, didn't know how to properly watch
film, wasn't a student of the game, was overly sensitive, and
would probably experience culture shock in the big city of
Pittsburgh.

The Steelers turned down 18 trade offers for the pick.
One team offered four regulars, a part-time fullback, and a
first-round pick. The Cardinals offered seven players, including safety Roger Wehrli, a member of the previous season's
All-Rookie team. Art Rooney Sr. was in fact showing interest
in a trade, and this worried Art Jr. The Chief spoke with the
general manager of the Atlanta Falcons and contemplated
an offer of multiple draft choices and a handful of veterans.
Art Jr. told him to ask for Claude Humphrey the next time
they called. The defensive end had been the third overall pick
of the 1968 draft, so when the Falcons called and the Chief
mentioned Humphrey, the talks ended.

Art Jr. felt he had talked his father out of making a surprise trade, but he began to worry about Chuck Noll. The
Chief called everyone together and made it clear they were

taking Bradshaw, and that ended the trade talk. So, on January 27, 1970, the Steelers drafted Terry Bradshaw. Noll told the media that Bradshaw was "the very best athlete in the country."

Any concerns?

"We were somewhat concerned about his competition, but when we got down to the Senior Bowl, he exhibited leadership qualities," Noll said. "He was not awed by the competition."

In the second round, the Steelers went back to North Texas State to draft wide receiver Ron Shanklin, whom they had scouted closely for three years.

With the first pick of the third round, the Steelers drafted a second foundational piece in the 1970 draft, 6'3" Southern University cornerback Mel Blount, who thought he should've been a first-round pick. Bill Nunn felt the same way, which is why he included Blount on his *Courier* All-America team. Blount became the first such honoree drafted by the Steelers since Ben McGee in 1964.

Blount arrived in Pittsburgh a few days later and one of the first players he met was center Ray Mansfield, who thought Blount was a new linebacker.

"My God," said Mansfield, "what a magnificent specimen."

Blount went upstairs to the eighth floor of the Roosevelt to meet with Noll. Blount told his new coach that he thought he would be drafted in the first round and that he saw himself as a starting NFL cornerback.

Looking out the window overlooking the city, Noll said, "I see championships."

5

THE PILLARS

THE PERFECT STORM that brought together the Rooney boys, Bill Nunn, and Chuck Noll resulted in the perfect start to a dynasty. In place on the field was the baddest man in the NFL, a quarterback with 82-yard Hail Mary capability, a 6'3" shutdown cornerback who would one day force an evolutionary rule change, a premier pass-rusher, and a strong, durable left tackle—pretty much all the parts necessary for the scripting of a football masterpiece. The drafts of 1969 and 1970, along with the UFA signing of Jim Clack, gave the Steelers seven Super Bowl starters and three Hall of Famers.

Among the leftovers from Bill Austin's team were Andy Russell, Ray Mansfield, Sam Davis, and Rocky Bleier. However, much work remained, particularly from a developmental standpoint in regard to rookies Terry Bradshaw and Mel Blount. Bradshaw signed ceremoniously at a folding table near where the 50-yard line would exist once the construction of Three Rivers Stadium was complete. As Bradshaw and Steelers officials walked out for the photo op, the construction workers stopped to applaud.

Because of lingering and nagging injuries, Bradshaw missed rookie camp in June and the College All-Star Game, but a four-day lockout/players' strike gave the rookies some alone time to make up for it. Bradshaw's unique delivery—with the index finger on the back point of the ball—caused a raised eyebrow, but Chuck Noll chose not to tinker with it.

The first preseason game rolled around. Bradshaw started the second half against Miami, and his rally from 13 points down fell short in a 16–10 loss, the Steelers' only loss that preseason. The Steelers beat the Vikings on the road and returned home for the first NFL game at the new stadium. The Steelers beat the Giants 21–6, and Bradshaw scrawled WINNERS over top of Noll's notes on the chalkboard. The Steelers then crushed the Patriots 31–3 in Shreveport, and the rest of the league began to take notice after a 20–6 win over the Raiders in their final preseason contest. Bradshaw threw two touchdown passes that game, including a 53-yarder to Ron Shanklin. Bradshaw also had an 89-yard touchdown run down the sideline called back because of a penalty.

"They're the most improved team I've ever seen in my life at any level," said Raiders coach John Madden.

Sportswriter Tex Maule went so far as to predict in *Sports Illustrated* that the Steelers, off a 1–13 season, would win their division. "The ultimate hex," wrote upstate New York sportswriter and admitted Steelers fan Joe Stein. "It's like breaking 13 mirrors while walking under a ladder. Teams usually go to pieces after Maule puts the evil eye on them."

Stein's warning proved prescient. The 4–1 preseason record may have been the best in Steelers history, but it didn't carry into the regular season as Bradshaw began a long NFL apprenticeship at quarterback. He started the 1970 opener against Houston, completed four of 16 passes, was tackled for a safety (the first of three consecutive games taking a safety), and was pulled in the fourth quarter to begin an 0–3 start.

Bradshaw and the Steelers won four of their next five games, but then the season collapsed. Bradshaw lost all confidence as the Steelers lost five of their last six and finished 5–9. "I would go home every night, and it was me and Johnny Carson," Bradshaw wrote. "Pathetic. I'd think so much about it, I'd start to cry."

He called his college coach and asked for film from his senior season in order to get his groove back, but he only studied the physical aspects of his throwing motion. Preston Pearson had to drive over to Bradshaw's apartment to teach him how to watch game film from a mental aspect.

Bradshaw would continue to struggle throughout his first four to five years in the league. Pittsburgh fans even cheered as he was being helped off the field with an injury in 1973. This enraged Joe Greene, who became—along with Art Rooney Sr.—Bradshaw's close confidant and morale booster. The friendships of those two men kept Bradshaw from falling apart and helped him grow into a legendary football player.

✦ ✦ ✦

Steelers QB Terry Bradshaw (12) watches from the sideline beside head coach Chuck Noll during a game in 1973. The four-time Super Bowl champion and Hall of Famer struggled through much of his first four years in the NFL.

Melvin Cornell Blount wasn't finding things any easier after a solid start. On October 18, in the fifth game of his rookie season, Blount replaced John Rowser in the starting lineup in Houston. Rowser injured his shoulder in a goal-line collision with O.J. Simpson the previous week in the Steelers' first win. Blount stepped in and intercepted his first pass to earn the job the following week. Blount escaped unscathed in a 7–3 Steelers win over the Oilers and started the rest of the season, but stood out more for his kickoff returns (29.7 yards per return).

Blount started 10 games in 1971 and for the most part was satisfactory. However, one game in 1971 began to define him—at least to fans. On November 14 in Miami, Blount gave up touchdown passes of 12, 86, and 60 yards to Paul Warfield as the Dolphins rallied from a 21–3 deficit to beat the Steelers. Blount had clearly been targeted.

"He'll be just fine," Noll told reporters.

"Warfield's beaten a lot of great ones in his day," said Andy Russell. "He beat another great one today."

"I'm not going to let it bother me," said Blount.

At least some were seeing Blount for what he was, or was going to be, but one of the Pittsburgh papers called him "the laughingstock of the Steelers' secondary." In succeeding games, Blount was booed so much the team halted its pregame introductions and Blount considered quitting.

Like Bradshaw, Blount turned to Carson, but in his case *Bud* Carson, who was hired in 1972 to coach the secondary. Blount—while experiencing public squabbles throughout the next few years with Carson—forever cited him as the person who turned his career around. At the end of the 1972 season, after not having allowed a touchdown pass all season, Blount was considered the most improved Steelers defender, and his career took off. He was the NFL Defensive Player of the Year in 1975, was credited for being Donnie Shell's primary mentor, was the cause of the "Mel Blount Rule" in 1978 that forever changed when defensive backs could contact receivers, and won his fourth Super Bowl ring early in 1980. Blount retired after the 1983 season as the Steelers' career interceptions leader with 57. The "magnificent specimen" that Ray Mansfield saw a few days after the 1970 draft missed only one regular-season game and one playoff game in his 14 seasons, playing in 219 games overall.

Late in Blount's career, when Olympic hurdling star Renaldo Nehemiah worked out for the Steelers at training camp, Nehemiah impressed onlookers with an Olympian-level vertical jump at the new measuring pole on campus. Blount, wearing wing-tipped shoes and a three-piece suit, stepped up and topped Nehemiah's jump by several inches.

"He was the most incredible athlete I've ever seen," said Jack Ham.

Blount and Bradshaw went into the Pro Football Hall of Fame together in 1989, with Blount paying homage to the guy who was responsible for bringing the foundational pieces together and building an organization for the ages, his presenter, Dan Rooney.

"He held everything together," Blount said during his induction speech. "He has great managerial skills and he's a good man. He's a good man for youngsters to try to be like. No one else meant so much in my life. He was the kind of guy you could go and talk to, not just as a football player but for any reason."

✦ ✦ ✦

The 1971 draft would be the first for the Steelers out of Three Rivers Stadium. The room was new, the desk was new, and so was the personnel director. The Steelers hired one of the BLESTO scouts, Dick Haley, but since an agreement had been

Steelers cornerback Mel Blount (47) and safety Donnie Shell (31) during a game in 1975, the season Blount was named Defensive Player of the Year. Jack Ham called Blount "the most incredible athlete I've ever seen."

in place that such scouts couldn't make lateral moves, Haley was officially hired to head player personnel. Art Rooney Jr. moved into one of three vice president roles, along with his brother Dan and Jack McGinley. Art Jr. was still in charge of personnel, but would travel less and coordinate more.

Chuck Noll missed a week of prep for what would become one of the greatest talent grabs in NFL history. Noll's father died, and he left for Cleveland immediately. He was brought up to speed by Art Jr. and Bill Nunn upon returning. Noll also talked to reporters, who knew the Steelers were looking hard at Frank Lewis, a wingback from Grambling with 42 career touchdowns. Noll was asked if he thought the Steelers, drafting eighth, would get Lewis.

"Maybe," Noll said. "If we don't take Jack Ham."

Ham was an All-America linebacker at Penn State, but the reporter had to stifle a chortle when he reminded Noll that 200-pound linebackers aren't normally drafted in the first round. "He's awfully quick and awfully fast," Noll said, before pointing to his head. "He's got it all up here."

✦ ✦ ✦

The Steelers hired Dan Radakovich to coach the defensive line in 1971, and he could take credit for being the first college or pro coach ever to see Jack Ham play. Not that "Bad Rad" remembered him.

Radakovich, the linebackers coach and architect behind the moniker "Linebacker U" at Penn State, had gone to a Westmont-Bishop McCort High School game in Johnstown, Pennsylvania, to recruit Westmont guard Gary Shafer. Ham, a 6'1", 165-pound junior offensive lineman, made no impression on Radakovich, who went back the next year to scout Bishop McCort linebacker Steve Smear.

Again, Ham made no impression on Radakovich. Ham had really only impressed the Virginia Military Institute and a local Division II school. So Ham went off to VMI's prep school, Massanutten, in Woodstock, Virginia, as a 6'2", 185-pound offensive guard/cover-2 cornerback.

Radakovich only heard about Ham because, when he went back to Bishop McCort in 1966, the head coach gave him a heads-up. He said that Ham could run and jump and possessed football intelligence. Another Penn State assistant, George Welsh, saw a Massanutten film but wasn't impressed with Ham.

About a month later, after the 40th and final scholarship had come open at Penn State, Radakovich and Welsh questioned Smear, who said Ham was his best friend and a good player.

Massanutten played seven games in 1966 against service academy prep schools and college freshman teams. Ham learned a lot of football and considered it a good experience. But after the year he realized he didn't want to live the military life and would attend Penn State as a student. He was granted a meeting with Radakovich, thanks to Smear, and the three of them met for brunch at the Corner Room on the Penn State campus. Radakovich had no memory of the meeting, but Ham remembered that Radakovich took one look at the skinny linebacker and asked, "Can you even tackle?" It was one of several brusque questions, and after Radakovich left, Ham turned to his buddy and said, "What's up with that guy?"

"That's just Rad," Smear said.

But Radakovich noticed some speed from Ham on film, and that speed, Rad and Welsh felt, was worth the final Penn State scholarship in 1967. When Joe Paterno found out that

Ham had accepted an offer, he scolded his two assistants for giving the last scholarship to someone who was going to pay his own way anyway.

Ham, of course, went on to become one of only two Penn Staters (Dave Robinson being the other) to end up in both the college and pro football halls of fame.

✦ ✦ ✦

Scouts around the league used to grumble about legendary Grambling coach Eddie Robinson telling Bill Nunn things he didn't tell the rest of them. Not that any of them needed to be told about Frank Lewis.

As a wingback in Robinson's wing-T offense, Lewis made 397 career catches and averaged 10.8 yards per carry. He was Hines Ward and Deebo Samuel before either was born. The Steelers coveted Lewis as a wide receiver because the abrupt trade of Roy Jefferson had left them with a WR corps comprised of only rookies in 1970. The Steelers needed a threat opposite Ron Shanklin, and Robinson told Nunn that Lewis was their man.

Of course, Nunn could see that with his own eyes. The primary receiver for QB James "Shack" Harris at Grambling was a two-time *Courier* All-American and played in the first football game at Three Rivers Stadium, where, against Morgan State, Lewis caught three touchdown passes for Grambling.

At 6'1", 196 pounds, Lewis was timed in the 100-yard dash at 9.4 seconds.

The Deep South was opening wide for the Steelers, and Art Rooney Jr. was off to pursue a couple of other players, both defensive linemen. One was nicknamed "Mad Dog." Dwight White wasn't rated highly by BLESTO, but Art Jr. had heard nothing but raves about White's intelligence and attitude from the East Texas State coach.

Another defensive lineman, Ernie Holmes, had been nick-named "Fats" as a child growing up in Jamestown, Texas, near the Louisiana border. His father, 300-pound Emerson Holmes, had young Ernie out working in his field one day when the coach at Texas Southern spotted him, talked to him, and offered him a football scholarship. Art Jr. saw Holmes on film and flew to Houston in 1970. He drove to Jeppesen Stadium with a Washington Redskins scout on a rainy night to watch Holmes play. Rooney claimed they were the only two White people in the stadium. He then learned that the Texas Southern coach was upset with the way the season was going, called his seniors "quitters," and changed all of their numbers to confuse NFL scouts. The two scouts walked over to the bench to figure things out, and the first guy they saw was Holmes. The player tried to get their attention by pointing to his number and shouting, "Fats! It's me! Fats!"

Rooney filed it away in his soggy notebook.

On his first day of spring practice at Penn State, Jack Ham was trying his best to keep tight end Ted Kwalick from releasing inside and getting up the seam. But Kwalick did just that—as All-Americans can and often do—and this drew the wrath of linebackers coach Dan Radakovich. He threw his hat at Ham, and then his whistle, and finally his clipboard. As he had the day he met Radakovich at the Corner Room, Ham looked around and asked to no one in particular, "What's up with that guy?" Ham's sophomore year in 1968 was better. It was the third year of the Joe Paterno era and the starter in front of Ham had moved on. Radakovich moved star middle linebacker Dennis Onkotz outside the first day of camp because he didn't think Ham was ready, but after three days Ham proved he was. Onkotz moved back inside, and Ham started the entirety of an undefeated season.

In 1969, Radakovich had grand plans for Ham as a coverage backer. Instead of keeping him on one side only, Ham was moved to the field side, where there was more room and thus more need for a linebacker who could cover.

Ham did more than cover backs and tight ends as the new "Fritz" backer. He covered slot receivers, too, such as Missouri's Mel Gray. The future three-time NFL first-team All-Pro didn't catch a pass in the 10–3 loss to Penn State in the Orange Bowl on the first day of 1970. Missouri's quarterback was asked after the game about Gray's goose egg and said, "I didn't see him the entire game."

In 1970, Ham, a senior, was a consensus All-American as the defensive captain. He was cited by Paterno as the catalyst for the turnaround from a 2–3 start. Penn State won its final five games, and Ham was named the finest defender in the East and MVP of the Hula Bowl.

As a three-year starter, Ham had played on two 11–0 teams and learned how to play linebacker in a complex cover-2 scheme. It helped immensely that he worked every day for three seasons against Kwalick—and any other flying object that came his way.

✦ ✦ ✦

The Steelers played their final game of the 1970 season in Philadelphia, and a season that once held promise at 4–4 ended with a 1–5 finish. Joe Greene was an all-world defensive tackle and in the finale had four sacks. Of course, he was being held every other play, and he warned the lineman in front of him that it had to stop. But it didn't, and that player had to be taken off the field on a stretcher. Mean Joe also warned the backup not to hold him, but the backup didn't listen, and he too left the field injured.

Out came the third guard to play opposite Greene. He was a rookie from North Texas State, a friend of Joe's, and Greene didn't want to hurt him. But the rookie held Greene, who became frustrated, and as the Eagles approached the line of scrimmage, he grabbed the ball and threw it out of bounds. Greene glowered at the official who brought out a new ball, and then picked it up and held it as if he was about to throw it. Andy Russell tried to calm Greene as the fans began to boo, but Greene heaved it into the second level of the stadium and walked off the field.

"It was like Bradshaw threw it," marveled Dan Rooney.

Chuck Noll didn't say a word to Greene as the Steelers ended the season 5–9 and would draft eighth at the end of the next month.

✦ ✦ ✦

Jack Ham considered himself "a frustrated strong safety" because he enjoyed playing pass defense so much, but he wasn't considered a great prospect. For one, eastern football lacked respect. And two, 238-pound Fred Carr and 225-pound Isaiah Robertson were considered the prototype linebacker prospects in 1971.

But a new age was unfolding. The NFL was beginning to look for coverage linebackers, and Chuck Noll was at the cutting edge of defensive football with an eye to his specialty, the back end. Ham had played cornerback at Massanutten and was the strong-side field backer in Penn State's cover-2 defense. He showed great vision and intelligence to go along with his speed, so Ham was a natural fit for Noll.

Still, even Ham felt throughout his college days that he might be too small to play in the NFL. Ted Kwalick, the great Penn State tight end, had felt the same way and pushed his weight up to 240 as he prepared for the NFL Draft in 1969. But Kwalick played poorly before getting his weight back down to 220 to become one of the league's greats. That lesson wasn't lost on Ham, who came to Pittsburgh for his pre-draft meeting with the Steelers at 215 pounds.

"It would be going too far to call Ham emaciated," Art Rooney Jr. wrote in *Ruanaidh: The Story of Art Rooney and His Clan*. "He was certainly fat-free."

Rooney thought Ham would be a project for the strength coach, and Ham did add 10 pounds before the start of the season, but Ham certainly didn't look like an NFL linebacker when Rooney met him prior to the draft.

At the meeting in Rooney's office, Ham didn't seem to care about the player names hung on the prospect board. That hadn't been the case with most players, particularly those who, like Ham, had their names listed near the top. Rooney wondered how Ham couldn't notice or whether he cared. Rooney let it go as Ham focused on their meeting. But, when Ham got up to leave, he reached up to straighten his name on the board. He smiled at Rooney and left. Great vision indeed.

✦ ✦ ✦

Art Rooney Jr. started draft day 1971 by writing Frank Lewis on the blackboard and underlining it three times. Lewis had shown great vision and explosiveness as a wingback at Grambling, and his legendary coach, Eddie Robinson, loved him. Bill Nunn loved Lewis enough to name him a *Courier* All-American twice. The Steelers had visions of the two Louisiana kids, Lewis and Terry Bradshaw, working together in the off-season and joining Ron Shanklin as one of the most dangerous pass offenses of the '70s.

Plunkett, Manning, Pastorini, and Riggins were among the names chosen before the Steelers picked eighth, and just before they made Lewis the pick, an assistant coach in the draft room shouted, "Hey, what about Jack Ham?"

Rooney told him they were sticking to their list, and that if Ham was still available in the second round, they would pick him then. And Ham was available. But when it came time for the 34th pick, the same coach shouted out for Bowling Green linebacker Phil Villapiano. Rooney wondered if the coach was joking before the Steelers drafted Ham.

"He's a winner," Chuck Noll told the media, and added that he appreciated "his brains...his intelligence," which was a credit to his preparation at Penn State.

"The transition was easy," Ham would say years later.

While scouting reports questioned Ham's size, those reports also included raves about his "leverage, vision, unerring anticipation.... Moving to the ball, he could not be blocked. He covered passes with the agility and speed of a defensive back."

Years later, when asked about a particular mismatch that a running back had on a young linebacker in coverage, Noll became testy. "Jack Ham had that assignment on every damn down, and teams knew it. People tried to exploit it and weren't able to. That allowed us to double-cover the wide receivers."

"When you watched Jack Ham on film, you felt like standing up and applauding," wrote Andy Russell.

Ham would finish his career with 32 interceptions, 21 fumble recoveries, 25.5 sacks, four Super Bowl rings, and one Hall of Fame jacket.

In the third round of the 1971 draft, the Steelers drafted running back Steve Davis, a serviceable reserve, and in the fourth round drafted a blocking tight end out of USC, Gerry "Moon" Mullins. Assistant coach Walt Hackett was Mullins' champion in the draft. The Steelers' defensive line coach saw Mullins as a future guard. However, Hackett never got to see his vision come to fruition. He died of a heart attack nearly three months after the 1971 draft and was replaced by Dan Radakovich, who actually did get to coach Mullins when he became offensive line coach in 1974. Radakovich, never shy, recalled walking through the USC facility with coaches one day, when he looked up at the photos of former Trojans who went on to NFL greatness. Mullins wasn't up there with the group, and this upset Rad. "You have the only guard in history that ever started and won four Super Bowls," he told the

USC coach. "You're supposed to be Offensive Line U and you don't even have his picture up there."

With an extra pick in the fourth round, courtesy of the previous year's trade of Roy Jefferson to the Colts, the Steelers drafted Dwight White, a defensive end out of East Texas State. White not only became a rookie starter on what would become known in 1972 as the Steel Curtain, he was an intelligent voice in the turbulent racial environment of the times.

The Steelers didn't realize the rich roll they were enjoying at the moment, but it didn't end with Lewis, Ham, Mullins, and Mad Dog. With the second pick of the fifth round, acquired from New Orleans for Don Shy, the Steelers drafted another blocking tight end, Larry Brown, out of Kansas.

Brown started out at Kansas as a tackle, moved to linebacker, defensive end, and then tight end as a senior. He caught two passes in his first two seasons with the Steelers, and in Super Bowl IX caught a touchdown pass. But it was blocking that would define Brown's career, particularly after he moved to right tackle in the middle of the 1976 season. Years later, Noll was asked which of his former players belonged in the Hall of Fame and the first name out of his mouth was Brown.

"And if Chuck would've listened to us and moved him to tackle earlier," said Nunn, "Larry Brown *would* be in the Hall of Fame."

"Talk to Steelers players from that era or later," said Radakovich. "In their opinion, Larry Brown wasn't just a great tackle, he was the best who ever lived."

"Larry Brown was the best offensive tackle I ever saw play the game," said Tunch Ilkin.

The Steelers also drafted future reserves Melvin Holmes and Ralph "Sticks" Anderson with additional picks in the fifth round, future reserve Craig Hanneman in the sixth round, and then in the eighth round they drafted a defensive tackle who became so good that he was convicted of shooting a cop and didn't miss a game. Ernie Holmes's name is still mentioned as A) the sometimes best Steelers defensive lineman, and B) an example of how forgiving Steelers management could be if the player was their sometimes best defensive lineman.

Better than Joe Greene? Holmes thought so.

"Joe Greene made a whole lot of people think they were better than they were," said Nunn.

It was Nunn, Greene, and future defensive line coach George Perles who helped Holmes get past his problems, particularly the day he shot at a helicopter and hit a police officer in the ankle after they trailed him on the Ohio Turnpike during a psychotic episode in 1973.

"He listened to Joe," Nunn said.

Holmes was eventually traded to Tampa Bay in 1978 for a couple of late-round picks.

In the 11th round of the '71 draft, the Steelers were just hoping to catch lightning in a bottle. Noll turned to Rooney to ask why the safety from Western Illinois with the great BLESTO computer numbers was still on the board. What did Rooney know about Mike Wagner?

Rooney told Noll that injuries had kept Wagner's production low as a senior, but that he hits hard and was a nice kid. Noll laughed. "Nice kids make good son-in-laws," he said. "I'd rather have tough guys."

Noll thought about it for a minute and said, "If he's smart, maybe we can do something with him," and then drafted Wagner—who would start two Super Bowls at strong safety and two Super Bowls at free safety—with pick No. 268.

Wagner became close with Ham, who provided the young safety with a defensive mantra: "It's not who takes the first step first, it's who takes the second step first."

Not done yet, the Steelers drafted another reserve, wide receiver Al Young, in the 13th round, and after the draft signed their starting free safety in two Super Bowls, Glen Edwards. He had been a running back out of Florida A&M who was known to Nunn but who was left off the *Courier* team. "Tough, fast, but trouble off the field," Rooney Jr. wrote in his memoirs. Edwards was the team's punt returner as a rookie in 1971, MVP of the 1974 team, warned the Vikings they "had better buckle up" in the tunnel before Super Bowl IX, and played in two Pro Bowls. He remained in Pittsburgh until the 1978 training camp, when he was benched for Donnie Shell, left the team, and was traded to the San Diego Chargers for a sixth-round pick.

In what's generally considered the second-best draft in team history, and among the greatest of all-time in the NFL, 11 draft picks along with free agents Edwards and Jim Brumfield made the 1971 team.

In Ham, the Steelers had their fourth future Hall of Famer in Noll's first three drafts. Those three drafts/post-draft signees included 15 Super Bowl starters.

6

THE PENN STATER

PENN STATE MAY have been without Jack Ham in 1971, but the Nittany Lions still ripped off 10 wins to open the season behind the backfield duo of halfback Lydell Mitchell and fullback Franco Harris.

In the 1970 and 1971 seasons combined, Mitchell rushed for 2,318 yards at 6.0 yards per carry with 32 touchdowns, and Harris rushed for 1,359 yards at 5.1 per carry with 14 touchdowns.

Art Rooney Jr.'s first visit to watch the Penn State backs seemed off to him. He liked Harris, the bigger back who could cut at full speed, but whenever Rooney asked Joe Paterno or members of his coaching staff about Harris, they turned the conversation to Mitchell. On his next trip, Rooney heard from the coaches that Harris was lackadaisical in practice, and again the conversations were steered toward Mitchell.

This puzzled Rooney, who thought Harris clearly had more size, power, speed, and seemed to make the big plays at the big times for Penn State. Unshaken, Rooney sought confirmation from Dick Haley, and the two agreed: there was no legitimate comparison between the two backs—Harris was clearly the better pro prospect.

Penn State finally lost in Game 11 at Tennessee and four weeks later played in the Cotton Bowl against Texas. That week, Harris came out for practice a few minutes late after being taped. This angered Paterno, and he warned Harris in front of the team that he would be demoted if it happened again. Harris felt the need to test Paterno, and the next day he sat inside and came out exactly three minutes late, on purpose. True to his promise, Paterno didn't start his fullback, which raised more questions with scouts.

According to Penn State historian Lou Prato, Paterno thought the action would stimulate the team. "In fact," Prato wrote, "it solidified the team behind Harris, and the Nittany Lions went out and upset Texas 30–6, in what is considered one of the turning-point games in Penn State's football history."

"I was very upset with the consequences of not starting in the Cotton Bowl," Harris told Prato. "I did get to play. I didn't have a lot of yards, but felt I had a really good game, in blocking and doing other things. Then because of that, when they were talking about me being drafted, they talked about Franco being a problem kid. I called Joe about that, and he said, 'Don't worry about it. If anybody calls me, we know you're not a problem.'"

✦ ✦ ✦

The Steelers' 1971 season didn't go nearly as well, but the promise was obvious. First-round pick Frank Lewis caught a 38-yard touchdown pass on the first play of the first camp scrimmage, and second-round pick Jack Ham, the coverage linebacker, was proving rugged against the run, too. He was also compounding his football intelligence by soaking in all that veteran linebacker Andy Russell had to teach him.

Rookie Mike Wagner earned his job almost immediately when incumbent strong safety Chuck Beatty was injured in the first preseason game.

Another newcomer provided a huge impact in 1971. Dan Radakovich spent 1970 coaching at the University of Cincinnati in order to attend law school, and Noll had agreed to allow him to continue his studies at night at Duquesne. This pleased Ham, and not just because he would have a friendly ear at the start of his pro career. "He's the best linebacker coach I ever had," Ham wrote in the foreword to *Football Nomad*, "and I watched him overhaul that defensive line and turn them into the Steel Curtain."

The first thing "Bad Rad" did with the Steelers' defensive line was make them faster. He got the 40 times and devised a plan. Joe Greene at 5.1 wasn't moving from left defensive tackle, but L.C. Greenwood ran a 4.6, and Rad watched him lap *everyone* in the 12-minute conditioning run the first day of camp. Greenwood had to be moved off the bench and put next to Greene at left defensive end. Rookie Dwight White ran a 4.7 at 235 pounds and was perfect for right defensive end. The displaced veteran ends, Lloyd Voss and Ben McGee, would rotate with Chuck Hinton at right defensive tackle. Another rookie, Ernie Holmes, ran a 5.1 at 270 pounds, and that grabbed Rad's attention. "A block of granite," he said of Holmes, who just needed to learn to keep his feet moving upon contact.

Another assistant told Rad that Greenwood wouldn't last a game, told him how Dick Butkus had knocked him out cold a few years ago on special teams. "Well, hell, Butkus does that to everybody," Rad said.

So after two weeks of camp, he took his plan to Noll, and Noll agreed and immediately made the moves. They would be dubbed the Steel Curtain three months later, but the line didn't come into its full potential until Holmes—who was kept on the taxi squad his rookie year—moved to right tackle late in the 1972 season. Even then, the line wasn't truly feared until 1973, or as author Roy Blount Jr. put it, "until the incident" with Holmes.

The week before the last preseason game, Rad recommended to Noll that he move Ham inside to replace 11-year veteran Chuck Allen. But two days later, Henry Davis, whom Ham was behind at left outside linebacker, showed up injured at practice, so Ham started at LOLB in that preseason finale—and intercepted Fran Tarkenton three times.

Noll was ecstatic about Ham's coverage skills, so Rad, seeing that his boss appreciated tough, well-coached coverage 'backers, told Noll about another Penn State linebacker, Dennis Onkotz, a 1970 third-round pick by the Jets who was coming back from a broken leg. The Steelers heard Onkotz had healed and in late September traded one of their excess veteran defensive tackles, Hinton, to the Jets for Onkotz.

Hinton had a big game the next week and was named NFL Defensive Player of the Week. That same week, Onkotz limped around the Steelers' practice field, far from healed. A defensive assistant put a newspaper clipping on Rad's desk with a note that read, "You traded the NFL Defensive Lineman of the Week for a one-legged cripple. Congratulations!" Onkotz never did play for the Steelers, but Ham had a position locked up and his Hall of Fame career was underway.

✦ ✦ ✦

In the 1971 opener in Chicago, the Steelers had a 15–3 lead late in the game but fumbled two consecutive possessions and lost 17–15. In a rage, Joe Greene fired his helmet, and it smashed into the crossbar and shattered. Greene was sick of losing, but by November he would tell reporters, "The Steelers are the team of the '70s."

Six rookies started in the home opener, and the Steelers beat the Bengals 21–10. The defense received a standing ovation after the game, and Greene earned his first game ball. He said it should've been given to Dwight White, the rookie stationed at the next locker.

Another rookie stood out the following week. In a 21–17 win over the Chargers, the young Steelers defense held throughout three goal-line stands in the final quarter to preserve the win. Jack Ham intercepted John Hadl at the goal line to uphold the second stand, and on the third, on fourth-and-goal from the 3, Ham came from out of seemingly nowhere to break up a pass by Hadl on what appeared to be a certain touchdown.

The Steelers lost their second, third, and fourth road games of the season to fall to 3–4. But back home, L.C.

Greenwood sacked quarterback Bill Nelson on third-and-11 at the Pittsburgh 30 and then blocked the ensuing punt for the turning point in a win over the Browns.

Greene, speaking a few nights later in Meadville, Pennsylvania—equidistant from Pittsburgh and Cleveland—said, "The way we're improving, we won't have any trouble beating the Browns for the next 10 years."

The defensive line had been dubbed "Steel Curtain" in a radio contest. It beat out "The Mean Green Machine," "Noll's Knockers," "The Bang Gang," and, mercifully, "God's Little Ackers." The winner was flown to Miami, but the Steelers lost there after blowing a 21–3 lead to the Dolphins, who would represent the AFC in that season's Super Bowl.

So many rookies were playing well, but No. 1 pick Frank Lewis was struggling with only two catches in 12 games while playing behind Ron Shanklin and Dave Smith.

The Steelers won their first road game in their final attempt of the season, 21–13, at Cincinnati, and now had a chance for their first non-losing season in eight years. Terry Bradshaw had been benched for the Bengals game, but entered and rallied the team to the win. He was now hoping to end his season on a positive note against the 7–5–1 Los Angeles Rams in the finale. The Rams were quarterback by 10-year veteran Roman Gabriel, to whom Bradshaw had been compared the day he was drafted.

"In 1962 I had an arm like that," Gabriel said leading up to the game. "But I'll take my head in '71. My arm's not that bad. He has to learn to read defenses."

In the game, Bradshaw threw two touchdown passes to Gabriel's one, but Bradshaw also threw four interceptions to

Gabriel's none, and the Rams won 23–14, as the Steelers finished 6–8, their third consecutive losing season under Noll.

✦ ✦ ✦

The 1971 Steelers allowed a 57.6 percent completion rate and 198 passing yards a game to rank last in the NFL. A cornerback would help in the coming draft, but middle linebacker was still a problem, and tight end was a weakness. The offensive line was coming together. The backfield was in the capable hands of Preston Pearson and fullback Frenchy Fuqua, but Chuck Noll certainly wanted more than capable from the position heading into 1972.

The scouting department was bolstered by the hiring of Tim Rooney (son of the Chief's brother, Duke) off the Villanova coaching staff. He was hired to start up the pro personnel department. Noll and Dick Haley had discussed the possibility of free agency one day in the NFL and wanted someone to track the development of all players throughout the league, as well as scout future opponents. The fact that Rooney had coaching experience would help in that regard.

In January 1972, Rooney watched film with the rest of the scouts, and they came to a consensus around one player, if he was available, at pick No. 13: Willie Buchanon, a cornerback from San Diego State.

There was far from a consensus on the alternative, and the camps lined up behind running backs Franco Harris of Penn State and Robert Newhouse of Houston. The camp led by Chuck Noll liked Newhouse, a bowling-ball type who was fast and strong. Harris, at 6'2", 220, was a fullback, but Noll wasn't looking for a lead blocker. He wanted split backs who could block for each other and catch passes and run inside and outside. Harris could do all of that, but Noll didn't like big backs. He thought they lacked agility. Newhouse, at 5'10", 205, was more Noll's style because he liked balance, quickness, and Newhouse's body control. Noll also didn't like the reports questioning Harris's moodiness and work ethic.

The debate raged in the draft room the day running backs were discussed. "Pure emotion took over, especially in my own case," said Art Rooney Jr., leader of the Harris camp. "Let's say I was carried away."

Art Jr. came prepared that day. He had asked George Young about the backs, and Young was a highly respected assistant with the Colts and had worked alongside Noll. Art Jr. knew Noll would listen to Young, who said, "Tell Chuck that question was settled over 2,000 years ago when Socrates said, 'A good big man is better than a good little man any day.'"

It was a precursor to the Planet Theory that Young used to build the Giants into a power in the 1980s, but back in 1972 Noll laughed it off and continued to argue that Newhouse should be at the top of the Steelers' running backs list.

On that note, the meeting ended. And with the offensive line to be discussed the next morning, Art Jr. knew he had to be proactive and come in with fresh info before opening the topic again. So he solicited the opinions of friends who had scouted both backs, and Art Jr. put their assessments on tape for Noll. But Noll merely responded that Art Jr. was asking leading questions.

Art Jr. believes Dan Radakovich ultimately convinced Noll to draft Harris. Radakovich was on the move again. The Football

Nomad was moving on to Boulder, Colorado, to coordinate the Buffs' defense. Noll asked him to stick around through the February 1 draft to watch film and write reports, and it proved helpful because Radakovich had coached Harris through two weeks of linebacker drills the spring of his freshman year at Penn State and called him "quick as a cat." Rad also watched Harris practice two years as a Penn State running back, and he too loved how the big man cut at full speed. Rad told Noll that Franco had some misunderstandings and was perhaps over-sensitive, but at his core was a good person, that Franco was a good student, smart and quiet. "If you draft him, you won't regret it," Rad told Noll. But Rad also wondered why Franco didn't look as good his senior year as the previous two years.

With the Steelers on the clock, Noll turned to Radakovich, who said, "Take him."

"Well," Noll said, "let's take the Penn Stater." Noll then turned to Art Jr. and said, "You'd better be right." Noll left to talk to Harris on the phone and came back and told Radakovich that Harris seemed to lack energy.

"Chuck, he's just a shy, quiet kid," Radakovich said. "Believe me. He's smart. You'll like him."

✦ ✦ ✦

Franco Harris was the 13th pick of the 1972 draft and became another structural pillar of the dynasty that was being built. He was so good that Chuck Noll even admitted he was wrong a year later. Noll walked in on Art Rooney Jr. and the scouts watching film of Chuck Foreman and again expressed his same concerns about a big back's agility. "But I'm probably wrong about this guy the way I was wrong about that Penn Stater last season," Noll said.

The interesting part of Franco's ancestry was that his mother, Gina, had been hiding in the mountains overlooking Pisa, Italy, when the Germans occupied her village. One day she woke up to see her village on fire. Her brother was killed by the Nazis, but she made it out. She told the *New York Times*, "It was my destiny to live. Just like Franco's destiny was to play for the Pittsburgh Steelers."

Art Jr.'s scouting report on Franco proved prophetic: "Outstanding body control. Strength to break tackles and the movement and speed to be a big threat outside or in the open field.... Would give us a big gun in the backfield."

But what about his below-average 40 time?

"You know better than to get me started on 40 times," Bill Nunn said in 2004. "Franco ran a 4.75 but very seldom got caught from behind. That's competitive speed. There are different kinds of speed."

Harris was helped in Pittsburgh by his old teammate Jack Ham, who also chided him relentlessly about Lydell Mitchell. But Ham, with a kind streak behind the teasing, had a great sense of humor that loosened Franco up. The Penn State tandem would prove to be huge for the Steelers in the coming years.

The Steelers also filled some depth issues in the 1972 draft by selecting right tackle Gordon Gravelle in the second round, pass-catching tight end John McMakin in the third round, and defensive tackle Steve Furness in the fifth.

One particular prospect remained at the top of the Steelers' draft board, and it was making Nunn ornery. The

Steelers really didn't have a need for a third quarterback, but when Nunn was asked by Noll why he was bothered, Nunn said, "That name up there," pointing to Joe Gilliam. "That's what's wrong with football."

Gilliam, the son of Nunn's former college backcourt mate, Joe Gilliam Sr., had a rocket-launcher of a right arm and threw with a pure and easy motion. Nunn and Redskins scout Bobby Mitchell had first-round grades on Gilliam, who purposely ran his 40 slower so that he wouldn't be moved to another position. The *Courier* had named him the Collegiate Back of the Year as a two-time All-American, but he was, after all, a Black quarterback.

Gilliam's mother was a bit worried about Joe Jr. in the NFL, but only because of the money. "Joey is indulgent," she said. But his father, Joe Sr., had been the QB coach of superstar QB Roy Curry, a former Steelers draft pick who was moved to wide receiver by Buddy Parker. So Joe Sr. called Nunn before the 1972 draft to ask if his son would be drafted. Nunn told him to call Dan Rooney, and he promised Joe Sr. that his son would be drafted.

Well, it was late in the second day of the draft, and Joe Sr. called Dan Rooney back to remind him of his promise. Rooney told him the Steelers would draft his son in the next round, and true to his word Rooney drafted Joe Gilliam Jr. in the 11th round.

"Yes I think color entered into the matter," Gilliam Jr. told reporters after the draft, "but there isn't anything I can do about that."

Would Gilliam play another position?

"I have only been taught the game at the quarterback's position," he said. "They will not ask me to play any other position."

Meanwhile, back in his office, Art Rooney Jr. took a call from an anonymous source who wondered why in the world the Steelers had drafted Gilliam. "This guy's into drugs," the caller told Art Jr., who hung up and hoped it was just a bad rumor.

✦ ✦ ✦

Franco Harris arrived late to training camp due to the College All-Star Game, but he would say later that he immediately felt the vibe of a winner. However, those winners weren't feeling that vibe from Franco. Vets wondered about his picking style and ponderous running nature. His position coach was one of those worriers.

"He gets there late and he's behind and I'm spending time with him, and boy, he doesn't look very good those first few weeks," said Dick Hoak. "We're all wondering, *What the heck?*"

"I didn't think he could make the team," said Ray Mansfield.

There was another new running back in camp. Well, Rocky Bleier wasn't exactly new, but his ability was. Drafted by the Steelers in the 16th round in 1968, Bleier went to Vietnam and in August 1969 was ambushed by Viet Cong. While crawling through a rice paddy, Bleier was shot in the left thigh. Later, grenade shrapnel penetrated his right leg and foot. He made his way to safety with the help of an unknown soldier who carried Bleier over his shoulder to a Medevac helicopter. Doctors told Bleier his football career was over, but Art Rooney Sr. felt beholden to Bleier and sent a postcard that read, "Rock. The team's not doing well. We need you. Art Rooney." Rooney told equipment manager Tony Parisi to keep Bleier's locker intact while he started on his painful road back to football the next summer. Those who saw Bleier run in 1970 were certain he would never play. But Bleier improved from awful to merely bad in 1971 and startled the team in 1972 by ripping off a 4.5-second 40. But even Bleier wasn't impressed with the new first-round pick.

"Lazy," Rocky said of his first impression of Franco.

Jack Ham told the veterans not to worry about Harris, and in the first preseason game Franco showed why by breaking out of a tackle behind the line and bolting 76 yards for a touchdown. It was a one-play masterwork of vision and explosiveness, traits that would mark Harris's Hall of Fame career. After the game, Chuck Noll told Hoak not to over-coach him.

"The scheme fit my running style perfectly," Franco told reporter Stan Savran years later.

✦ ✦ ✦

The Steelers opened the 1972 season by beating the Raiders, but then lost to the Bengals 15–10 on five Horst Muhlman field goals. At St. Louis, the Cardinals blocked a punt with 3:03 left to take a 19–18 lead, but Terry Bradshaw's 38-yard touchdown pass to Frank Lewis with 66 seconds left was the game-winner. A loss to the defending champion Cowboys evened the Steelers' record at 2–2, as first-round pick Franco Harris was sitting on 79 yards rushing at 3.0 per carry.

With Preston Pearson injured, Harris got the start the following week against Houston, and the rookie rushed for 115 yards. For the next 11 years, the only games he missed were due to injury.

Of course, not every game was perfect. The following week against the Patriots, Franco rushed for only 27 yards but promised himself, "No more ups and downs." And he embarked on a streak of six consecutive 100-yard games to tie Jim Brown's NFL record.

It wasn't just the running game propelling the Steelers through a 5–1 midseason run. In the 33–3 win over the Patriots, QB Jim Plunkett was sacked six times before Dwight White knocked him out of the game with a forearm shiver to the head. "They never quit coming at you," Plunkett said. It was also a coming-out party of sorts for Ernie Holmes, who, in rotating with Ben McGee at right defensive tackle, was dominating offensive linemen. "Watch the guards he plays against come off the field," said Chuck Noll. "They're always limping. He hurts people." Before the game Noll had decided to trade starting flanker Dave Smith and start Lewis opposite Ron Shanklin. It all added up to a blowout, with a trip to "the Rockpile" in Buffalo up next. O.J. Simpson rushed for 189 yards, with the help of a 94-yard touchdown run, but the Steelers' offense carried the day in the Steelers' 38–21 win. Bills coach Lou Saban was impressed with Bradshaw. "He's come a long way. So has the team."

Bradshaw had one of his best games the following week, and the defense held Muhlman to five points in a 40–17 thrashing of the Bengals. The two Franks, the Steelers' last two first-round picks, had big games. Lewis caught two touchdown passes and Harris rushed for over 100 yards. "Franco Harris broke more tackles in the Chiefs game than I have seen any back do in a long time," Noll said. That was in response to a question Noll had been asked about the improvement of his offensive line. "If you get a great back, all of a sudden you've got a good line," he said.

Jack Ham also had a big game against the Chiefs. His two fumble recoveries in the fourth quarter sparked the rally for the 16–7 win. Ham made seven solo tackles, three behind the line, had three unassisted tackles, and broke up a big pass play. He was named NFL Defensive Player of the Week and even received a standing ovation in church that night.

Bradshaw continued his up-and-down roller coaster ride by throwing three interceptions against the Chiefs. Later that week, the Steelers acquired cornerback John Dockery, who had played for the Jets in Super Bowl III. Dockery said of his new surroundings, "This team is easily as good as our Super Bowl team." He explained the difference was that his former team had come together around Joe Namath, and the Steelers didn't have that. "Bradshaw is not Namath—yet," Dockery said.

The four-game win streak ended in Cleveland, but the 7–3 Steelers rebounded with home wins over the Vikings and Browns. Franco provided some playoff foreshadowing by scooping up a Bradshaw fumble and running 80 yards against the Vikings. It was called back, but Franco's instincts impressed his running backs coach. "He has a knack," said Dick Hoak. "He always runs to the ball."

The Steelers needed to win their final two games on the road to clinch the division title. The first, a 9–3 win at Houston, is considered Joe Greene's greatest game. With the Steelers' offensive line beat up, Bradshaw out with a dislocated finger and Terry Hanratty home injured, rookie Joe Gilliam entered the 3–3 game at quarterback. On the sideline watching, Greene told Andy Russell that the 1–11 Oilers couldn't score another point, that the defense would have to win the game. To that end, Greene blocked a 25-yard field goal at the end of the first half and then went in at halftime and told the offense to just give him one field goal. They gave him two, and Greene set both of them up. On the first, he fought through three blockers to strip-sack QB Dan Pastorini and then recovered the fumble. On the second, Greene nearly intercepted a handoff in blowing up the play and causing a fumble at the Houston 13 for the six-point lead. Just in case Pastorini had any ideas about a late touchdown, Greene sacked him on third down and again on fourth down. Greene even helped Pastorini up and said, "Keep cool, kid. Everyone has days like this."

Not everyone had days like Greene's. He recorded five sacks, forced two fumbles, recovered one, blocked a field goal, and received the game ball from Russell on the flight home.

One more win and the Steelers would clinch their first title of any kind in team history. At San Diego, Franco rushed for only 34 yards, but the Steelers intercepted John Hadl four times—twice by Ham—and Ray Mansfield and Jim Clack hoisted Noll onto their shoulders in celebration. This time, on the flight home, Russell gave the game ball to the Chief as 5,000 fans awaited their arrival at the airport.

✦ ✦ ✦

The Steelers were making history and so was Kent State, a small MAC school that was coming together over its football team almost two-and-a-half years after four students were massacred on campus by government troops. The Golden Flashes needed one more win late in 1972 to not only claim their first MAC title, but to play in their first-ever bowl game.

There was a problem, though. The quarterback had broken a team rule and would be suspended for the regular-season finale unless he could "run, roll, and crawl" the 100-yard field 100 times. The QB said no, that he would take his punishment and sit the game out. Kent State wasn't expected to win the game without him, so the defensive captain made an appeal.

"Look, asshole," Jack Lambert told the quarterback, "do the drill. I'll do it with you. It's going to be tough, but if you don't finish it, I will kill you."

The QB did the drill. He vomited halfway through, but Lambert dragged him to the finish line. Once there, Lambert looked down disgustedly at the quarterback and said, "I think I'll kill you anyway."

✦ ✦ ✦

The Steelers were 3.5-point favorites over the Raiders in the first round of the AFC playoffs at Three Rivers Stadium, and the Steelers were making Las Vegas look smart with their 6–0 lead late in the fourth quarter. But we all know what happened next: Ken Stabler tightroped the sideline 30 yards for a touchdown with 1:17 left and a 7–6 Raiders lead. The

Steelers matriculated the ball to their 40-yard line and faced fourth-and-10 with 22 seconds left and no timeouts. Their coach remained calm.

"He still thought we'd win," Terry Hanratty said after watching Chuck Noll on the sideline. "He called those final pass patterns very calmly. He knew something would break. It was weird."

The Chief wasn't as optimistic. He put his cigar out and got up to leave his box. A security guard tried to console him by bringing up next year. The Chief nodded. He wanted to talk to his players in the locker room, so he and six friends got on the elevator while Terry Bradshaw was in the huddle calling 66 Option.

The Chief, of course, missed what many consider the greatest play in football history as Bradshaw's pass to Frenchy Fuqua was broken up by Jack Tatum. The deflection was scooped up by Franco Harris and run all the way to the end zone for the first playoff win in franchise history.

"I was always taught to go to the ball," Harris explained.

In the locker room, Noll hugged Franco and told him it was the greatest play he ever saw. To the team, Noll told them he was proud but veered quickly to talking about next week. To the press, Noll said, "If Frenchy didn't touch the ball, and Tatum didn't touch the ball, well, the rule book doesn't cover the hand of the Lord."

Luck ran out the following week in the person of Larry Seiple. A star running back, pass receiver, defensive back, and punter at the University of Kentucky, the Miami punter had caught 41 passes for the Dolphins in 1969 and run six fake punts to that point in his career, each time successfully picking up the first down. Seiple did it again to turn around the AFC Championship Game for the undefeated Dolphins. Before taking off on his first carry of the season, Seiple saw every defender but Barry Pearson turning to set up a return. So Seiple took off. He avoided Pearson and gained 37 yards to set up the tying touchdown, as the Dolphins went on to the first and thus far only perfect season in NFL history.

✦ ✦ ✦

For as much capital as the Steelers had invested in their receiving corps, first-round pick Frank Lewis was forever dealing with a nagging injury, second-round pick Ron Shanklin stopped improving, and third-round pick John McMakin caught only 21 passes as the "receiving" tight end his rookie season. So, the general consensus was that in the 1973 draft the Steelers would need a wide receiver, tight end, and an interior offensive lineman to groom behind Ray Mansfield. But Bob Smizik of the *Pittsburgh Press* believed the team's primary need was a cornerback to replace John Rowser.

Smizik was right on the mark as the Steelers drafted cornerback J.T. Thomas, the first Black starter at Florida State. With Thomas in hand, the Steelers that day traded Rowser to the Broncos.

The Steelers believed they drafted a "can't miss" prospect in the second round, but right after defensive back Ken Phares was selected, the Chief got a call from one of his sources that Phares had a bad knee. Steelers scouts countered that Phares's coach had convinced them the knee was healed. The Chief countered that his source was very well connected.

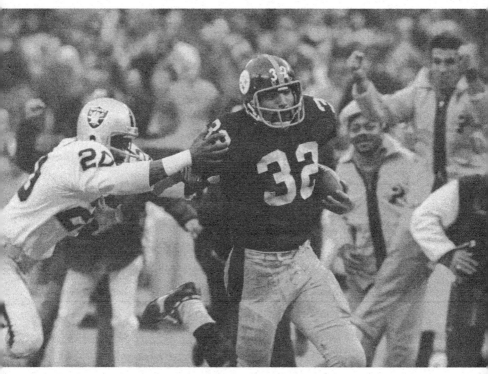

Franco Harris's "Immaculate Reception" against the Oakland Raiders on December 23, 1972, gave the Steelers their first playoff win in franchise history and marked the beginning of a run of Steelers dominance in the 1970s that resulted in four Super Bowl titles.

Once Phares showed up, he was reexamined, and Chuck Noll was told he was healing properly, that the surgery had been a success. But on the second play of the first drill of rookie camp, Phares's knee collapsed, and he never played again. It resulted in a thin draft, but also in the Steelers bringing prospects in before the draft for physicals, which led to BLESTO doing the same, which led to the NFL Combine, which led to the draft being moved into the spring.

The Steelers did find, in 1973, one sleeper prospect in linebacker Loren Toews, who was drafted in the eighth round. Art Rooney Jr. tells the story of a Boy Scout approaching him in the stands on a "Good Deed for the Day" event during the 1972 Cal intra-squad game in Berkeley. The Boy Scout asked Rooney what he was doing, and Art told him he was scouting. "Are you watching Toews? He's my brother," the Boy Scout said. When Rooney saw Toews on his BLESTO prospect list, he began taking a particular interest, primarily because of the Boy Scout.

That Boy Scout grew up to become University of Washington All-America lineman Jeff Toews, a second-round pick of the Dolphins who spent seven years in the NFL. Loren Toews grew up to start for the Steelers in a Super Bowl and spent 10 years in the NFL.

✦ ✦ ✦

The 1973 season was the next step for the Steelers. They were coming off their first division title and first playoff win in franchise history, and even though they didn't win more games, or advance further in the playoffs, that season continued the process of grinding the unit into arguably the greatest football team of all-time.

At training camp, the continued development of halfback Rocky Bleier was noted for his additional 20 pounds and 129 yards on 20 preseason carries in three games. And then there was the helicopter that flew past the St. Vincent College training facility with teammates teasing their big guy with "Easy, Fats." Ernie Holmes understood the humor, one time telling a young offensive lineman, "Son, you keep holdin' me like that, and we're gonna have another Ohio Turnpike out here."

"I feel sorry for whoever is playing in front of him this year," said Holmes' roommate Joe Gilliam.

The 1973 season opened with four consecutive wins, a loss at Cincinnati, and then four more wins. But a dreadful three-game losing streak followed. The quarterback carousel had devolved into three-part chaos as Terry Bradshaw still hadn't developed consistency in his fourth season.

One writer noted after watching the quarterbacks leave meetings with Chuck Noll that "Bradshaw looked whipped, Gilliam looked mad, and Hanratty was just smiling and shaking his head."

Joe Greene realized where his bread would be buttered and became more of a champion of Bradshaw's early in 1974 as the two foundational pieces came together as unit leaders for an unprecedented championship run throughout the remainder of the decade.

Greene clearly had been a foundational leader all along, but after the '73 season ended in Oakland with a 33–14 playoff loss, Greene told writer Phil Musick, "Something's missing. We lack that thing you can't see, that one intangible that all football teams who are winners have. Something is missing."

As reserve lineman Craig Hanneman told author Roy Blount Jr. on the sideline, the Steelers were about three bricks shy of a load.

7

THE BRICKS

THE NO. 1 overall pick of the legendary 1974 NFL Draft was Ed "Too Tall" Jones, who played for Tennessee State, the defending Black college national champion. Jones was a two-time All-American, but only after switching sports. He went to Tennessee State as a basketball player, and after a couple of years switched to football. The equipment manager wasn't prepared for a 6'9" defensive lineman and gave him a uniform that was too short. Or, in other words, the player was Too Tall.

Jones and another intriguing defensive prospect, middle linebacker Waymond Bryant, played in the 1973 Thanksgiving Day game against rival Alabama A&M, led by a receiver named John Stallworth. Bill Nunn counted two other scouts at the game, and he hoped they were there to see the TSU players because he was there to see Stallworth.

Stallworth grew up two hours south of the A&M campus in Tuscaloosa, Alabama. As a child, Stallworth thought he had contracted polio and, while in a hospital bed, vowed to be remembered for his achievements. At Tuscaloosa High, Stallworth was a running back who dreamed of playing for the big school in town. But Alabama coach Bear Bryant thought Stallworth ran too upright, so Stallworth went to Division II Alabama A&M in Huntsville, near the Tennessee border.

Stallworth was tall and thin and no doubt hit the hole too high, but he became an exceptional wide receiver at A&M, and Nunn wanted to see him play against one of the best Black college football teams in the country. Stallworth caught 13 passes that day and was so good Nunn became obsessed with the other two scouts at the game. Nunn knew, at that point, that his ploy of leaving a player off his *Courier* All-America team had become a tip-off as to whom the Steelers *really* liked.

Teams had already heard about Stallworth. In fact, he had been invited to participate in the Senior Bowl in less than two months. Before then, Stallworth had a pro day in Huntsville. Nunn had timed him in the 40 the previous year at 4.6, but on this day Stallworth was suffering the effects of a hip pointer and ran a 4.8 for a group of disappointed scouts. Nunn and the others went back to their hotel, but the next day Nunn told them to go on ahead to the airport without him, that he wasn't feeling well. Nunn, though, was feeling fine. He just wanted to time Stallworth again.

The great scout showed up at Stallworth's dorm room, and the surprised wide receiver—who knew only one NFL scout by name, this one—agreed to run again. For this run,

Nunn took him to a better track, and after Stallworth ran, he asked Nunn how he did. All Nunn said was, "It was okay."

Nunn had one more errand to run. He had done a solid for the A&M coach six years earlier, so that coach agreed to let Nunn take film canisters of Stallworth home. Nunn, in particular, wanted the film of the Tennessee State game, and he got it. This was the game that Nunn worried the other two scouts in attendance that day would show their bosses.

Nunn brought the film home to Pittsburgh and showed it to Dick Haley and Art Rooney Jr., who thought Stallworth looked like the great Don Hutson.

Nunn then showed the film to Chuck Noll, who called Stallworth a definite first-rounder.

Nunn showed the film to WRs coach Lionel Taylor, and the QBs coach, and the Chief, and Dan Rooney. The film was practically on a loop in the Steelers' offices, and after a month Art Jr. told Nunn that he *had* to send the tape back to A&M. Nunn knew better. He and the rest of the scouting department told Noll that Stallworth, while having first-round talent, could be had in later rounds, so Nunn knew better than to let the "Don Hutson tape" fall into the hands of other teams.

Art Jr. went to the Senior Bowl with Stallworth foremost in mind. On film, Art Jr. saw "a tall, skinny kid who caught every ball anywhere near him." The time he had on him was 4.6, and even though no one else had witnessed the A&M–Tennessee State film, the Steelers' scouting department worried that the Senior Bowl would be Stallworth's coming-out party.

But at the Senior Bowl, Art Jr. couldn't believe his good fortune when he saw the coaches using Stallworth at cornerback.

And what Art Jr. really appreciated was that Stallworth took this curious coaching decision with a good nature.

✦ ✦ ✦

Art Rooney Jr. already had one sleeper in his back pocket for the 1974 draft. And after hearing the story from Tim Rooney about Jack Lambert and the Kent State QB, Art wanted to take the short drive and find out for himself whether he might have a second sleeper. Lambert grew up in Mantua, Ohio, where he worked on his grandfather's farm. He lost his front teeth on the basketball court, and even contemplated playing the sport in college because he wasn't getting much interest from college football coaches.

Lambert was a quarterback and cornerback at Crestwood High, and his coach called him the fourth-fastest defensive back of his four starters. Not much to go on. And little wonder that the coach, Gerry Myers, couldn't scare up any interest for Lambert from Myers's alma mater, Miami (Ohio). But Myers did think highly of Lambert.

"He didn't get his speed 'til he got to college," Myers said. "And no one ever completed anything deep over him. His first step was always correct. He always knew the angles. And, God, would he hit 'em. First they stopped throwing curls in front of him, and then they just stopped throwing to the split end in general. He was intense, dedicated. He used to say, 'I don't know where I'm gonna play someday and I don't care, but I will play.'"

Miami thought Lambert was too small to play linebacker and too slow to play in the secondary. Wisconsin showed some interest, as did a few MAC schools, but no scholarship was offered. Lambert's basketball coach at Crestwood knew Kent State coach Dave Puddington and told him Lambert was young for his grade and hadn't started to mature, that he might become a player. Puddington reluctantly gave Lambert a scholarship, and he arrived at Kent State as a quarterback. In 1971, when eligible to play, he was moved to defensive end.

Don James, who would later coach Washington to a national championship, became Kent State's coach in 1972 and moved Lambert to linebacker. Lambert took off not only as a player (233 tackles and first-team MAC that season), but as a leader, as his teammates at the time, Nick Saban and Gary Pinkel, would surely attest from their eventual head-coaching seats. They played with Lambert on the 1972 Kent State team that won the MAC but lost to John Matuszak, Freddie Solomon, and coach Earl Bruce of Tampa in the Tangerine Bowl.

So Art Jr. took the drive. He knew what his cousin Tim Rooney thought about Lambert. Tim had heard the suspended-QB story from a Kent State coach while visiting in August 1973. Tim was actually there to see Gerald Tinker, an Olympic sprinter/Kent State WR. Lambert was just learning to play linebacker, and Tim thought he looked like a physical reject because of his skinny legs and poor 40 time. But James told Tim to take a good, long look at him, and Lambert was on BLESTO's prospects list, so Tim watched and liked Lambert's upper-body strength and instincts. He gave Lambert a draftable grade in order for the Steelers to take another look later. Bill Nunn, in fact, went to see Lambert and wasn't impressed. "I didn't reject him, but I didn't give him a second-round grade," Nunn said. "I thought he was too thin."

In the 1974 draft, the Steelers added four future Hall of Famers to the team, including middle linebacker Jack Lambert (58), who joined Joe Greene (75), L.C. Greenwood (68), and Jack Ham (59)—all future Hall of Fame inductees from earlier drafts—to help forge Pittsburgh's Steel Curtain defense.

Art Jr. talked to the Kent State coaches and watched practice, but heavy rain forced the team off its muddy field and onto the gravel-strewn parking lot. Art watched Lambert drop into coverage, show off his peripheral vision, lateral quickness, awareness, and leadership. He noted in his scouting report that Lambert weighed only 195, but "all sinew" and "mean as hell." What got Art Jr. excited was a touch-tackle scrimmage during which a running back broke through the line and the only way Lambert could stop him down was to dive full out and take him down into the gravel. It wasn't that single act that impressed Art Jr. so much as the nonchalance Lambert took in picking the gravel out of his body throughout the remainder of practice. Lambert had to feel pain, but appeared unfazed. "There was nothing more I needed to see," Art Jr. wrote.

✦ ✦ ✦

"Oh, Mr. Otto! Mr. Otto!"

Gene Upshaw and Art Shell were mocking their teammate, legendary center Jim Otto, but for what reason—before this Week 3 game in 1974—Otto could not fathom. Until he heard a voice coming from the Steelers' side of pregame warm-ups and then he knew.

"Mr. Otto! It's me, Mike Webster! I made it!"

Otto could only smile and say, "Way to go, kid!"

As a boy growing up in northern Wisconsin, Webster could take pride in two highlight moments: 1) he had successfully defended his mother from an armed intruder as an eight-year-old, and, 2) he had met Jim Otto.

As a junior at Rhinelander High, Webster wrote out his goal of becoming an All–Big 10 defensive tackle. As a senior in 1969, Webster called Otto from his family's potato farm in Tomahawk, Wisconsin. Otto had grown up 40 miles south in Wausau and had become an idol of young linemen throughout the state. Otto agreed to meet him, and Webster got to the point. He wanted to know how to get to the NFL. Otto told him to work hard, keep his nose clean, play with desire, and make everyone around him proud.

Webster could do all of that. In fact, his tolerance for pain became folklore back at his high school. During one game, Webster's thumb had been pushed so far into its socket that only the nail was sticking out as Webster ran around asking for teammates to pull it out. A doctor used special pliers to pull the thumb out and Webster reentered the game soon thereafter.

Webster played collegiately at Wisconsin, so he played against Minnesota with linebackers coach Woody Widenhofer and against Colorado with defensive coordinator/linebackers coach Dan Radakovich.

Football Nomad "Bad Rad" was returning to the Steelers after a two-year stint at Colorado, and he was coming back as the new offensive line coach. He had impressed Chuck Noll with some innovative ideas about technique, so after 15 years as a defensive assistant Bad Rad took over the Steelers' offensive line in 1974.

While at Colorado, Rad's defense went up against Wisconsin and Webster in the second game of 1973. In film prep, Rad watched all of Webster's junior games, the opener of his senior season, and then reviewed the narrow Colorado win in Madison. Rad considered Webster the best center in the country; however, BLESTO ranked Webster 11th at his position. He was, at 6'1", 218, too small.

The numbers didn't compute, but of course the computer didn't know Webster the way his line coach at Wisconsin,

Charlie McBride, did. McBride was close friends with George Perles, the former Michigan State defensive line coach who was now with the Steelers, and McBride told Perles that Webster was the best offensive lineman in the Big 10, if not the country. McBride sent films to Perles, who watched Webster play against the top prospects and thought him dominant. Perles loved Webster's ability to consistently gain leverage and convinced the scouting department to take a look.

Art Rooney Jr. was amazed at what he saw and called the small-but-powerful Webster "an exception" in the same way that bumblebees confound the laws of physics by flying.

The Steelers paid close attention to Webster in the all-star games, which sent Dick Haley running into Art Jr.'s office to rave about Webster's Senior Bowl work. Haley had a better comp than a bumblebee. He said that Webster hits like Rocky Marciano. Tim Rooney came into the office with another reel, and then *he* fell in love with Webster.

Radakovich went to the Senior Bowl with Webster as his primary assignment. In the game, Webster dominated middle linebacker Waymond Bryant of Tennessee State. Bryant would become the No. 4 overall pick, by the Bears, but would be out of the league after four seasons. "I still wonder what the Bears scouts had been drinking when they were watching the Senior Bowl film that year," wrote Radakovich.

Noll was impressed with all that his people were telling him, and when he watched film even he thought Webster was a first-rounder. But at 218 pounds, Webster could be had later in the draft. No one disagreed with *that* assessment the way they had—and would again—with the decision to draft Stallworth later.

✦ ✦ ✦

Lynn Swann was closer to a college football superstar—an acclaimed-by-the-public superstar—than any other player over whom the Steelers were fawning early in 1974. Swann had speed, soft hands, and a gracefulness that we can assume was honed by his background in ballet. Mom had wanted a girl in the worst way and had no boy's name chosen when she went to the hospital, so the third and last of her three children was named Lynn, after Dr. Lynn Curtis. *Lynn* means a love of life, and the double letter at the end of his last name, Swann was told, indicated a special extra power—like Jimmy Foxx.

Lynn was born in Alcoa, Tennessee, but his father, an airplane maintenance worker, moved the family to the San Francisco Bay Area when Lynn was two. They lived a lower middle-class life, and Lynn attended a Catholic school, Junipero Serra, on academic scholarship. He was a track star and won the state title in 1970 with a long jump of 24'10".

At USC, Swann gained 1,203 yards of total offense in helping the Trojans win the national title in 1972. In 1973, Swann posted more great receiving stats, but these numbers weren't impressing the Steelers: 5'9", 173, 4.65.

As scouts like to joke, Swann was "small but slow." Yet the Steelers wanted a game-breaking wide receiver, and Art Rooney Jr. went out to watch him. He recalled being driven around the practice field by USC coach John McKay in a golf cart, and McKay told him Swann "is one of the greatest competitors that I've ever had. He has uncanny jumping ability and he has an ability to make the big plays at the big time."

Still, that size. That speed. But a week before the draft, Art Jr. received a new time on Swann from a BLESTO scout in Los Angeles: 4.56. Rooney thought that better matched Swann's playing speed on film and agreed with BLESTO's decision to move Swann from 10th on the wide receiver list to first.

Sometimes it's a matter of forcing the time to match the tape, and even Bill Nunn believed that Swann had cheated at the start of his updated 40. None of that mattered to the Steelers' wide receivers coach. "That sumbitch gets open and catches the football," said Lionel Taylor.

✦ ✦ ✦

The Steelers went into the 1974 draft with Lynn Swann, John Stallworth, Jack Lambert, and Mike Webster identified as prospects other teams would underrate. The Steelers normally lost such players, but, as Art Rooney Jr. put it, "On this occasion the stars in the heavens were properly aligned for us."

So was the film of Don Hutson Jr., but first the Steelers had to worry about beating Dallas in a coin flip for the 20th pick so they could choose Swann.

Why Swann and not Stallworth? That's what Chuck Noll still couldn't figure out. But his scouting department—consisting at the time of Art Jr., Dick Haley, Bill Nunn, Tim Rooney, and Bob Schmitz—convinced Noll to wait on Stallworth, that Swann was the better-timed receiver from the bigger school and had made big plays in big moments. Noll sighed and let Art Jr. talk him into waiting the same way he had talked him into drafting Franco Harris over Robert Newhouse.

So, after the Steelers lost the first of two coin flips, they won the second against the Cowboys and drafted Swann. The Cowboys admitted after the draft that Swann was their target, so the decision to draft Swann first was a wise one. But in the second round, Noll wanted Stallworth again. The scouting department again talked Noll into waiting because there were a couple of good—and much-needed—linebackers on the board, and, besides, the Steelers already had taken a wide receiver to work into the lineup with Frank Lewis and Ron Shanklin.

But which linebacker? One ran a 4.6, and Lambert a 4.8. The conversation went on until there were scant seconds left on the clock, and Noll left it up to his linebackers coach, Woody Widenhofer. He took into account Lambert's demeanor—his recklessness, aggressiveness, and physicality—and how he might only have appeared slower because of his high-top shoes. Widenhofer thought it all added up to, if not a better linebacker, surely a better special teamer *this* year, and so he—and they—chose Lambert.

Before the draft ended—and possibly during those interminable 35 picks the Steelers had to wait for their next pick—Lambert called Widenhofer and asked if he could drive to Pittsburgh on weekends to study film and learn the defense before rookie camp. He didn't make 593 career tackles and have his jersey No. 99 retired at Kent State with his good looks, so Widenhofer, who was looking forward to taking some time away from football, sighed and told Lambert yes.

Noll, who had wanted Stallworth in the first round, and again in the second round, didn't have a pick in the third round, thanks to the previous year's trade for Tom Keating. So the wait was particularly painful. "This is a huge gamble," Noll said to Art Jr., before addressing the rest of the scouting department: "You guys blew it," Noll said. "He will be gone."

It was a two-hour wait, but when the Chargers, badly in need of a wide receiver to team with second-year QB Dan Fouts, chose wide receiver Harrison Davis from Virginia, the Steelers chose Stallworth with pick No. 82. The scouting department was ebullient. Their bet had paid off. "We got lucky," thought Nunn, who knew that it took more than luck. A lot more.

The Steelers had another pick in the fourth round, and Noll thought it a perfect spot to draft Webster, whom Noll considered a first-rounder. But when his scouts told him that a short, 218-pound center could be had even later in the draft, Noll didn't argue, and the Steelers selected 6'2" UCLA cornerback Jimmy Allen.

Allen went to UCLA out of the volatile Watts neighborhood in Los Angeles after picking football over swimming and an Olympic dream. Dan Radakovich, then at Colorado, had recruited Allen hard when he left Pierce Junior College in Los Angeles, so Rad couldn't disagree with the selection, even though he, the O-line coach, preferred Webster as well.

By the time pick No. 125 rolled around, two centers had been drafted, one—Mark Markovich of Penn State—by the unlucky Chargers. So the Steelers drafted Webster to complete their Murderers' Row draft of four future Hall of Famers. It was the pinnacle of draft success. To that point in NFL Draft history, only one team, the Cowboys in 1964 with Mel Renfro, Bob Hayes, and Roger Staubach, had grabbed as many as *three* Hall of Famers in one draft.

✦ ✦ ✦

Randy Grossman was the same size as Mike Webster, 6′1″, 218, but Grossman was a tight end and Webster was a center. So even though Grossman had led 9–1 Temple with 39 receptions, 683 yards, and four TDs, and was named third-team All-America, he was still waiting to be drafted as the Steelers completed their selections. The Steelers' scouts were already out on the road pursuing free agents as Grossman slumped in his seat at a local TV studio in Philadelphia.

A three-year starter at Temple, Grossman had been invited to the television station's draft day set, along with William Johnson, another local college star who, while in high school, dyed his shoes a different color and became known as Billy "White Shoes" Johnson. He was a Division III receiver at nearby Widener University, and he and Grossman sat in front of the TV cameras in agony as the long weekend droned on without their names being called—until the 15th round. That's when Johnson was drafted by the Houston Oilers.

As for Grossman, he waited on set all the way through the last pick without being drafted. Discouraged, he left for a bar, and that's where he heard from his parents that the Steelers had been calling. Grossman accepted the Steelers' offer and spent the next eight seasons in Pittsburgh. He caught 119 regular-season passes and four Super Bowl rings. He caught everything and anything. His hands rarely let him down, and his touchdown catch in Super Bowl X tied the game at 7–7.

Not bad for someone overlooked in the draft for a perceived lack of athleticism.

"Randy Grossman couldn't run the 40," said Bill Nunn, "but he was 4.3 out of his breaks. He was quick to separate."

Before the Steelers finished signing what they hoped would be an unusually large crop of free agents due to a possible player strike, news got back to them that Lynn Swann, their first-round pick, had been arrested.

Out celebrating with family members, Swann was arrested and jailed by San Francisco police for what he claimed was "the crime of being Black." He was booked for resisting arrest and battery. Swann said the police destroyed a college All-Star wristwatch and hit him on the knees with nightsticks when they learned he was a football player. He fought the charges and was acquitted by a jury in July. His two brothers and a cousin were also charged, and they all sued the city for $2 million for false arrest. Four police officers filed a countersuit for $200,000, but Swann, party of four, received $143,090 and the cops received a total of $15,000.

The better news was that the Steelers had found a player who would become a fifth Hall of Famer out of draft week 1974. Yes, it took a few days to sign Donnie Shell, an outside linebacker who projected to safety in the NFL. Shell was deployed mainly on special teams, and Dan Radakovich called him the best special teams player he had ever seen in 50 years of coaching.

Different coaches at South Carolina State had told the Steelers the same line: "He'll knock your jock off." But Nunn, kingmaker of Historically Black Colleges and Universities such as S.C. State, couldn't get Shell on the Steelers' draft list. Nunn was told the transition from linebacker to safety would be too difficult. Shell was an in-the-box force linebacker at S.C. State, so, yes, the transition was difficult to project. And Shell couldn't prove himself in the de facto Black college national championship game—the Orange Bowl Classic—after a blood clot in his thigh forced him to sit out the second half. Still, Nunn liked his footwork, reaction time, and football character.

Nunn had told Shell's coach, Willie Jeffries, that Shell would fit the personality of the Steelers, so Jeffries called Nunn a few days after the draft to tell him Donnie had received offers from Denver and Houston. Jeffries also wanted Shell to play in Pittsburgh because of what Nunn had said about Chuck Noll's lack of prejudice.

So Nunn called Shell. "He asked if I was aware I hadn't been drafted," Shell said. "I said I was keenly aware."

Shell recalled the sequence of events some 47 years later after being elected to the Pro Football Hall of fame: "I talked with Jeffries, and he said, 'You need to go to Pittsburgh, man.' I said, 'Coach, why do you say that?' He said, 'They like self-motivated players and hard workers, and you fit right in with them.' So I signed with Pittsburgh."

In his first scrimmage, Shell acquired a nickname that stuck. He hit Franco Harris head-on during a simple off-tackle run. The coaches seemingly all asked in unison, "Who was that?" Dwight White said it was a "Torpedo," and a legend was born.

Of course, Shell wouldn't make the first-team in Pittsburgh until injuries opened up a spot during the 1977 season. He played so well that the Steelers traded Glen Edwards for a sixth-round pick during the off-season, moved Mike Wagner over to free safety, and Shell was the starting strong safety until he retired after the 1987 season.

✦ ✦ ✦

The greatest draft class in NFL history reported for a four-day rookie minicamp. WRs coach Lionel Taylor watched Lynn Swann and liked the rookie's route-running, his burst after the catch, his jumping ability, and the fact he was a quick learner. And he thought John Stallworth might be better.

In yet another coincidence for this pair of future Hall of Fame rookie receivers, both wore No. 22 in college. Swann, as the first-round pick, was given the number in preseason, but by summer was told he had to pick another number. He chose 88 and Stallworth used both numbers in wearing 82.

The next step was training camp, and it proved to be a continuation of rookie minicamp due to a player strike that kept the veterans out for a month. That meant the first Oklahoma drill of the summer was a showdown between rookies Mike Webster and Jack Lambert, with Webster showing off his strength and leverage in getting the upper hand. "Mr. Webster is one helluva fine center," Lambert told reporters.

Webster also continued the habit he had developed in college of sprinting from the huddle to the line of scrimmage, and after practice would make 50 more snaps and hit the blocking sled. Reporters couldn't help but spot him. "Mike Webster is a center," was the simple but astute verbiage in the suburban *Beaver County Times*.

Four days in, Stallworth went to the hospital with cramps during the morning practice. He was given fluids intravenously and released. By the time he got back to camp, the team was into its second practice, and Stallworth became worried he would get cut. So, in taking advice from a friend back home, Stallworth took a good look around to soak in the vibration of camp and made some mental notes. His position coach, Taylor, walked over and told Stallworth to "get the fuck off my field."

Yep. Stallworth knew it. He was getting cut. He walked about 25 yards away and stopped to take in a bit more. Taylor said it again, "Get the fuck off my field."

Figuring that was it, Stallworth went up to the locker room and soon the team followed. No one talked to him. He went to dinner, and someone there told him Chuck Noll wanted to see him.

Yep. It's over. This would be Stallworth's last night. He wondered if they would let him sleep there. He went to see his head coach, and Noll advised him to take more fluids, go out with the guys, and have a few beers. Stallworth was puzzled on many levels, but he went, had some beers, and woke up in the dorm. He realized he had survived, and he felt even better when Taylor told him to relax, that he was going to make the team, that he had been considered a No. 1 draft pick and that No. 1 draft picks make the team. "Just slow down, do what you do, continue working to get better," Taylor advised.

✦ ✦ ✦

The Steelers traded for QB Leo Gasienica in July to give them a needed camp arm, but Joe Gilliam crossed the picket line (with Ernie Holmes, Gordon Gravelle, and Steve Furness), and Chuck Noll became excited watching him throw. Of course, Bill Nunn was happy, too. And everyone was happy watching

Lynn Swann and John Stallworth run down those deep throws from Gilliam.

But to slap them with a cold blast of reality, Lionel Taylor reminded his hot-shot rookie receivers that they won't be able to do this once Mel Blount gets off the picket line. Blount lived in the New Orleans area and went to the Steelers' opening preseason game there. He saw that Stallworth was Gilliam's favorite receiver, and Stallworth caught his first glimpse of Blount, who had worked his way to the sideline. *He can't be a cornerback,* Stallworth thought. *Not that big.*

Gilliam had moved ahead of Terry Hanratty and began threatening Terry Bradshaw for the No. 1 job after throwing a 14-yard TD pass to Stallworth in the 26–7 win over the Saints. Bradshaw broke ranks and reported two days later. Against the Bears, Gilliam threw a 67-yard touchdown pass to Stallworth in the Steelers' 50–21 aerial show.

The vets showed up en masse behind player rep Rocky Bleier, and the Steelers beat the Eagles 33–30 as Gilliam again played well. Bradshaw injured his forearm in the game and began to legitimately worry about his job. Joe Greene disliked Gilliam and began taking a special interest in Bradshaw's status. While on strike, he told Bradshaw not to talk to the media or get involved with the union, that he, Greene, didn't want outside forces pulling the team's threads. His concern paid off as the Steelers became closer, giving them another reason to appreciate the 1974 players' strike.

The team was coming together, and the rookies were learning at a rapid clip. Like Jack Lambert. Noll surprised the team's veterans and also reporters when he threw around the words "fantastic" and "sensational" to describe Lambert's camp. Not that it put Lambert in a good mood. When asked to stand up in front of the team and sing his college fight song, as rookies traditionally do, Lambert said, "Kiss my ass."

There was also the day Stallworth blasted his boombox in the locker room. Lambert hated it and told Stallworth to shut it off. Ernie Holmes loved it and said leave it on. Words flew, and that night someone cut the cord to the box. Stallworth saw it the next day and began an investigation. When he learned it was Greene who cut the cord, the investigation ended without further comment. Stallworth had bigger things to worry about. Like Mel Blount.

✦ ✦ ✦

Bad Rad was back in the lab concocting an offensive line for Chuck Noll. Radakovich felt that, with rookie Mike Webster, there were seven quality players, and the seven should rotate in games.

Rad was certain that Jon Kolb and Moon Mullins would start. Kolb locked down the left tackle job in 1971 while Mullins would play right guard or right tackle, depending on the development of Gordon Gravelle. Sam Davis was the left guard, while Ray Mansfield would alternate at center with Jim Clack. The group was small. They averaged 247, and by season's end the average was closer to 237. Late in the season, Rad watched Clack and Mullins weigh in at 222 and 218. Rad called them his seven dwarfs, but the group remained in rotation through the end of the 1975 season, or two rings.

Rad also had the jerseys tailored and tightened so they couldn't be grabbed. To that end, he made sure the jerseys stuck to the shoulder pads with double-sided tape.

Rad had some other business in camp. He and Lionel Taylor worked with the tight ends—Lionel on receiving skills, Rad on blocking. Taylor told the new OL coach to pay particular attention to Larry Brown, who was entering his fourth year at tight end. It took Rad 15 minutes of the first practice with vets to see Brown possessed incredible blocking prowess. He told Brown he would be first-team—either tight end or right tackle—for the next 11 years.

Brown had never heard a coach say anything like that, so he may not have believed Rad. And after the first preseason game with Dallas, Brown did a TV interview and said this would be his last summer, that he was entering dental school. This shocked Rad, and he and Lionel went to see Brown, told him again he would play until he's 40, that he would move to tackle "when his 4.6 speed became 4.9."

That wouldn't happen for three more years.

✦ ✦ ✦

The vets arrived, and Jack Lambert became a backup outside linebacker. But he was moved to first-team middle linebacker the week of the fifth preseason game after Henry Davis suffered a concussion. With Lambert in the middle, the Steelers beat the Redskins 21–19 and finished their preseason with a 45–14 thrashing of the Cowboys. The Steelers were 6–0, an appropriate record for a once-in-a-lifetime rookie class playing in a rookie-dominated preseason.

Against the Cowboys, Joe Gilliam threw another touch-down bomb to John Stallworth and nailed down the starting QB job. The *New York Times* called Gilliam, "the NFL's most significant player this season." Noll was certainly enamored by Gilliam's buggy whip of an arm, but Gilliam wouldn't prove to be nearly as significant as the rookie class that would produce six Super Bowl starters over the next six years. The lineup was also about to be infused with Rocky Bleier. The fifth-year vet would become a starter in Week 6.

The Steelers started the 1974 season 1–1–1 with Gilliam regressing each week. His poor decision-making turned a win into a tie at Denver, and then the Steelers were shutout at home against the Raiders.

Stallworth and Lynn Swann were playing the second and fourth quarters, and throughout the season Lionel Taylor repeatedly showed them film of the Week 3 hammering they took from Jack Tatum and George Atkinson of the Raiders.

Mike Webster was the long-snapper, occasional guard, and a member of the short-yardage and goal-line units. While he became discouraged enough that season to consider quitting, the veteran in front of him, Ray Mansfield, was telling friends he had met his replacement. "He wants it so badly," Mansfield said of Webster.

In the sixth game, the Steelers beat the Browns, but Gilliam threw poorly. And he wouldn't stop throwing poorly. His disregard of the running game began to infuriate Chuck Noll, and Noll met with his offensive-line coach, Dan Rada-kovich, who preferred Terry Bradshaw at QB because he could and would audible to a running play. Rad had been complaining to Noll every week since the Denver tie, and

Noll finally made the move at 4–1–1 to replace Gilliam with Bradshaw.

Gilliam passed Rad in the hallway after learning of the demotion and asked, "Rad, were you part of the lynch mob?"

"Not only was I part of it," Rad said, "Joey, I led it."

Bradshaw, in spite of a hiccup or two the rest of the season, eventually locked down the job by primarily handing off to the new backfield duo of Bleier and Franco Harris. Gilliam had helped Noll make the decision easy when he began arriving late for meetings. Also, players were hearing rumors and seeing evidence of drug use. Gilliam's next start would be the 1975 regular-season finale in which he went 2-for-11 and was intercepted twice before being yanked. It was his last start. His career was over at 25; his life would be over at 50.

✦ ✦ ✦

Terry Bradshaw still couldn't show much consistency, and the offense struggled in a 13–10 loss to Houston on December 1. Joe Greene watched the next night's game, on Monday night, and became so enraged by the poor offense, as compared to what he was seeing from the Dolphins on TV, that the next morning he went to the stadium, attended a meeting, and packed his stuff. The team was 8–3–1, but Greene told Andy Russell he was going home and not coming back. Greene walked out of the stadium with WRs coach Lionel Taylor in pursuit. Taylor sat in Greene's car and eventually talked him out of it.

The Steelers won the next two weeks with Greene becoming more familiar with his new cocked position between opposing interior linemen. In the playoffs, the Steelers held

O.J. Simpson to 49 yards rushing in a 32–14 win over the Bills, setting up an AFC Championship Game matchup in Oakland against the Raiders. In anticipation, a group of rookies sought boxes from the equipment manager so they could begin clearing out their lockers, just in case they lost.

Greene heard about it and asked the rookies why they needed boxes. No one answered. He asked again, in a harsher tone. The rookies looked at each other and decided that no one actually needed the boxes for anything, and the matter ended.

The Raiders had their longest run of the game on their first play—for four yards. With Greene angled between the center and guard, the Raiders tried to run at Ernie Holmes and Dwight White behind Art Shell and Gene Upshaw, but could muster only 29 yards on 21 carries.

"I've never been hit so hard," Marv Hubbard said after rushing for six yards on seven carries.

But with Bradshaw struggling, the Steelers needed a blocked 38-yard field goal by Jack Lambert to keep the game tied 3–3 at halftime. Then Cliff Branch beat Mel Blount for a 10–3 lead in the third quarter. Franco Harris' eight-yard touchdown run on an inside trap tied the game, and a Jack Ham interception return to the Oakland 9 set up Bradshaw's TD pass to Lynn Swann for a 17–10 Steelers lead.

But Branch beat Blount again, this time for 42 yards as Lambert saved four points on a touchdown-saving tackle. Bud Carson benched Blount for Jimmy Allen, which would spur Blount not only into some pre–Super Bowl hissing at Carson, but no doubt inspired him along the way to winning NFL Defensive Player of the Year the following season.

Lynn Swann (88) makes a leaping catch over the middle against the Cowboys in Super Bowl XIII in January 1979. Both he and wide receiver John Stallworth (82) were drafted by the Steelers in 1974 and went on to Hall of Fame careers.

A George Blanda field goal cut the Steelers' lead to 17–13, but J.T. Thomas intercepted a pass a play after his holding penalty had negated a sack. Harris then ran 21 yards for the clinching score in the final minute, and the Steelers were going to their first Super Bowl.

✦ ✦ ✦

The Steelers reached the Super Bowl with 14 rookies and half a roster made up of Black players. Half of those Black players were from Historically Black Colleges and Universities. The group was loose, and late in the first week Dan Radakovich brought his offensive line in for one final day of Vikings film study. The group felt confident, and Rad felt they might even be bored. So he put on the 1956 Penn State–Syracuse game for comic relief.

"Hey, that's Rad," one of the linemen said in pointing out the Penn State linebacker. That linebacker was struggling that day. He was losing most of his battles to a Syracuse running back named Jim Brown. The linemen enjoyed the show and filed out of the room in a good mood.

The Steelers left for New Orleans a few days later and were given run of the city by Chuck Noll until practices began on Wednesday. Dwight White went out with Joe Greene and came down with a lung infection and spent the week in a hospital. He lost 18 pounds but showed up on gameday and played nearly the entire game. In fact, White downed Fran Tarkenton in the end zone to give the Steelers a 2–0 halftime lead. Glen Edwards, who had told the Vikings to buckle up in the tunnel before the game, had rocked a Vikings wide receiver at the 5 to pop up a Tarkenton pass that Mel Blount intercepted to preserve the slim first-half margin.

In the second half, Franco Harris ran nine yards behind Moon Mullins for a touchdown, while the front four was busy batting and intercepting Tarkenton passes. L.C. Greenwood batted two passes and White batted another, which Greene intercepted. Greene also forced and recovered a fumble, but the Vikings were still within 9–6 thanks to a blocked punt/touchdown in the fourth quarter.

Terry Bradshaw finally delivered the title on a four-yard laser to Larry Brown with 3:31 left. The play, suggested on the sideline by Joe Gilliam, put the first Lombardi in the trophy case. Franco finished with 158 yards rushing to win the game's MVP award. The Vikings offense was blanked by a Steelers defense that allowed 17 rushing yards on 21 carries, an average of 29 inches per carry.

Ten of the Steelers defensive starters that day played in a Pro Bowl. The only starter who never did was Ernie Holmes, who at times was viewed, even by Greene, as their most dominant player.

After the game, veteran TV broadcaster Curt Gowdy said of the Steelers, "They're still a very young team. I would say their best years are still ahead of them. A team that may not have reached its peak, and their future opponents are going to have some trouble."

8

AFTER THE GOLD RUSH

IT'S 1987, AND Dan Rooney has fired his brother, Art Jr., whom Art Sr., the Chief, continued to blame for passing on the Pittsburgh-born and -bred Super Bowl QB Dan Marino. Obviously, a price had to be paid for the poor drafting that left the display case at Three Rivers Stadium still holding only four Lombardi trophies. With one quarterback after another being booed off the home field, and losing seasons returning as the norm, the era seemed postapocalyptic to fans in Pittsburgh.

"The Marino thing," harrumphed Art Jr. while surveying the damage several years later. "My dad blamed me until his dying day for not drafting Marino. But it really wasn't my fault."

Of course, as Art pointed out, "Noll was the main guy. My dad was the glue. Dan was a phenomenal businessman and great with the league. My thing in personnel was to draft the best available athlete, and that fell right in line with what Chuck believed, so we got along great, but he was the main guy." And, yep, it was Noll's call to draft defensive tackle Gabe Rivera in the 1983 draft instead of Marino, the local legend who was tall, strong-armed, and had lightning in his release.

"Noll loved Marino," Art said. "And we had him rated higher than Miami did. And those rumors about Danny? My dad knew every cop in Western Pennsylvania, and we really looked into it, but there was nothing serious, nothing like narcotics or anything like that. Dan was just an Oakland kid who got around. He had a great college career, was a little down his senior year, but so was Franco, and we still drafted him. We had Bradshaw, of course, and we'd drafted [Mark] Malone in the first round in 1980, but what most people didn't know is that our other backup, Cliff Stoudt, was the fair-haired boy of the organization. Yeah, Chuck scouted him himself. He had a real good arm, real nice size, could move okay. Still, even with all that, Noll liked Marino so well, and so did I. We really took a long look at him, and in the end it was between him and Rivera and Dave Rimington, a center from Nebraska. Well, we crossed Rimington off first because Chuck said he had bad knees, and he was right. Then Chuck said, 'This team was built with defense,' you know, with Joe Greene being his first pick and all, and that 'we can do it again.' So we took Rivera. I said fine since I wasn't real passionate about drafting Marino. After the draft, [Don] Shula called Chuck and asked him what he thought about Marino, and Chuck gave him the most positive scouting report he could.

"But my dad never forgave me, and he wouldn't hear anything about Chuck having the last word. I think it might've had to do with Marino getting really friendly with my dad, and besides, how would anyone know the kid we drafted was going to break his back? But even in his last year my dad would see me and he'd say, 'You should've taken Marino!'"

✦ ✦ ✦

With the Steelers off back-to-back losing seasons for the first time since Chuck Noll's earliest years, Art Rooney Jr. was fired and replaced at the top of the personnel department by Dick Haley. Bill Nunn also retired from full-time work but remained with the organization.

Art Jr. had worked with Noll in drafting only five Pro Bowlers in the 12 drafts following the legendary draft of 1974. And none of those five—Robin Cole, Tunch Ilkin, David Little, Mike Merriweather, or Louis Lipps—came close to making the Hall of Fame.

"We still had BLESTO, and it was still very good," Art Jr. said. "And we put in a computer system in 1979 that Tom Modrak said was one of the best things we ever did. One of the things I've been thinking about is that I was always so passionate about the draft, and when I started working with Coach Noll, he said he didn't want arguments, only discussions. But I'll tell you, those discussions got pretty passionate. The stories about our arguments about Franco and those guys, they're all true.

"But what happened? Why in the hell didn't we just keep going from there? Sure, we began drafting late, but we drafted late in '74, too. I thought I did a pretty good job. Bill Nunn was a very good scout by then. Like I said, BLESTO was still strong. But we never did draft another Hall of Famer until I was out of there.

"Why? The only thing I've been able to come up with is that after the '74 draft we didn't have those passionate discussions. They were discussions, but they weren't passionate. Maybe we all thought we were big shots. We still worked as hard as anyone, but the passionate discussions weren't there. We had one with Bradshaw. My dad wanted to trade the pick. He just wanted to do the proper thing, but I was so sold on Bradshaw. We just had great coaches and great arguments.

"I have gone over it and over it. The set-up we had was still very good, but maybe we all had too much phony respect for each other. Aw, phony's probably too strong of a word, but something was missing. I guess it was those passionate discussions we used to have."

✦ ✦ ✦

At 6–10, the 1986 Steelers posted their worst won-loss record since 5–9 in the 1970 season that was recognized as Year 2 of Chuck Noll's rebuilding plan. But there weren't any foundational pieces in place as they prepared for their first draft without Art Rooney Jr.

The 1987 Steelers would be drafting 10th and were looking to revamp a secondary in which 35-year-old Donnie Shell was still the best player. The Steelers were also hoping to add a foundational linebacker to play inside. The Steel Curtain was officially retired in 1982 when the Steelers began evolving into a 3-4 alignment. When Jack Lambert suffered an injury in 1984 that led to his retirement after the season, Noll replaced him with David Little and veteran outside 'backer Robin Cole.

Cole, 32, would need to be replaced in 1987, and possibly the hope was, with another of the famed Penn State linebackers, Shane Conlan. At least that was the thinking in the lead-up to the 1987 draft, because the guy they really wanted, a safety named Rod Woodson, had turned in a stunning performance at the NFL Combine.

"If you were making a highlight tape and showing somebody how to do a particular drill," Steelers scout Tom Donahoe told *Steelers Digest*, "you would've shown them Rod Woodson doing that drill."

By that, Donahoe meant *every* drill. The 6', 202-pound Woodson ran a pair of 40s that ranged on various watches from 4.24 to 4.34. He flew 12 feet in the standing broad jump, ran 3.98 in the short shuttle, and made several diving catches while working with the wide receivers. He was viewed as a potential two-way player after what *Pro Football Weekly* called a "scintillating" workout that experts believe moved him into the top five of the draft.

"That workout probably took him right away from us," said Noll.

The Steelers stopped worrying about Woodson right then. Noll even told defensive coordinator Tony Dungy not to waste time attending Woodson's postseason workout as the Steelers began hoping for Conlan, or even Penn State running back D.J. Dozier. The Steelers figured Woodson would go anywhere from No. 3 to No. 6 in the draft and on their board had him rated No. 4.

Woodson was primarily a safety at Purdue, with some experience at cornerback. In his last game, the Old Oaken Bucket against rival Indiana, Woodson started at tailback and rushed for 93 yards. He also played wide receiver, catching three passes for 67 yards. Woodson made 10 tackles that day, forced a fumble, and averaged 23 yards on a pair of kickoff returns and 10 yards on three punt returns. He was a do-it-all type of athlete who also held the NCAA record in the 60-meter hurdles and had qualified for the 1984 Olympic Trials in the 110-meter hurdles. Noll said he was "head and shoulders" above the rest of the draft's defensive backs.

The Steelers shrugged and looked elsewhere as Conlan's stock seemed to be falling a bit as the draft unfolded.

The Browns surprised everyone by taking a different line-backer, Mike Junkin, out of Duke, and then the Cardinals reached for QB Kelly Stouffer at No. 6 as Conlan became a very real possibility.

For the Bills at pick No. 8.

But that meant Woodson was still falling, and if he didn't make it to pick No. 10, defensive tackle Jerome Brown would. Of course, Brown went ninth to the Eagles, and the Steelers had their next foundational player fall into their laps at No. 10.

"I'm in love with him," Noll famously said at the post-pick press conference.

Personnel director Dick Haley announced that Woodson would be a cornerback, and Woodson confirmed that the Steelers were very surprised he was available. "I could hear it in their voices that they were surprised," he said.

"I was a college scout when he was coming out," Donahoe said in an interview 35 years later. "We didn't think we had any shot to get him because of the career that he put together. But he got into trouble right before the draft. I can't remember exactly what it was, so we probably should've vetted him more than we did, but we didn't think we could get him and the draft started and he started sliding. So when we saw that his name was going to get to us, it was a no-brainer. We had got enough work on him that we were comfortable picking him, and he had an unbelievable career."

In the second round, the Steelers grabbed another 6', 200-pound cornerback in Delton Hall, who was considered a reach by the experts because he had started only one full season at Clemson. But the Steelers targeted him even though he had broken his jaw wrestling in his dorm a week before the draft.

"Physically, these guys are prototypes," Dungy said of the just-drafted cornerbacks whom he envisioned replacing Harvey Clayton, John Swain, and Lupe Sanchez.

In the third round, the Steelers, looking to groom a replacement for 35-year-old John Stallworth on the other side of Louis Lipps, drafted Charles Lockett, who was compared to Lynn Swann because of his body control and study of ballet.

Still in need of that inside linebacker, the Steelers eyed Penn State's Donnie Graham in the fourth round, but he was drafted by the Bucs. So the Steelers went back to their value board, and that meant a third defensive back—hard-hitting Thomas Everett, a true free safety who was fast enough to play cornerback if needed. He had beaten out Woodson for the Jim Thorpe Award, and his coach at Baylor, Grant Teaff, compared him favorably to a defender he had coached a few years earlier. "He played at a level equal to or above Mike Singletary as a senior," Teaff said of Everett.

"Christmas in April," was how Dungy described his plethora of new defensive backs. "We felt we had to add some size to our defensive backfield, and some speed."

Dungy wasn't done opening his presents. In the fifth round, the Steelers drafted inside linebacker Hardy Nickerson, a 6'2", 230-pound, high-intensity hitter from Cal. And in the sixth round, they drafted Penn State defensive tackle Tim Johnson and a light outside linebacker who had impressed them with his play in an all-star game, 6'2", 225-pound Greg Lloyd out of Fort Valley State, a Black college in Georgia.

"They used to have a small-college Black all-star game, and Greg played in the game," said Donahoe. "He was not a graded player by BLESTO, so we had no information on him. But we were watching the tape, and Greg, I think, made three interceptions in the game, so we pinpointed him and said this might be a guy we need to check out. That spring I was scouting in Georgia and stopped at Fort Valley. We were probably the first team that got on Greg."

In the 10th round, the Steelers added fullback Merril Hoge of Idaho State to put the exclamation point on their best draft in 13 years.

The consensus reaction to the Steelers' haul at the time was to compare it to the 49ers' draft in 1981, which also landed a top-10 safety/cornerback and two others within the top four picks: 1) Ronnie Lott, 2) Eric Wright, and 3) Carlton Williamson. The 49ers went from 6–10 in 1980 to Super Bowl champs in 1981 with the help of that single draft. So optimism was running high in Pittsburgh following the 1987 draft.

"The Steelers have to believe their draft luck has changed," longtime beat reporter Vic Ketchman wrote in *Pro Football Weekly.*

Here's how *PFW* draft expert Joel Buchsbaum broke down the Steelers' haul: "Woodson may have been the best athlete in the entire draft.... Hall is another big, fast, physical cornerback who lacks technique.... [Lockett] is a poor man's Lynn Swann.... [Everett is] small, ran a 4.6 or 4.7, and gets burned at times because of his aggressive tendencies, but no defensive back in the country made more big plays last year.... [Nickerson is] a tough, emotional inside linebacker who should do well on special teams.... [Lloyd is] undersized, but active, a Steeler-type outside backer. He did some good things in the [Heritage] Bowl and has gotten bigger and stronger since then.... Tim Johnson is an undersized pass-rusher who could also be used on the nose or inside linebacker.... [Hoge] catches the ball well but lacks speed and isn't a great blocker."

In summation, Buchsbaum wrote: "For defensive coordinator Tony Dungy, Christmas came on April 28th. However, most of the team's offensive coaches will have to wait another year for their presents."

✦ ✦ ✦

Rod Woodson was born in Fort Wayne, Indiana, raised in an all-Black neighborhood where he was bullied for his biracial ethnicity, but the neighborhood grew to respect him as his athleticism blossomed at Snider High School.

In one game as a sophomore, he touched the ball six times and scored five touchdowns as a slot back and return specialist.

Steelers cornerback Rod Woodson (26) gets by Browns running back Tommy Vardell (44) during an interception return on September 11, 1994. Selected 10th overall in the 1987 draft out of Purdue, Woodson was widely considered the best athlete in his entire draft class.

He was always a defensive back, but became a tailback his junior season after the senior got hurt. As a senior, Woodson rushed for 9.8 yards per carry and scored 12 touchdowns to not only make the all-state team, but the 1982 *Parade* All-America team. Later that school year, he successfully defended his state titles in the low and high hurdles.

He mixed both sports in one of his more memorable plays at Snider. In the playoffs against Lafayette Jefferson, Woodson ran a reverse and hurdled the last defender to score a touchdown.

Woodson's football ability was noticed nationwide, but he chose nearby Purdue over Michigan because he wanted to study electrical engineering. He eventually switched majors and graduated with a degree in criminal justice. On the field, he was a star from the beginning. He became a two-time NCAA All-American, a three-time All–Big Ten performer, and set 13 school records.

"He could've played any position," said his coach Leon Burtnett. "He could have played running back in the NFL. He was the complete package."

Woodson was that on the track as well. In 1987, the year the Steelers drafted him, Woodson had the fourth-fastest 110-meter high-hurdle time in the nation, behind No. 1 Roger Kingdom by only .08 seconds. So using the Olympics as leverage during his 95-day holdout with the Steelers was no joke. But back then, Olympians couldn't be professional in another sport, and that's what the Steelers' defensive coordinator told him when he went to watch Woodson run in a meet at North Carolina. Dungy told Woodson, "You can run track and probably be world-class, or you can play corner and be one of the best that ever played."

Woodson bought the pitch and signed with the Steelers in October 1987.

✦ ✦ ✦

The 1987 rookie season was something of a struggle for Rod Woodson as he served primarily as a return specialist in his eight games. But sixth-round pick Greg Lloyd couldn't even play special teams. On the second day of training camp, a tight end rolled up on the back of his left knee and tore Lloyd's ACL.

"I had surgery at Divine Providence Hospital, and the first person I saw when I woke up was the Chief," Lloyd recalled. "I was like, 'Does the Chief really know me?' But he came in, called my name, and said I was going to be okay. It was really kind of cool."

After rehabbing and returning in 1988 at full strength, he injured the knee again in the second preseason game. While chasing Eagles QB Randall Cunningham, Lloyd felt the knee pop and was out seven weeks. When he returned, the Steelers were 1–6 and playing at home against the Broncos. Lloyd didn't start but got in the game, and his first career tackle was Tony Dorsett. Lloyd also recovered his first fumble that day and was called for his first personal foul. He smacked QB Gary Kubiak hard in the face following a teammate's sack and, subsequently, was hit with his first ejection. He also served up his first one-finger salute in the NFL while exiting the field.

It was a foreshadowing of his personality. His T-shirt—I WASN'T HIRED FOR MY DISPOSITION—is well remembered, just as well as Lloyd remembered a childhood that honed his anger.

"I started playing when I was six years old," Lloyd said in a 2007 interview from his Dojo in Fayetteville, Georgia. "The coach came by my house and asked my aunt, who raised me, if I could play football. I never played football, but, cool, I'll play. I was athletic. One of the first things he did at practice was he got on his knees and said, 'I want to see who can knock me over.' All the guys ran into him, hitting him, and I'm going, 'I don't want to hurt him.' At six. At six I'm already thinking

I don't want to hurt him but I knew I could knock him over. He was a pastor. I knew I'd hurt him, and I was the only one who hit him and knocked him on his butt. And I remember him looking at me and saying, 'You're my linebacker.' I was that way all the way up until I got to college.

"But when I was playing football, the anger that I had back then was that I didn't have no parent. I had parents, but, my mom and dad, they split [in Miami, drove the kids to Fort Valley, Georgia], and just said, 'Here, take care because we can't do it.' They did that to five of my brothers and sisters, me being the youngest at two years old. How can you leave innocence for somebody else to take care of for your own selfish good? I couldn't understand that. So as I got older I was the best kid in everything, but there was nobody there to go, 'Way to go, Greg,' other than a coach. All my other friends, they sucked. They sucked at football, and their parents were there saying, 'Hey, way to go.' And I'm going, 'You sucked.' And so when I went to play football, and I see this parent jumping up and saying, 'Come on, Johnny!' I'm finding out who is Johnny. I'm looking around for her boy because she's making an awful lot of noise, and I would look at him and say, 'I'm going to knock Hell out of him. I can't wait to knock Hell out of him.' And I'd go and knock him out. Same way in college.

"I went to college in Fort Valley, which is about an hour and 15 minutes from where we're sitting right now. My home was 1.36 miles from my college, and my aunt never came to see me play football. I played baseball in my backyard. The high school baseball field was in my backyard. She never came to see me play. I always had to prove myself to people, regardless that I have no parents, that not only am I a good player, but I'm a good person. And after a while you get tired of it."

Lloyd played fullback and linebacker in high school and was once ejected for breaking a quarterback's leg. He went to Fort Valley State (Division II) and was named all-conference three times. He earned a degree in electrical engineering, but his other big moment occurred in the Heritage Bowl, where he impressed two teams: the Steelers and the Cowboys. In fact, Lloyd was told by the Cowboys they were going to draft him. But Steelers scout Tom Donahoe had watched the tape of the Heritage Bowl and had to go to Fort Valley to check Lloyd out for himself. At one point during the workout, Donahoe looked down at his watch and asked Lloyd if any other teams had been down to work him out. Lloyd said no, that the Steelers were first. He didn't hear from them again until draft day.

"Greg's an interesting character," said Donahoe. "I love the guy, but he's challenging to deal with, to say the least. I'll say this about Greg: as much as he might frustrate people during the week, on Sunday there was nobody better."

The injuries put Lloyd's career on delay, but he didn't need much practice time to impress the Steelers' coaching staff.

"His rookie year, he got hurt right away at training camp," Donahoe said. "I remember that night going over to his room in the dorm, and the guy was despondent. It was like his world was over and it ended. I said, 'Greg, you'll come back. We've got good doctors, good rehab. You'll be fine.' So he comes back the second year and he had an unbelievable training camp. So even though he tore up his knee again, the coaches

Steelers linebacker Greg Lloyd watches the action during Pittsburgh's 29–9 divisional playoff victory over Cleveland on January 7, 1995. Injuries stalled Lloyd's rookie year, but by 1994 he was a perennial Pro Bowler and anchor of one of the NFL's most feared defenses.

couldn't wait to get their hands on him, based on what they saw early that second preseason. So he came back and he was in there and kept the spot for a long time."

His sixth-round status no doubt motivated him.

"That anger was there because I came from a little old Black college right here in Fort Valley," Lloyd said. "I'll fight you 'til I got no fight left in me. And I think after a while my teammates began to appreciate that and they respected that and they realized that, 'Don't come over here and line up in front of Greg in practice and not buckle your chin-strap up, because he's going a hundred miles an hour.' And then everybody adopted that mentality, and when everybody adopted that mentality, guess what we did? We didn't win the Super Bowl, but we had a Super Bowl mentality. We were in three AFC Championship Games and a Super Bowl. There's no way in between that we shouldn't have won two Super Bowls."

✦ ✦ ✦

Back in 1969, the Steelers got it all started by drafting Joe Greene, Jon Kolb, and L.C. Greenwood. They grabbed a Hall of Fame team leader for the middle of the line, an underrated full-time starter at left tackle for nine seasons, and a slithery, game-changing pass-rusher.

In 1988, the Steelers came close to matching that. They only missed on the pass-rusher. And what a miss it was. "Let's face it, we're all shocked," TV draft analyst Paul Zimmerman said after the Steelers drafted pass-rusher Aaron Jones out of Eastern Kentucky with the 18th overall pick.

Jones was 6'5", 261 pounds, and had nine sacks his senior season. That's solid production, but not enough to justify his prediction to Pittsburgh reporters of 18–20 sacks his rookie season.

The Steelers' second-round pick, Dermontti Dawson, became that Hall of Fame team leader in the middle of the line. "Dermontti was an undersized guard at the University of Kentucky," said Donahoe. "I remember going to scout him, and it had rained that day and they practiced in the gym. Guys were slipping and sliding all over the place except for Dermontti. He was like on ice skates on an icy surface and everybody else was on the ice in street shoes."

Dawson had the look of a champion, a high-pedigreed, Kentucky-born thoroughbred.

At perennial track-and-field power Bryan Station High, Dawson won the state championship in both the shot and discus as a junior and senior. College recruiters told him to add the javelin and he could make an Olympics run.

He wasn't playing football as a sophomore, but Dawson still caught the eye of University of Kentucky football coach Jerry Claiborne at the state track-and-field meet. Claiborne contacted the Bryan Station football coach and asked why Dawson's name wasn't on the list of football prospects. Marc Logan and Cornell Burbage were. The two future NFLers were also on the Bryan Station track team and talked their buddy Dermontti into going out for football his junior year.

"I'd love to have gone to the Olympics," Dawson said in 2006. "But you don't make any money in the Olympics from track and field."

So off to the University of Kentucky he went with his buddies. Dawson moved into the starting lineup at right guard his junior season. It was a relief because the previous year Claiborne had tried to make him a defensive tackle. Fortunately, that experiment failed, because playing guard in Kentucky's trapping offense was the perfect way to catch the attention of Chuck Noll.

The Steelers didn't see Dawson play center until the Senior Bowl. They already knew he was a long-snapper, so the versatility and the fact they had timed him in the 40 at 4.8 added up to a fairly high Steelers grade on Dawson.

The problem was the New York Giants really liked Dawson, who, at 6'2", 282 pounds, had below-average size for a guard and the move to center was still just a projection. So the Giants of George Young and Bill Parcells went bigger. They went Planet Theory and drafted 6'5", 291-pound tackle Eric Moore with the 10th pick and 6'7", 305-pound tackle Jumbo Elliott with the 36th pick. The Steelers chose Dawson with the 44th pick, the second interior offensive lineman in the draft behind Randall McDaniel.

"When Ron Erhardt [the offensive coordinator with the Giants in 1988] became the offensive coordinator of Pittsburgh," Dawson said, "he said, 'Daws, we liked you. We were going to take you in the first round, but Bill got cold feet and went with Eric Moore.' [Erhardt] said, 'We should've taken you.' Although I was small, I was strong and fast, which makes up for size. Plus you can't determine a man's heart. And I took pride in not getting beat. That was my worst fear."

"He was an undersized guy, but he had amazing athletic ability and explosion, and we were really looking for a center," said Donahoe. "The year we drafted him we took Dermontti and Chuck Lanza because we were determined to get at least one center out of it, and Dermontti had played guard primarily in college.

"He was a unique player, and what he enabled our offense to do with a center who could run and move laterally and get out in space and block in front of screens, quick throws to the outside, he set a rare standard. And now a lot of teams are doing that with their centers and trying to find guys who are more athletic and can do it. But Dermontti was really the first of that type of center who could get out in space and do what he did."

Lanza, chosen in the third round, lasted only two years and never made a start. He's remembered as the center who replaced Dawson (altitude sickness) in Denver and made the poor shotgun snap that hit Bubby Brister in the shin and was fumbled away, ending the Steelers' upset bid and their surprising run in the 1989 playoffs.

The other lineman drafted by the Steelers in 1988 was left tackle John Jackson, who was taken in the 10th round and started full-time for the Steelers from 1989 to 1997 of what was a 14-year NFL career.

✦ ✦ ✦

Art Rooney Sr. died on August 25, 1988, at the age of 87, and the pall hung over the Steelers throughout their worst season since 1969. They finished 5–11 as the heat from fans—and eventually Dan Rooney—enveloped Chuck Noll.

Of the young foundational pieces, Rod Woodson continued his early career struggles, and Greg Lloyd was injured again. Only Dermontti Dawson enjoyed what could be considered success in 1988, and he started only five games.

Dawson was injured in his first start. In a Week 4 game at Buffalo, Dawson started at left guard, but Art Still, a Bills defensive end and his wife's uncle, fell on his knee near halftime. Dawson missed the next eight games with a sprain. When he returned, the Steelers were 2–10, and that was two losses after Dan Rooney had declared a bottoming out and their quarterback, Bubby Brister, had suggested they punt on first downs.

"All we're doing is standing in each other's way," said Woodson.

But defensive coordinator Tony Dungy was exasperated by Woodson's inconsistencies. "He's got so much talent," Dungy told author Sam Toperoff. "He can make mistakes and still recover. He can take that little peek into the backfield and still be able to close ground on a deep receiver. In college, he could relax; he knew he could always catch up. Here, that's not always the case. He's not used to playing under discipline, not used to playing against the great receivers in the game."

Noll repeatedly took responsibility for the team's ills, but even the great Mike Webster was struggling. He snapped a ball over the punter's head to set up a Browns touchdown, and Webster's next long snap resulted in punter Harry Newsome's sixth block of the season, this one for another Browns touchdown in a blowout Steelers loss.

Coming up for the 2–10 Steelers were the 3–8–1 Chiefs in what was being dubbed "the Aikman Bowl." A line of questioning ensued, and when Noll was asked about the possibility of tanking for QB Troy Aikman, he exploded. "If I ever thought about losing a football game," Noll said, "I'd have me put in jail."

Into this environment came the smiling "Cookie Monster," the young and chipper Dawson. "A regal presence," wrote Toperoff. "Not a talker but an intense listener and observer," and, no doubt, Toperoff concluded in *Lost Sundays*, a future team leader.

None of this was lost on the head coach. "I haven't seen many players in all my years here who can explode off the ball any better than Dermontti," Noll said the week of Dawson's return from injury.

Dawson would finish the season at right guard and was perhaps the lone beacon of sunshine at Noll's end-of-season presser. "Dawson's a young man who just keeps making progress," he said. "I believe he has an outstanding future in this league."

Noll was a big part of the reason. While interior offensive line coach Hal Hunter would be fired at the end of the season, Dawson years later credited Noll, the former guard, with teaching him proper hand usage. That hand usage was a big part of Dawson's regal stature as he grew into a polished pro. Defensive-line coach John Mitchell would chastise rookies with warnings that, "If you don't get your hands up any quicker than that, Dermontti Dawson is going to knock you right through that snow fence over there when he gets here."

Dawson credited Webster, in his final season with the Steelers, for teaching him how and when to use finesse and/or power, among other things. "I learned a lot from Mike," Dawson said. "Mike would be in the weight room early in the morning. And he wrote everything down. Even though he'd been in the league 15 years, he just wanted to reinforce and make sure he knew the game plan, what everybody did and what their blocking assignments were. I tried to emulate that. And also, Mike, as soon as he got out of that huddle he was sprinting up to that line because you're the leader and it starts with you. I tried to emulate that as well."

Dawson also emulated "Iron Mike" by starting 170 consecutive games. He made the Pro Bowl every year from 1992 to 1998, was named to the All-Decade Team of the 1990s, and was eventually voted into the Hall of Fame. Kent Stephenson, who coached NFL offensive lines—including Pittsburgh's—from 1985 to 2000, called Dawson the best center to ever play the game.

✦ ✦ ✦

Of course, Dermontti Dawson came out of 1988 a guard, but with Mike Webster leaving for Kansas City as a free agent, the center position was wide open at the start of 1989.

Chuck Lanza was the presumed replacement, but Dawson was the team's best long-snapper, so Chuck Noll approached him in the hallway at St. Vincent College during training camp to ask him if he would compete with Lanza for Webster's job.

"He was asking you, but at the same time telling you," Dawson recalled.

Dawson, of course, won the job and later called the position switch the turning point of his career.

That season, he had a new position coach in Ron Blackledge. Hal Hunter had been forced out—along with LBs

Dermontti Dawson (63), blocking for Neil O'Donnell (14) in a 1995 game against the Patriots, moved from guard to center in 1989, replacing Hall of Famer Mike Webster. Dawson went on to start every game at center for the Steelers for 10 years. He was inducted into the Hall in 2012.

coach Jeb Hughes and special teams coordinator Dennis Fitzgerald—by Dan Rooney. The team president gave Noll an ultimatum of resigning or firing the three coaches. Noll thought long and hard, but eventually decided to stay. He also asked Tony Dungy to take a demotion to secondary coach so the Steelers could hire Joe Greene's former coach at North Texas State, Rod Rust, as the new defensive coordinator. Dungy opted to leave, and John Fox was hired as secondary coach.

The moves proved to be a godsend to Woodson as he entered his third season.

"He really taught me a lot, Rod Rust," Woodson said. "Tony taught me a lot about playing corner in this league and being positive all the time, but Rod Rust really challenged me as an individual to pick my game up and study film and make the game slow down. It became easy watching film and studying throughout the week, so when gameday comes you just let your talent take over."

Woodson said it took him only a few weeks of watching film with Rust before a light came on. "I just started to believe in everything I saw," he said. "Went to seven straight Pro Bowls after that."

Rust and Fox had another young cornerstone piece to groom that season in second-round pick Carnell Lake, who was drafted out of UCLA as a linebacker. Dick Haley had gone to UCLA to talk to Lake for only a couple of minutes, and Lake thought the only interesting bit of information he passed along to the Steelers' director of player personnel was that he had met Joe Greene as a child while traveling with Lake's godfather, and Greene's friend, Roy Jefferson, through Texas.

Jefferson was a close friend of Lake's father while both attended the University of Utah. All Haley said was, "It was nice to meet you," and Lake didn't hear from him again until the Steelers drafted him with pick No. 34 early in the second round.

Of course, at 208 pounds, there was little chance of Lake playing linebacker for the Steelers.

"I was a true linebacker," Lake said. "I lined up over tackles and tight ends and held my point."

He was a three-year starter at UCLA and led the Pac-10 in sacks as a junior. He covered tight ends as a senior, benched 330 pounds, and ran a 4.42-second 40 at the Combine. He drew comparisons to college linebacker/pro cornerback Lester Hayes from Dungy, now with the Chiefs. Dungy said at the time that he projected Lake as a cornerback, which, by Super Bowl XXX, turned out to be the case.

"I'd like to tell you we were that smart, but I'm not sure," Donahoe said of accurately projecting Lake's position switch. "Projections are interesting because most of them don't work. Donnie Shell worked. Carnell Lake worked. There have been some others, but a lot of projections in the NFL don't work, so you're always a little bit nervous.

"Now, the thing that stood out so much about Carnell when we looked at him was he was such a good athlete and he had such unbelievable play speed that we thought he could make the transition from linebacker to safety, and then, to take it a step further, the year that Woodson got hurt and Carnell was our strong safety, he volunteered to go out and play corner. He was not a natural corner and he struggled some with it, but he enabled us to stay competitive. And we never did put Woodson on IR, and he eventually ended up coming back to play in the Super Bowl that year. But the thing that set Carnell apart is he's a team guy. He'd do anything for the team. And Carnell was a big, strong guy, and he could run with anybody."

Lake continued to learn secondary play from one of the UCLA cornerbacks after the Combine and felt he was ready for Steelers training camp in 1989. "I felt confident enough to hold my own," Lake said. "And any corner with the Steelers, especially Rod Woodson, I watched him like a hawk."

Donnie Shell had been replaced at strong safety in 1988 by Cornell Gowdy, but Rust urged Noll to cut Gowdy, and so the job of strong safety, next to free safety Thomas Everett and behind cornerbacks Woodson and Dwayne Woodruff, was all Lake's.

Was it still his after a 51–0 loss to the visiting Browns in the opener?

"Well, I did get burned," Lake said. "But the fact is I had a great game. They had me covering [Eric] Metcalf a lot, and he was quick as a cat. Not many people could cover him, but I covered him and put some good hits on him. I walked away from the game saying I could do this."

Lake and the Steelers were bludgeoned again the following week, 41–10, at Cincinnati, but the young players grew and the team rallied to make the playoffs that season. "It was one of the great coaching jobs by Coach Noll," said longtime running backs coach Dick Hoak.

It was a positive way to end a most negative decade.

9

A CLEAN BREAK

IT WAS 1992, and Chuck Noll had just resigned following a historic 23-year run as head coach. Noll's last team went 7–9, his fourth losing season since 1972, but the group wasn't far from making a run.

The defense was clearly ascending behind future Hall of Famer Rod Woodson and 2021 Hall of Honor inductees Greg Lloyd and Carnell Lake. On offense, the Steelers had come away from the 1990 draft with an intriguing haul: QB Neil O'Donnell, RB Barry Foster, and TE Eric Green. Two of their 1988 draft picks, future Hall of famer Dermontti Dawson and left tackle John Jackson, were their best offensive linemen. There were other talented players about to be joined by more as new coach Bill Cowher and just-promoted director of football operations Tom Donahoe prepared for their first draft together in 1992.

The Dallas Cowboys, picking 13th, wanted an important piece of that Steelers draft. The coach of the Cowboys, Jimmy Johnson, called his former star tackle at the University of Miami, Leon Searcy, to tell him the Cowboys were going to trade up for him. A Cowboys rep showed up at Searcy's home in Orlando, Florida, with a contract and jersey, but he left after Searcy received another phone call, this from Cowher, who told Searcy he would be his first-ever draft pick at No. 11 overall.

The massive Searcy had been a three-time national champion at Miami and would eventually start at right tackle for the Steelers, but his rookie season was spent behind two-time Pro Bowler Tunch Ilkin as the 35-year-old played his final season with the Steelers.

The Steelers had youth at linebacker with Lloyd and Hardy Nickerson, both 27, and Jerrol Williams, 25, but 1990 Pro Bowler David Little was 33, and the Steelers wanted to groom his replacement at inside linebacker.

Drafting 10th in the second round, 38th overall, the Steelers awaited the Cowboys' back-to-back picks. The Steelers were hoping to draft Penn State inside linebacker Mark D'Onofrio, but the Packers took him 34th. That left the Steelers with a projection for the position, and after the Cowboys drafted WR Jimmy Smith and DB Darren Woodson, the Steelers were able to select Clemson defensive end Levon Kirkland and hope he could play inside linebacker in the NFL.

"He was so unusual in college," recalled Donahoe. "He was a rush defensive end, and his movement was exceptional, along with his size and range. He could rush the passer and he could chase down plays in pursuit. We just thought this guy's not going to be big enough in the 3-4 to play defensive end, so what we wrestled with, with Levon, was whether he could play linebacker. So when we went down there to work him out, we had him do all the linebacker drills, and he looked like a natural. That reminds me of the time Aaron Donald worked out at Pitt, and somebody had him do linebacker drills. I came back from the workout and told everybody that not only can this guy play defensive tackle, he can play inside linebacker because he moved around like Levon could move around. You get a guy that big with change-of-direction and the ability to bend and just the lateral quickness, those guys who have explosiveness in their body, they have a chance to be really good players."

Kirkland was a 6'1", 240-pounder who ran a 4.84-second 40, but his competitive speed was faster. He had been recruited to Clemson out of tiny Lamar High School in central South Carolina. As a junior, he was Lamar's top offensive threat as a wide receiver, tight end, and return specialist, and as a linebacker he intercepted seven passes and returned six for touchdowns. His stock grew in the playoffs when the coach told the team that college scouts would be in attendance. Kirkland nodded and "just balled out." The state's two biggest colleges noticed, and Kirkland turned down South Carolina to enter Clemson as a 205-pound freshman. His goal was to add 15 pounds each year, and by the time he joked with Pittsburgh reporters that he was "down to 495" in 1999, it was fair to say he'd accomplished his goal.

Kirkland set a Clemson freshman record with 5.5 sacks, and as a sophomore won the 1989 Gator Bowl MVP award against Major Harris and West Virginia. Kirkland was a

Butkus Award finalist as a junior in 1990, and he left Clemson in 1991 as a 240-pound edge-rusher with 19 career sacks.

The Steelers moved Kirkland behind Little as a rookie, and Kirkland took the job a year later. As his weight grew into the 275–280 range, he obviously became a fierce run-stopper, but it was his ability in coverage that caused football experts to label him a "freak."

"In a lot of ways I think I kind of redefined the position," Kirkland said after his playing days ended. "Being a big man like I was and doing some of the things I did on the field was kind of unique.... I knew the angles pretty well and I was very patient as a cover man, so I knew the things that I could do and the things I probably shouldn't do. When I called Cover-2, it was really hard to beat me deep because that was my responsibility. As far as covering somebody man-to-man, I just took away half the field, or took half their body. I played a lot smarter than people realized. Plus, I really worked on catching the ball—making interceptions—every training camp. I played wide receiver in high school and had some interceptions in college. It was more of a surprise for them and not so much for me."

✦ ✦ ✦

Before the 1990 season, Rod Woodson appeared on the cover of the team's publication, *Steelers Digest*, in a Superman outfit, replete with cape and *S* on the chest. Third-round pick Joel Steed must've been confused because he assumed the guy who was beating him up every day in practice was the Superman.

"He might as well have had an *S* on his chest," Steed said of Dermontti Dawson.

Dawson had yet to play in a Pro Bowl when Cowher arrived, but along with Cowher came new offensive coordinator Ron Erhardt. He had coordinated the New York Giants to two titles but was demoted after Bill Parcells left. Erhardt went looking for another coordinating job, hopefully one that would emphasize the running game. Cowher was his huckleberry, and so Erhardt became Dawson's. Right away Erhardt looked to involve the mobile center in more pulling, which became Dawson's trademark as his career took off.

But poor Steed. He was getting killed by Dawson in his rookie camp, and Steed, a 6'2", 281-pound nose tackle with short arms and tiny hands, began to worry Steelers coaches, who began thinking they had overdrafted Steed in the third round. He was looking like his NFL Combine profile said he should look. Steed's Combine numbers were rather poor. His 20-yard split of 3.0 seconds (of a 5.22-second 40) was his high mark at 35th percentile. By comparison to the other athletes at the Combine, Steed was small, slow, and weak.

"You have to be careful in scouting that you don't give the Combine numbers too much credit or you don't kill guys who don't have great Combine numbers," said Tom Donahoe. "When you watched Joel's college tape, you saw how strong he was and how difficult he was to block. He could take on blockers, he could defeat blockers, he could handle double-teams, and really that's what you're looking for in a nose tackle in the 3-4. Joel wasn't difficult to take based on his work ethic."

Gerald Williams, 29, was the starting nose tackle, but he could move to defensive end in a 3-4 alignment if Steed could develop as a true nose tackle. Steed did start four games in place of Williams in 1992, but the team's run defense fell from 3.4 rush yards allowed per carry in 1991 to 4.2 in 1992. The 1993 camp began the same way, with Dawson putting young Steed against the proverbial snow fence seemingly on a daily basis. But during the trip to Barcelona, Spain, for an exhibition against the 49ers, the teams practiced together the week of the game, and Steed looked like a new man. He was going up against Jesse Sapolu, who would play in the Pro Bowl at the end of the season, as well as the next, but Steed was beating him up. That's when the Steelers realized just how good a center Dawson was.

Steed went on to play in only one Pro Bowl (1997), but he became a vital cog in the Steelers' decade-long dominance against the run. After another outstanding season in 1998, Steed underwent knee surgery and played the 1999 season with pain in both knees as the run defense staggered. The Steelers allowed 4.3 yards per carry, and Steed retired following the season. It took the Steelers two years to recover their defensive identity by making nose tackle Casey Hampton their No. 1 draft pick in 2001.

"People didn't realize how good Joel Steed was," said Dawson. "Joel made me better as the years went on."

✦ ✦ ✦

Along with Leon Searcy, Levon Kirkland, and Joel Steed, there was one more key piece from the first Cowher-Donahoe draft, and Darren Perry, selected in the eighth round out of Penn State, was the only rookie to start the 1992 opener.

"As good as we were in the secondary," said Donahoe, "we needed a safety who could make the calls, get all those knuckleheads lined up properly so that they could take advantage of their athletic skills, and Darren was the ideal guy for that. Ideal. He was like a coach on the field."

The Steelers were worried a bit about Perry's size and speed (5'11"/190/4.81), but when they scouted him at Penn State and continued watching tape, "His playing speed and his reaction time were exceptional," Donahoe said. "He was that way his whole career."

With Thomas Everett holding out (eventually traded) and Gary Jones injured, Perry started at free safety in the opener as a rookie, and it was a big game. The Houston Oilers were defending division champs in their run-and-shoot passing heyday.

The Oilers jumped out to a 14–0 lead, but Cowher called a fake punt on fourth-and-15, and the Mark Royals pass to Warren Williams broke for 44 yards to the Houston 1 to set up a touchdown. Perry then intercepted Warren Moon on the next series to set up a field goal, and an interception by Larry Griffin set up another Steelers touchdown.

The Steelers defense dominated the second half. Rod Woodson stuffed a third-and-2 running play and later intercepted his second pass to set up a Neil O'Donnell touchdown pass for a 29–24 Steelers lead. Moon drove the Oilers to the Pittsburgh 14, but on second-and-1, his pass intended for Ernest Givens was intercepted by Griffin. The Steelers ran out the final 2:09, and the new regime celebrated a big first win.

"The thing you have to remember about my rookie year," said Perry. "This system was new to everybody, so we were all on equal playing fields. If I didn't know it, chances are no one else knew it either."

Cowher brought with him some all-star defensive coaches, too. New defensive coordinator Dom Capers had been incorporating exotic blitz packages since his Philadelphia Stars reigned as the USFL's No. 1 defense. By 1991, he was the secondary coach of a Saints defense that allowed the fewest points in the league. And new secondary coach Dick LeBeau had taken concepts from Bill Arnsparger to design the zone blitz as the defensive coordinator of Sam Wyche's Bengals in the mid-1980s. At the end of LeBeau's fifth season there, 1988, the Bengals led Joe Montana's 49ers 16–13 late in the Super Bowl. But on a second-and-20, three Bengals defensive backs collided and allowed a 27-yard pass to Jerry Rice. It set up the game-winning touchdown with 34 seconds left. The Bengals went 8–8 the next season, rebounded with a playoff berth in 1990, and went 3–13 in 1991. Wyche and his staff were fired, and LeBeau was hired by Cowher in 1992.

The young Steelers defense had been taught well by Rod Rust. Woodson and Co. learned how to think on their feet, and when Rust left after one season, his linebackers coach, Dave Brazil, retained the matchup zone concepts. So the Steelers were receptive to innovations from LeBeau and Capers that could complement what Rust and Brazil had taught. And Cowher set ego aside for his two brilliant assistants.

Woodson later raved about how LeBeau taught him the angles that allowed him to play safety at the end of his career.

Carnell Lake appreciated how LeBeau, a former cornerback, grew his defenses from the perspective of a defensive back. The young defensive players were clearly happy with the changes. And the offensive players—well, after two years of Joe Walton's overly complicated tight-end offense, everyone who didn't play tight end was ecstatic about the hiring of Erhardt.

Cowher also lessened the intensity of practices from Chuck Noll's fever pitch. Every Friday when Noll was the coach, the No. 1 defense went against the No. 1 offense at the goal line. There were no passing plays or gimmicks. "There was no brother-in-lawing it, either," said Greg Lloyd. No, they were running the ball, in pads, and if Noll didn't like the execution, he made them run it again—the same play.

"Oh, so now we know where it's going," Lloyd recalled. "And I hear everybody on the other side of the ball going, 'You've got to be kidding me.' We could've put 11 guys in that hole if we wanted to.

"One thing people didn't know about those days: when teams played us, it was a black-and-blue game. We were physical. We were very physical. And practice was crazy. You played the game on Sunday, and on Monday you didn't even feel like you played a game."

Cowher not only tempered the physicality of practice, he brought a semblance of team unity to what had become an offense vs. defense mentality. At one point, after Lloyd blew up a receiver in practice, Cowher called the team together and had them take a knee. He admonished Lloyd and told the team why it couldn't continue in this manner. It became a galvanizing moment.

✦ ✦ ✦

The Houston Oilers were called America's Wild-Card Team for good reason in the late 1980s and early 1990s. They had been to the NFL playoffs seven times, all as a wild-card, but in 1991 finally broke through with their first division championship since the NFL-AFL merger. So the win by the Steelers in the 1992 opener in Houston was a key win and set Bill Cowher's new regime up for a 3–0 start. It also gave credence to Dick LeBeau's zone-blitz schemes, which coordinator and coach heartily incorporated. In the rematch, a battle of 5–2 division leaders, the Steelers ran a 4-1-6 dime most of the game. An injury to Moon allowed the Steelers to rally from a 13-point deficit and win 21–20. The use of Rod Woodson in the slot was a particularly tough matchup for the Oilers, who couldn't block him on the blind side, and he knocked Moon out of the game in the third quarter.

The win concluded a regular-season sweep of the Oilers and confirmed that LeBeau's scheme—designed to stop the popular West Coast offenses—worked well against the run-and-shoot, too.

But could it stop the K-Gun? The 6–2 Buffalo Bills were next for the 6–2 Steelers in what loomed as the Sam Wyche show. In the 1980s, Wyche spawned both the no-huddle offense and LeBeau's zone blitz, and here it was in living color in Week 10 of 1992 with the upstart Steelers and the two-time defending AFC-champion Bills.

The Bills utilized the no-huddle with Jim Kelly, three WRs, a Hall of Fame RB, and—the big difference from the Oilers—a tight end. The Bills would be more physical than the Oilers, but defending the run-and-shoot had provided the Steelers with a blueprint for stopping the Bills. At least that was the hope. However, the dime defense couldn't stop Thurman Thomas the way it could stop Lorenzo White. Thomas gained 155 yards on a whopping 37 carries as the Bills took what the Steelers' defense gave them in an easy win. A third-quarter Steelers touchdown cut the deficit to eight, and the Bills took a knee inside the 10 in the final seconds of a 28–20 Bills win.

The following week, Woodson's blindside blitz forced an Erik Kramer fumble to set up the game-winning touchdown in a 17–14 win over the Detroit Lions as the Steelers embarked on a four-game win streak. A pair of losses to NFC teams was followed by a 23–13 win over the Browns, giving the Steelers the AFC Central Division with an 11–5 record.

The Oilers made the playoffs as a wild-card for the fifth time in six seasons, but blew a 35–3 second-half lead in Buffalo in a historic collapse to the Bills. The rally had its effects in Pittsburgh, where defensive coordinator Dom Capers was resting comfortably at home on a bye. But the comfort turned to panic when he was forced to scrap a game plan he had finished at halftime. The greatest rally in NFL history forced Capers to redo his game plan for a Bills team that would be without Kelly.

Capers leaned even more heavily on LeBeau's zone blitzes, and those concepts confounded the Bills—for a while. "What the Steelers were running was like Chinese to me," Bills center Kent Hull told author/analyst Ron Jaworski. "I directed our offensive line, and I looked at it like 'A-B-C.' The only problem was it turned out to be the Chinese alphabet. We simply didn't know who to block."

The Steelers defense dominated early, but their offense was abysmal. Bruce Smith strip-sacked Neil O'Donnell to set up a tackle-eligible touchdown pass by the Bills for a 7–3 halftime lead. The Bills of QB Frank Reich had only 121 yards at the break, but late in the first half Woodson left with concussion symptoms after taking a blast during a punt return. He was replaced by "One-Eye Blind" Sammy Walker, and the Bills went right at him on their first drive of the second half. When the Steelers toyed with safety help, the Bills attacked the opening created by that. Richard Shelton had a chance to stop the drive, even score, but dropped an easy interception. On the next snap, Reich beat Carnell Lake's blitz off the slot to hit James Lofton for a 17-yard touchdown pass and 14–3 lead late in the third.

The Steelers opened the second half with a drive into field-goal range, but holder Mark Royals fumbled the snap, and the Bills recovered at their 31. Woodson returned but broke his hand a few plays later and was done for the day. It didn't take the Bills long to add 10 points for a 24–3 win, their fifth straight over the Steelers.

The Bills went on to play in their third consecutive Super Bowl, but the Steelers had announced their presence.

"The Steelers were the first team we went up against where we were going to have to counter what they did to us," Bills WR Steve Tasker told Jaworski. "This was the first defense we played against that could control a game."

✦ ✦ ✦

In sorting through the offense, the Steelers liked what they had up front. None of the interior trio of Duval Love, Dermontti Dawson, and Carlton Haselrig missed a snap. They teamed with John Jackson and Tunch Ilkin to lead Barry Foster's 1,690 rushing yards. Ilkin would be replaced by Leon Searcy in 1993.

The wide-receiving corps did need some help. The Steelers had picked up Chargers castoff Yancey Thigpen in the middle of the 1992 season but didn't know what they had in him, so they went into the 1993 draft wanting to add to the trio of Jeff Graham, Ernie Mills, and Dwight Stone.

The Steelers also wanted to continue adding pieces to their defense, particularly since they were playing five and six defensive backs against the top AFC teams. Joel Steed was improving at nose tackle, outside linebacker Kevin Greene was signed in free agency, and Jerry Olsavsky and his protégé Levon Kirkland were replacing free-agent Hardy Nickerson and the retired David Little at inside linebacker.

Tom Donahoe entered his second draft with the idea of adding depth, with an eye at an eventual replacement for cornerback D.J. Johnson, who was entering the final year of his contract in 1993.

The 1993 draft was outstanding but not flashy. The Steelers drafted cornerback Deon Figures out of Colorado in the first round and all 10 picks made NFL rosters. Only fifth-round pick Marc Woodard and eighth-round pick Alex Van Pelt were released by the Steelers, but they played elsewhere.

After Figures, the Steelers traded a fourth-round pick to move up five spots in the second round to draft Chad Brown, an outside linebacker at Colorado who projected as an inside linebacker for the Steelers.

In the third round, they drafted Georgia wide receiver Andre Hastings, and in the fourth round they took defensive end Kevin Henry out of Mississippi State. Lonnie Palelei was a fifth-round guard, Willie Williams a sixth-round cornerback, and in the seventh round they drafted depth reserves Craig Keith (TE) and Jeff Zgonina (NT).

The defense was certainly helped by the additions of Figures, Brown, and Williams. Henry became a starter in 1996, but the other three became prominent members of a defense that led the Steelers to the pinnacle of the AFC in 1994 and 1995.

"All three of those guys helped us," said Donahoe. "Remember, Deon Figures got shot. It really hurt his career. He had very good ball skills and good cover skills, and we thought he was going to be a starting corner."

But the gold ribbon pick was Brown. Donahoe said Brown reminded him of Jack Ham. "Bigger and a little different style player," Donahoe said, "but as far as the athletic ability—run, cover, rush the passer, playmaker—that's the guy we thought of when we talked about Chad Brown."

Figures was a 6', 192-pound cornerback who was timed in the 40 at a rather pedestrian 4.62 at the NFL Combine. But he was coming off a six-interception season (12 career), won the Jim Thorpe Award as the nation's best defensive back, and was also one of the nation's top punt returners. His biggest collegiate moment occurred his sophomore season in the Orange Bowl when he intercepted Notre Dame QB Rick Mirer to seal Colorado's 1990 national championship.

Figures grew up in Compton, just south of downtown Los Angeles, in Crip country. He wasn't in the gang, but he went to school with rival Bloods and knew the terrain well. But while he got out of his childhood in one piece, Figures lost a step—and thus his career—when he was forced into South Central Los Angeles on a May night in 1995. A construction detour forced him off the freeway, and suddenly a shooter appeared out of the dark. Figures ducked, the shooter fired through the car door, and Figures took off not knowing he had been shot—until he brushed his hand against his pants and felt blood. He drove to a hospital where his sister worked, and heard later there were 16 shootings in South Central that night. After extensive surgery, Figures's knee never fully recovered. The young cornerback who had become a starter on the NFL's best defense in 1994 couldn't regain the step his 40 time told us he couldn't afford to lose.

Brown was another heartbreaking story, but only because the Steelers couldn't afford to keep him after his breakout 1996 season. Brown was a 6'3", 236-pound linebacker with a poor 40 time of 4.85 but outstanding agility times. He was also productive at Colorado. In spite of three different injuries, he finished his senior season with 15 tackles for loss and was named second-team All-America and unanimous first-team All–Big Eight. He played inside his first two seasons and outside his last two, in which he compiled 14 sacks. He finished his career with 369 tackles (242 solo) and 38 tackles for loss.

Brown came under the tutelage of another future head coach on Bill Cowher's staff, linebackers coach Marvin Lewis. He brought Brown in for a film session before the draft. After they watched outside linebackers, Lewis grilled Brown on his understanding of the inside position. Brown responded so well the Steelers signed outside linebacker Kevin Greene in free agency a few days later and began teaching Brown the inside position. He was the third-down pass-rusher as a rookie and then became the starter next to Kirkland after Olsavsky injured his knee in the seventh game of the 1993 season. Brown started the rest of the season and had three sacks. He improved to 8.5 sacks in 1994, but in 1995 struggled with a high ankle sprain and dipped to 5.5 sacks. His breakout occurred in 1996 when he moved outside full-time to replace an injured Greg Lloyd and piled up 13 sacks.

And then Brown was gone. The Steelers opted to re-sign Lloyd in 1997, and Brown left for Seattle in free agency. He couldn't say no to the money, but years later said he remained unknown in that city even after making the Pro Bowl twice. "It was like playing in the Canadian League," he said.

✦ ✦ ✦

In 1993, the Steelers took one step forward. And two steps back.

Forget the latter for a minute and listen to the late, great Kevin Greene to understand the step forward:

"One of my favorite memories involved the Buffalo Bills rolling into a *Monday Night Football* game at Three Rivers Stadium," Greene said in 2006. "We were having a great day, and I could tell by the end of the first quarter they were overwhelmed. The crowd was rocking. The Steeler fans were just cranking out really loud, so Greg [Lloyd] and I just started yelling at Jim Kelly and Thurman Thomas, just yelling, 'Yeah, do you hear that? We're coming after you! We're gonna get you! Oh yeah!' Kelly and Thomas were back there, and we were yelling and screaming, just intimidating them. That, coupled with the crowd, was working on them. I could look in their eyes, in Jim Kelly's eyes, and Thurman Thomas's eyes, and I could just see they were overwhelmed and they were just lost. The way I read their look, they were like, 'Oh, God, what are we doing here? These animals are really, really serious.'"

The signing of Greene in free agency, along with the growth by Joel Steed, Levon Kirkland, and Chad Brown and the maturing of Rod Woodson into the NFL Defensive Player of the Year should've meant more for the 1993 Steelers than a one-and-done playoff appearance.

They opened the season with a loss to the Steve Young–led 49ers, but a loss in the second game was curious. Off a 6–10 season and a 30-point loss to the Packers, and headed for a 5–11 season, the Rams crushed the Steelers 27–0. The final blow was a 29-yard touchdown run in the fourth quarter by rookie Jerome Bettis as the Steelers fell to 0–2.

A four-game win streak was followed by a loss in Cleveland, but the Steelers rebounded with a 23–0 ambush of the three-time defending AFC-champion Bills. It was everything Greene described above as the Steelers pummeled Kelly. He was taken to the locker room at halftime, and Woodson admitted later that he felt sorry for him.

Defensive end Kenny Davidson knocked Kelly out of the game, but the real culprit was Dick LeBeau, whose expanded zone blitz concepts—specifically his increased use of three-under/three-deep coverages—thoroughly confused the Bills. That expansion was built largely on LeBeau's use of strong safety Carnell Lake in a precursor of what LeBeau would do with Troy Polamalu a decade later.

Kent Hull, the Bills' great center, defined the Steelers this way: "They're dropping back tackles and blitzing linebackers. Some guy goes by you who wasn't your guy and you just froze. The zone blitz was absolutely the nemesis of the K-Gun offense. That defense just stopped what we were able to do."

In that game, the Bills punted on eight of their 10 possessions. On the two that didn't end with a punt, the Bills lost a fumble and threw incomplete on third-and-17 with a concussed QB to end the first half.

Utter domination.

But the two steps back were awaiting in losses to the Oilers two weeks later (23–3) and then in the rematch at Three Rivers Stadium three weeks after that (26–17). The Steelers lost at Seattle, beat Cleveland to make the playoffs, but lost in the playoffs to the Joe Montana–led Chiefs.

The Steelers had added a Hall of Fame piece in Greene, had seen the Hall of Famers on hand—LeBeau, Woodson, Dermontti Dawson—perform at their peak levels, watched the rapid development of youngsters Joel Steed, Levon Kirkland, Chad Brown, Leon Searcy, and Darren Perry, and watched the great draft picks of the late 1980s—Lloyd, Lake, John Jackson—move into their prime years. And yet the Steelers won two fewer games in 1993 than in 1992.

Pieces were still missing.

10

BLITZBURGH

WHERE DOES THIS chapter begin and end? Was it early in 1998 when the Steelers were poised to run the Broncos out of Three Rivers Stadium but instead threw an interception to the eventual Super Bowl champs? Was it early in 1996 when Neil O'Donnell threw to a wide open Larry Brown—twice—for interceptions in Super Bowl XXX? Was it early in 1995 when Tim McKyer was beat on third-and-14 by Tony Martin?

"The '94 team was better than the Super Bowl team," was where Greg Lloyd started.

To reset: the 1994 Steelers lost in the AFC Championship Game, at home, to the 9.5-point underdog Chargers. The 1995 Steelers lost Rod Woodson in the opener but went to the Super Bowl where they lost to the Cowboys on perplexing interceptions by O'Donnell. In 1996, Lloyd was injured in the opener and missed the rest of the year.

"Come back the following year in '97 and lose to Denver, in Pittsburgh, in the AFC Championship Game," Lloyd said. "One of the best runs I ever had in my life."

And yet, no ring.

"And who do you blame it on?" Lloyd asked. "We give all the glory to the quarterback when we win. We give all the glory to the coaches when we win. But when we lose, who gets it? Who are you going to put it on? Are you going to put it on the back of who?"

Of course, O'Donnell is the easy target. And Bill Cowher took his share of blame. And Tom Donahoe was ousted after a power struggle with Cowher in 1999.

Who was to blame?

"I never said," Lloyd continued, "because the fact of the matter is that they're my teammates, and what happens in-house stays in-house. We can sit back and look at the film and let the country and all the readers and the writers make the decision, but the fact of the matter is we won as a team, we lost as a team. That's how I saw it."

Lloyd was the face of the "Blitzburgh" nickname that became synonymous with the Steelers defense in 1994. That year they sacked opposing quarterbacks 55 times, which stood as a team record until 2017 (56). It was the second-ranked defense in 1994, third-ranked in 1995, second-ranked in 1996, and sixth-ranked in 1997. It was the Blitzburgh Era, and it came and went in a blur. Kind of like their pass rush.

✦ ✦ ✦

Tom Donahoe enjoyed another solid draft in 1994 with a haul that included Super Bowl starting pieces Charles Johnson, Brentson Buckner, Jason Gildon, Bam Morris, and Myron Bell.

In 1995, the Steelers added Mark Bruener, Brenden Stai, and Kordell Stewart.

"I think Kordell was an interesting pick," Donahoe said in 2022. "We thought that Neil O'Donnell was going to have a good year that year, but we were probably going to lose him because he would get an offer we wouldn't be able to match. So we wanted to try to get a quarterback in there just to buy some time and develop in case we did lose Neil. But of those guys, the guy that probably helped us the most was Bruener because Bruener was not a great receiving tight end—he didn't run great—but as a point-of-attack tight end for a team that wants to run the ball, I don't know that you could've had a better player than Mark Bruener. He blocked everybody."

Bruener was the 27th overall pick in the 1995 draft. A 6'5", 249-pound University of Washington tight end, he caught 90 passes for 1,012 yards as a three-year starter and four-year letterman. He wasn't fast (a 4.89-second 40 at the NFL Combine) but he was agile, strong, and could block.

"We knew we'd get some receiving out of him, but it was going to be more short-to-intermediate stuff," Donahoe said. "And, again, back then, tight ends were not used in the passing game the same way they are today. It was a different style and a different type of football. But Mark could block anybody. He could block anybody that you put him up against. He could single-block him and he could get him off the line of scrimmage."

Bruener had replaced the talented but enigmatic Eric Green, who had left in free agency. Green was the Steelers' first-round pick in 1990 but never lived up to his physical (6'5"/274/4.84) abilities. He caught 198 passes and scored 24 touchdowns in five seasons, but he's better remembered for the meeting he called to make a "Super Bowl Shuffle"-type video before the loss in the 1994 AFC Championship Game.

"We were being tremendously cocky at the time," said Levon Kirkland, "and it backfired on us."

The Steelers went 12–4 in 1994 and beat the Browns for a third time to advance to the AFC Championship Game as heavy favorites against the Stan Humphries–led Chargers. The Steelers had lost to the Chargers in a meaningless regular-season finale after the Steelers had locked up the No. 1 seed in the playoffs. The loss only figured to add motivation for the Steelers in a January 15 game played at an unseasonably warm (for Pittsburgh) 60 degrees.

The Steelers accepted the opening kickoff and drove for a touchdown and held a 10–3 halftime lead that became 13–3 early in the third quarter. But the Steelers were struggling on offense. After rushing for 136 yards in the regular-season finale—while resting some players the entire game and most for a half—the Steelers were being stuffed on the ground by the Chargers of coordinator Bill Arnsparger. The Steelers averaged only 2.5 yards per carry and were held to a field goal after a first-and-goal at the 6 early in the third quarter.

Still, the Steelers' 13–3 lead seemed safe—until lightning struck.

Twice.

The first strike was a 43-yard touchdown pass to tight end Alfred Pupunu that cut the lead to 13–10 with 8:03 left in the third quarter. After three consecutive Steelers series ended with punts, they were stunned by the second bolt from the powder blue. A tackle for loss by Levon Kirkland and an illegal procedure penalty by the Chargers set up third-and-14 with less than six minutes remaining. The Steelers blitzed, and the Chargers gave QB Stan Humphries just enough time to loft the ball toward the end zone. Tony Martin ran past nickel cornerback Tim McKyer and hauled it in for another 43-yard touchdown and a 17–13 lead with 5:13 left.

Neil O'Donnell drove the Steelers to a first down at the San Diego 9 on the strength of three passes to Green for 47 yards. But Barry Foster lost a yard, O'Donnell threw incomplete, and then O'Donnell threw to fullback John L. Williams for seven yards to set up fourth-and-goal at the San Diego 3 with 1:08 remaining. The fourth-down pass for Foster was batted away by linebacker Dennis Gibson, and the season was over for the shocked Steelers.

"The most disappointing play in my years playing there was when Tim McKyer got beat on third-and-14," said Rod Woodson in 2006. "I think we had the best team and should've been in the Super Bowl three years in a row."

McKyer had to be helped off the field after collapsing in tears. The 1994 season was his only one with the Steelers.

"San Diego was the loss that hurt," said Kirkland. "I don't know if we underestimated them, but I think we gave them lot of material to play us well. I think we had a better team than we did the year we went to the Super Bowl. Our defense, instead of two good cornerbacks, we had three because Deon Figures, before he got shot, played very well for us. And our blitzing package was really dominating, killing people. The offense was clicking on all cylinders, and we felt we had a pretty good team. And we felt we had a chance to go to the Super Bowl, but, man, we really motivated San Diego to play to our level and we gave away too many big plays. We kind of had to learn the hard way how to get to the Super Bowl. Every year was like a step to get to the Super Bowl, until we finally got there.

"The funny thing was, we had a great mix of veterans and young guys, but nobody said anything at that [video] meeting, because I don't think we had too many guys who'd been in that situation. To us, we were just confident. But I think that was a little premature. I guess nobody wanted to buck the system. That was a big-time mistake on my part."

✦ ✦ ✦

Barry Foster established the Steelers' single-season rushing record with 1,690 yards in 1992, but he also that season set the team record with 390 rushing attempts and 426 touches. It's possible that workload was the reason he was out of football in 1995, the doomed fourth-and-3 pass against the Chargers his final play. With 1994 third-round pick Bam Morris entering his second season and Erric Pegram signed in free agency, Foster was traded to the Carolina Panthers. He failed his physical and retired at age 26.

Pegram was joined in the 1995 offensive mix by Mark Bruener. He replaced Eric Green at tight end, and Yancey

Thigpen showed Pro Bowl form opposite 1994 first-round pick Charles Johnson. They gave the Steelers their best pair of wide receivers since Louis Lipps and John Stallworth in the mid-1980s. The offensive line endured a bit of a shakeup with free agent Tom Newberry replacing departed free agent Duval Love at left guard and rookie Brenden Stai stepping in at right guard for Todd Kalis.

On defense, another rookie, Brentson Buckner, stepped in for departed free agent Gerald Williams. He joined "Big Play" Ray Seals and Joel Steed to form what the Steelers felt was their best defensive line since the days of the Curtain. The linebackers were the envy of the league. Kevin Greene, Levon Kirkland, Chad Brown, and Greg Lloyd put the Blitz in Blitzburgh, and Dick LeBeau was now the defensive coordinator.

Of course, 1993 first-round pick Deon Figures had been shot in the spring, and then his mother died in August. This would not be his best season, but Willie Williams had developed into a quality starter and replaced Figures on opening day against the Detroit Lions.

And then the *Titanic* hit the iceberg.

Their best player, perhaps the greatest athlete ever to don the uniform, Rod Woodson, went down for the season with a torn ACL late in the first quarter of the opener while trying to tackle the shiftiest runner in NFL history, Barry Sanders.

The Steelers beat the Lions on a Norm Johnson field goal as time expired, but they were reeling. Figures played a bit, but still wasn't ready, so Woodson was replaced by Alvoid Mays, a veteran they had picked up in the off-season to replace Tim McKyer in sub-packages. Mays started in a Week 2 win over the Oilers, but the Steelers lost four of their next five, and the team that felt it should've danced in the Super Bowl the previous season was 3–4 and taking on water.

Bill Cowher called his Pro Bowl strong safety Carnell Lake into his office. He asked Lake if he wanted to play cornerback throughout the week and see how he would progress, see if it was a possibility for the next game. This was Chuck Noll asking Dermontti Dawson if he might volunteer for a position switch. Lake could only do the same and volunteer for the move. He did. And it worked. The Steelers won their next eight games to clinch the division title.

Lake's worst game was the 49–31 win over the Bengals, who took a 31–13 lead by picking on him.

"I was learning on the run," Lake said. "But I think I learned fast enough where we solidified the secondary, which was really all we needed that year because defensively we were so strong. I just made sure that I paid attention to what Dick was telling me, what Rod was telling me, and Cowher had a talk with me in Cincinnati. I was having a tough game and he said cornerbacks have to have short memories. That little kind of off-the-cuff remark like that off the sidelines really stuck with me. That little comment put me at ease and after that I played very well."

In the playoffs, Buffalo receiver Andre Reed boasted before the game that the Bills would pick on Lake, but Lake intercepted a pass and recovered a fumble in the Steelers' 40–21 win. It was the end for the Bills, who wouldn't win another playoff game until 2020.

Next up were the Colts, who have never beaten the Steelers in the playoffs. This would be their closest attempt as the Steelers needed dime-back Randy Fuller to swipe away a ball off the belly of Aaron Bailey, who was lying prone in the end zone as Jim Harbaugh's Hail Mary fell to him. The Steelers let out a sigh of relief and headed to their first Super Bowl in 16 years, where they would play their old Super Bowl rival.

✦ ✦ ✦

The Steelers were 13.5-point underdogs to the Cowboys, who were looking for their third title in four years. They had the big three of Troy Aikman, Emmitt Smith, and Michael Irvin, but the Steelers had Rod Woodson. He was back, thus becoming the first player ever to return in the same season in which he had suffered a torn ACL. Irvin became the object of Woodson's motivation when he asked, "How can a guy who just had surgery on his knee run on the autobahn?"

Woodson not only ran with Irvin, he broke up a pass and celebrated by pointing to his knee. "With all due respect," Woodson said in 2006, "Michael was a great receiver in this league, and one day he will be in the Hall of Fame, but he wasn't the fastest guy in the NFL at that point, really ever. He was an outstanding player in his own right, but, yeah, that was a challenge and the reason I pointed to my knee to say, 'Yeah, I had the surgery, but I'm fast enough to keep up with you,' at least for a couple plays. In the end, they won the Super Bowl, and that's all that really matters."

The Steelers had rallied from a 13-point fourth-quarter deficit to put a legitimate scare into the Cowboys. A Neil O'Donnell pass was intercepted by Larry Brown to set up a Cowboys touchdown for the 20–7 lead. But a 46-yard Norm Johnson field goal early in the fourth quarter was followed by a surprise onside kick recovered by Deon Figures. Nine plays later Bam Morris was in the end zone, and the Steelers trailed only 20–17 with 6:36 remaining as the pro-Steelers crowd in Tempe, Arizona, came alive. A Levon Kirkland sack set up third-and-17 and an eventual punt, and the Steelers got the ball at their 32 with 4:15 left.

Two plays later, O'Donnell again found the wide-open Brown for an interception. This one was returned to the Pittsburgh 6, from where Smith ran four yards for the championship-clinching touchdown.

For Smith, who would go on to become the NFL's all-time leading rusher, his 49 yards (2.7 average) was his low of the season. For the Cowboys, their 56 rushing yards (2.2 average) were their fewest in over two years. Their total offensive output of 254 yards was their second-fewest of the season. With Woodson playing only 12 snaps, the defensive performance by the Steelers was remarkable. Captain Kirkland led the way with 10 tackles in what the rest of the country viewed as a breakout performance by the Steelers' buck inside 'backer.

"That was my breakthrough game," Kirkland said. "That game really helped my confidence a lot. Before that time I was doing a lot of things undercover. You didn't hear a lot about me because we had so many great guys on defense. Really the job I did was moreso the dirty work, and there weren't a lot of highlights. When you're stuffing running backs, people don't realize how important it is until you've got a guy who can't stop the run. People who knew the game and studied the game gave me my props, but I think playing in that Super Bowl, and playing as well as I did, that really helped get the word out, and it really helped my confidence a whole lot."

As for Woodson, he wonders if his rushed return for the game was the beginning of his end in Pittsburgh. He played the following season with an injury that he felt was due to overcompensation, and then he wasn't offered much to return as a free agent, so he departed in 1997.

"I was healthy enough to get out there," Woodson said. "It wasn't the smartest thing to do, but even in retrospect I thought I was going to spend my whole life in Pittsburgh as a player, so I never knew if we'd make it back to the Super Bowl. I needed to try to play in that game. I was probably 45–50 percent healthy at that point."

The Steelers shocked their fans on draft day 1996 with the blockbuster trade for 255-pound running back Jerome Bettis, the former No. 6 at Notre Dame who was known for his powerful long runs for the Irish. He was the 10th pick of the 1993 draft by the Los Angeles Rams and was voted NFL Offensive Rookie of the Year after rushing for 1,429 yards. He was known then as "the Battering Ram," but the nickname changed to "Bus" in Pittsburgh as he embarked on a Hall of Fame career that made this trade perhaps the best in team history. To acquire Bettis and the Rams' third-round pick (OLB Steven Conley), the Steelers traded a 1996 second-round pick (TE Ernie Conwell) and a 1997 fourth-round pick (OG Jerome Daniels). The Rams were coming off 5–11 and 4–12 seasons and decided that "Ground Chuck" was the issue. So they got rid of coach Chuck Knox and man/bus running back Bettis.

"We looked at the tape and studied it," said Donahoe. "We felt it was more their offensive line than it was Jerome, so we went ahead and made the trade. Jerome came in, and I think Jerome was just as valuable for the Steelers in the locker room as he was on the field. He's one of their great players of all-time. I'm prejudiced for the guy. Loved the guy because of what he did for the Steelers when I was there and what he did for the Steelers later on. How can you get a better leader and better guy than Jerome Bettis?"

Bettis became everything the Steelers hoped for in the trade. He rushed for 1,431 yards in 1996 and won NFL Comeback Player of the Year.

However, it wasn't enough to get the Steelers over the hump, especially since they lost QB Neil O'Donnell in free agency, and a three-man replacement derby was eventually won by 34-year-old journeyman Mike Tomczak.

The Steelers also lost the heart-and-soul of their defense when Greg Lloyd suffered a torn patellar tendon in the opening-day loss in Jacksonville. Lloyd missed the season and was replaced as an edge rusher by Chad Brown, who had a career-high 13.5 sacks that set him up for a huge payday in free agency, which the Steelers wouldn't match.

The Steelers also lost talented right tackle Leon Searcy in free agency prior to 1996. The first pick of the Donahoe–Bill Cowher era wouldn't effectively be replaced until the drafting of Marvel Smith four years later.

Searcy's departure is a lesson in why players shouldn't take personally what's said during contract negotiations. In fact, Cowher had called Searcy to tell him just that, and to not listen to whatever his agent was telling him about what management was saying. But Searcy's agent, Drew Rosenhaus, was intent on procuring a huge offer, so he had Searcy listen on another phone line as the Steelers negotiated against his flaws. Searcy heard the Steelers' unknown negotiator tell Rosenhaus that Searcy's play lacked consistency and that he was too young to be asking for such a big contract. After 20 minutes, an enraged Searcy hung up and told Rosenhaus to find him a new team. And he did. Searcy signed a mega-deal with the Jaguars and became the highest-paid offensive lineman in the league.

"Did my agent set me up?" Searcy asked in *Steelers Takeaways*. "He probably did. Maybe he used me."

The Steelers made the 1996 playoffs as a wild-card and beat the Colts again, but lost in the fog in New England, marking the end of the line in Pittsburgh for the great Rod Woodson. "They felt that with all of the injuries I wasn't worth keeping around," Woodson said in 2006. "At first I took it personally, but once I left and got away from it, and was a couple years removed from the Steelers, I realized they just had to do what was best for that company. Every company has to do that. The only way, as an employee, we can say you were wrong, especially as an athlete, is to go out and produce somewhere else. But I still talk to Bill Cowher, and I'm glad they eventually won the Super Bowl."

Cowher, in the 2021 book *Polamalu*, contemplated which player—Woodson or Troy Polamalu—was the greatest he had coached. Before Polamalu came along in 2003, Cowher easily answered the question with Woodson.

"What Troy did," Cowher said, "he changed the game with his ability to disguise, his ability to anticipate, to take some chances even though he understands where his responsibility is. A strong safety to me can be a lot more impactful. But you're talking about the greatest player? No question Rod Woodson was just a special player at his position. It's hard to pick, but my point was both of those guys, I put them in the same breath. They didn't play the same position, but they both had the same effect on the game."

Woodson's contract expired in 1997 after he underwent another knee surgery to remove a bone chip and scar tissue. The Steelers offered the 32-year-old a five-year contract at an average of $2 million per year. He said no, and the second offer was $2.7 million with a smaller bonus and more incentives. He turned that down, too, so the Steelers signed 31-year-old cornerback Donnell Woolford. Woodson left for San Francisco, and the next day Dan Rooney, in the *New York Times*, compared the loss to that of Franco Harris at the end of his career.

Woodson struggled with his knee in San Francisco but eventually regained his elite status at free safety and won a Super Bowl with the Ravens.

Did the Steelers realize he would've moved to safety as he got older? Did they realize he could've afforded a lost step at that position? "I used to play with Bill Cowher my last couple years," Woodson said. "I'd do some scout team and mess around at safety, and I'd say, 'Hey, this is my natural position, Coach. I'm telling you that's my natural position.' And it was. Safety is a natural position for me because I can go back there and look at the defenses, call out our defensive sets or our coverages, and get people set up. I think I had almost as many interceptions as a safety in five years as I had in 12 years as a corner. I really enjoyed safety. I really, really enjoyed it.

"The memory I have from Pittsburgh is that we had so many athletes. Our defense was always physical and one that was in the top of the league seven out of the 10 years I was there. I remember how deep we were at linebacker. At one point we had Kevin Greene, Greg Lloyd, Levon Kirkland, Chad Brown all on the same team. We had some players on defense. You try to tell guys how talented we were and never won a Super Bowl, they always question that until I say all the names. Once I say all the names, they say, 'Oh, yeah, you guys had some players.' We had a whole bunch of players on that defense."

11

PAYING IT
FORWARD

THE 1997 STEELERS won their division behind the best year
of future Hall of Famer Jerome Bettis's illustrious career.
He gained a career-high 1,665 yards at 4.4 per carry to make
the Steelers the No. 1 rushing team in the NFL. They squeaked
past the New England Patriots 7–6 in their first playoff game
and hosted the wild-card Denver Broncos at Three Rivers
Stadium for the right to play in another Super Bowl.

The Steelers were leading the Broncos 14–10 late in the
first half as Bettis was chewing up the NFL's 16th-ranked
run defense with 49 yards on 11 carries. The Steelers were
second-and-2 at the Denver 35 and ripe to add to their lead
by halftime.

But the Steelers got cute and called a pass. Kordell Stewart,
finishing his first season as the full-time starting quarterback,

was intercepted at the goal line by Ray Crockett, and the Broncos, behind John Elway, drove for a touchdown. After getting the ball back, the Steelers were forced to punt, and then Elway drove for another touchdown. The Broncos led by 10 at halftime.

The sequence silenced the crowd, and the Broncos went on to win 24–21. Then they beat the Packers in the Super Bowl.

The Steelers? They tried to regroup but lost Greg Lloyd, Jerry Olsavsky, Yancey Thigpen, and John Jackson after the season. The previous year they had lost key starters Rod Woodson, Chad Brown, and Brentson Buckner from their defense.

✦ ✦ ✦

In 1998, Carnell Lake was injured, Joel Steed lost his effectiveness, and Levon Kirkland gained weight as the team sagged to 7–9. They went 6–10 in 1999. It marked the end of an era. Blitzburgh was over. It was time to rebuild a team that had so much promise but couldn't win a title.

"There are no regrets," said Lloyd. "When I got here, the team wasn't very good. We had some good players, great coach, but the team wasn't very good. I didn't know about losing. I didn't come from a place where you lost. The Steelers were like 5–11, 6–10. We were the group of guys who got drafted and started playing. We got the Steelers back on track to being recognized as a championship team, a team in the playoffs, a team that can win a Super bowl. Even though Super Bowl XXX we lost, we had put the work in. They kept putting the pieces of the puzzle together, and 10 years after we played in the one that we did, Pittsburgh put it together and they won. So for that I'm grateful. For a long time I kind of regretted the fact we weren't the guys who could bring that No. 5 in. But to have helped usher it in, it was kind of cool knowing that."

"Greg was accurate with that," said Tom Donahoe. "I think that people came in, they knew there was a culture. We were fortunate that our veteran guys were among some of our best workers, so they set the standard for the young guys. I think anytime you have a culture like that, they have a chance to be successful for a long time. Coach Cowher built that culture, and it took him well into the 2000s. Those kinds of players make it work.

"You go back to Woodson, Dermontti, Lloyd, Lake, Kevin Greene, Bettis, Searcy, Joel Steed, those guys worked. It wasn't like they just played on Sundays. Those guys were serious about their craft. They worked hard every day. They practiced hard. You never had to say to those guys, 'Hey, how about taking a day off today?' They probably would've had a fight with Cowher if he'd have told them that. They loved to practice and they loved to play.

"I used to love to go to practice. Those guys were so good. They really got after it. That's probably why the Steelers were able to do as well as they did for a long period of time."

✦ ✦ ✦

Liane Faneca tells the story of how her two-year-old son, Alan, would run across the room to greet family with "flying hugs" that would knock adults off their feet. Kent Stephenson, Alan Faneca's first pro line coach, calls that "country strong."

"You know how when you shake hands with someone who's never lifted a weight in his life," Stephenson said, "and he about breaks your hand? That's country strong. Just a powerful human being."

That's how Faneca entered the NFL—country strong. He had been the primary puller for an LSU team that ranked as one of the nation's top rushing offenses in 1997. But getting to LSU was a story unto itself for "Big Red." At age 15, on Christmas Eve, during his freshman year at Lamar Consolidated High School in Houston, Texas, Faneca experienced his first epileptic seizure. He didn't know it was a seizure. He was at his great grandmother's house with the rest of the Faneca family, and he thought it was a nightmare. But he awoke with adults hovering over him and wondering what was wrong. He thought it was Christmas morning and wanted to open presents, but when told what occurred, he wandered around the house crying uncontrollably. He realized he was okay and calmed down, but the seizures didn't stop. In the ensuing days and weeks he had a couple more, and by then Liane already had doctors' visits arranged. After months of testing, he was told he had epilepsy and the doctor answered all of his questions. Alan would just need to take medication and he would be all right. But then Alan asked the really tough question: what about football?

The doctor rather flippantly told him he could play football, too. Alan felt the need to explain the game to the doc, the position he actually played and how much head-bangin' was involved. "I know what football is," the doctor said. "Go have fun. Go do it."

Alan didn't ask again, and then he shot up the following summer and entered his sophomore season at 6'4", 260. And, yes, he was country strong.

Two years later, as a freshman at LSU, teammates noticed that strength right away. Faneca was instructed on the first day of practice to hold the blocking dummy in a drill. All-America tight end David LaFleur ran into it and Faneca didn't budge. LaFleur recalled it as "the hardest hit I've ever had." After LaFleur left LSU as a first-round draft pick, he called Faneca the best offensive lineman he had played with at LSU.

Faneca felt that Hal Hunter—son of the former Steelers OL coach—turned him into a complete lineman, and that's what Tom Donahoe saw when he went to LSU to scout the player who interested Bill Cowher greatly in the 1998 draft.

LSU in 1997 averaged 257 rushing yards per game and 5.4 rushing yards per carry in rolling up a 9–3 record and No. 13 national ranking. The Tigers were led in rushing by Kevin Faulk, a back who would be drafted in the second round by the Patriots. LSU's No. 2 rusher was Rondell Mealey, who would be drafted by the Packers. Mobile QB Herb Tyler was the No. 3 rusher, and "the Diesel," Cecil Collins, was No. 4.

"It wasn't just because they had good backs," said Donahoe. "Alan keyed the running game. He was pulling in front of fast backs 30–35 times a game, and he was effective in space."

And when Faneca made contact, "they went flying," Donahoe said. Of course, Faneca was country strong, so it only made sense. And it made sense to Donahoe that he begin evaluating Faneca. The Steelers' director of football operations was a member of the college advisory draft board, so when Faneca submitted his paperwork as 21-year-old junior, Donahoe went right to work. And he didn't have to twist Cowher's arm. His line was quickly falling apart. With the free agent loss of left tackle John Jackson, Cowher was forced in 1997 to play his best guard, Will Wolford, at left tackle opposite right tackle Justin Strzelczyk. Dermontti Dawson was 32, but Jerome Bettis was only 25, so another line had to be built, and quickly.

Cowher saw not only strength and mobility in Faneca, he saw aggressiveness, durability, physicality, tenacity, mental toughness, and a great work ethic. This was his guy, so the 6'5", 322-pound Faneca became the Steelers' first-round pick, No. 26 overall, in 1998.

Since the Steelers already had a young right guard in Brendan Stai, they moved Faneca to second-team left guard, where he had practiced a bit at LSU but never played. Not that it matters when you're country strong.

The plan was to ease Faneca into the starting lineup behind Roger Duffy, Dawson's backup at center. But in the fourth game of 1998, the piecemeal offensive line was obliterated by injuries to Wolford and then to replacement tackle Jim Sweeney, another backup center. Sweeney had been forced to tackle because rookie Chris Conrad, a third-round pick, was inactive that day and Paul Wiggins, a third-round pick the previous year, had been suspended for a banned substance. Former first-round pick Jamain Stephens was inactive, so the Steelers turned first to Sweeney and then to Duffy to play right tackle. Stephenson huddled with tight end Mark Bruener to discuss his next position should one more injury occur.

All of this opened the door that day for Faneca, and the Steelers didn't close it on him until he left in free agency after the 2007 season. By the time Faneca left, he had won a ring (helped by his key block on the longest run in Super Bowl history), made the Pro Bowl seven times, been named first-team All-Pro six times, and was eventually elected into the Pro Football Hall of Fame.

The block Faneca made to spring Willie Parker for his record 75-yard touchdown run in Super Bowl XL is the play most Steelers fans remember best, but only two weeks earlier Faneca had pulled and wiped out three Broncos in springing Bettis for a touchdown in the AFC Championship Game.

There was also the game from which Cowher tried to have Faneca named AFC Offensive Player of the Week. "He had two blocks that I don't think I've seen in a long time in this league," Cowher said. "I've never seen a game by an offensive lineman any better than that."

One of those blocks on poor Adrian Ross of the Bengals occurred as the Steelers grinded the final 5:54 off the clock. "I actually saw him knock the helmet off the guy," said Bettis. "It was a serious hit."

Faneca didn't win Player of the Week. Again, he was a guard. But he could play tackle. Three weeks later he started at left tackle in another one of those OL mishmash emergencies. He was in and out of the position throughout the remainder of what may have been his best season.

"My year out at left tackle was the easiest year I've had in my career on my body," Faneca said at the end of his career. "You're never on the backside of a play when you're a guard, but when you're a left tackle and you're on the backside, you really are on the backside. You're sealing a guy off or you're chasing down a linebacker and sealing him off. I never felt fresher than after that season at left tackle. I still give my left tackle buddies hell for stealing all the money. They're just out there cheating. But, no, it never crossed my mind to stay out there. I wasn't having near as much fun as I was at guard."

The Hall of Fame guard was presented at Canton by another member of the Steelers' 1998 draft class, Hines Ward. "He's a Hall of Famer, it's just a matter of when he gets in," Faneca said. "The reason I picked Hines was that he and I had so many conversations and so many discussions over the times. We just really bonded over those moments. We grew up together. We came in together out of college together and grew up in the Steelers organization together, bringing the team along to where we were. We just had a really good bond and that's where it ended up. I wanted somebody who represented me and kind of the same mentality. Hines and I have a lot of the same characteristics and mentalities that got us where we are. We're very similar, and that's how we became who we are as players."

Hines Ward also spent his early childhood in Louisiana, moved out of state at the age of seven, and developed a difficult medical condition that didn't prevent him from playing football. But it should have. Ward was nine when he fell off his bike and lost the anterior cruciate ligament (ACL) in his left knee. It wasn't sprained. Wasn't torn. It was lost. Gone. "Just something I've had to overcome," Ward said.

216 ON THE CLOCK: PITTSBURGH STEELERS

That's what Ward does. He overcame being raised by a single parent who worked multiple jobs and virtually raised himself in the Atlanta suburb of Forest Park. "It gave him a lot of focus," said childhood friend and college roommate Corey Allen. "He's always had a very high individual focus."

Allen played on the same baseball team with Ward and called him the best center fielder he had ever seen. But they played against each other in football, and Allen warned his middle-school teammates to watch for the halfback pass.

"He had probably 150 yards rushing," Allen said. "He was killing us. I was at safety on one side of the field, and in the fourth quarter we're up three points. And, of course, 40 yards in Hines throws the halfback pass. We all bite on the fake. He's laughing. You could see him smiling the whole time. That still bothers me to this day, that when you played against him he's laughing the entire time. You can literally hear him laughing and joking. He never liked a mouthpiece, so you can always see that Cheshire Cat smile, and that just used to irk me whenever I played against him. I hated to see that smile. It's a nasty little smirk."

Ward was an all-state basketball player, too, but he was the No. 1 football player in Georgia and was offered scholarships by Notre Dame, Florida State, Tennessee, and Nebraska. He turned them down, along with a $25,000 offer from the Florida Marlins to play baseball. Ward chose Georgia to stay home with his mother, and he went there as a quarterback.

But Georgia needed a running back in 1994, so Ward played there as a freshman and gained 425 yards at 5.5 yards per carry. His sophomore year he floated between positions.

It was a jack-of-all/master-of-none situation in which he was the second-team quarterback, second-team running back and second-team split end and flanker. This frustrated him greatly, especially after he didn't play at all against Clemson. He considered transferring, but by the end of the season Ward was the starting quarterback. He passed for 413 yards in the Peach Bowl against Virginia in a Georgia loss that had more to do with Virginia linebacker James Farrior's blocked punt than anything Ward did or didn't do.

Georgia changed coaches after the game, and Ward approached new coach Jim Donnan and asked that no matter where he played to keep him at the one position. Donnan agreed but didn't live up to his promise. He played Ward primarily at wide receiver, where, as a junior, he caught 52 passes for 900 yards and was named to the All-SEC team. As a senior, Ward caught 55 passes for 715 yards. He also carried the ball 57 times and threw eight passes under Donnan and finished his career with 3,870 all-purpose yards, second in school history to Herschel Walker.

Ward came within 82 passing yards of becoming the first SEC player with 1,000 yards passing, rushing, and receiving. He also became the first college graduate in his family. Not that any of it helped him on draft day 1998. He went from catching 12 passes for 154 yards in his final game to catching a medical red flag at the NFL Combine.

"People told me I'd be a late-first, early-second [round]," Ward said. "But nobody wanted to take a chance on me because I didn't have an ACL in my knee. It was frustrating because to this day I've never had a problem with it."

"He never had one," said Tom Donahoe. "So we figured, look, he's never had one—he's *never* had one—and he's played without it, so what are we worried about? And we took him."

Ward was the fourth player chosen by the Steelers in the 1998 draft. They drafted Alan Faneca first and moved up to draft defensive tackle Jeremy Staat second. In the third round, the Steelers received the go-ahead to draft fourth and chose linebacker Leonard Little. The Rams protested, saying they were still on the clock, and the NFL agreed. The Rams then drafted Little, and the Steelers chose Fresno State offensive tackle Chris Conrad. Twenty-six picks later, with the last pick of the third round, the Steelers chose Ward.

"People were scared of the knee," Donahoe said. "It probably didn't help that he played several positions, either, and I don't think Hines ran a real fast time (4.55–4.61 pro day). He wasn't a vertical guy. He was more of a possession guy. But, again, you talk about guys who make your running game go, Hines Ward made it go."

Ward's blocking skills were evident at Georgia. "He liked to be aggressive," Donahoe said. "He liked to mix it up."

After the draft, Bill Cowher said he wanted to get Ward "settled down at receiver." But Cowher couldn't help himself when he said later, "What's exciting for me is all the things you can do with Kordell Stewart and Hines Ward in the lineup at the same time. I've got a couple months to think about it. That's dangerous."

At Ward's first practice, veteran cornerback Dewayne Washington learned right away the type of receiver the Steelers had drafted. Washington lined up over Ward in bump-and-run coverage, but Ward knocked Washington on his ass.

"It threw me for a loop," Washington said in *Steelers Takeaways*. "He came at me even though he was a rookie, just to prove himself. That tells you about the guy's mentality. He figured it out Day One."

Ward made his mark on special teams as a rookie, but in 1999 the Steelers drafted another receiver, Troy Edwards, in the first round. So Ward prepared with extra verve—aka a chip on his shoulder—and won the starting job in 1999. He caught 61 passes, and yet the Steelers drafted Plaxico Burress in the first round in 2000. So Ward alternated with Edwards in 2000, and his production dipped to 48 receptions.

The Steelers didn't draft a receiver in 2001, and Ward enjoyed a breakout season. He caught 94 passes for 1,003 yards, and the rest of the league began finding out what Washington had learned at Ward's first practice: defensive backs don't like being hit. One DB after another complained publicly after scraps with Ward. In the case of Jets safety Victor Green, the girlfriend complained. Browns DB Earl Little threatened to kill Ward. Defensive end Eric Hicks was embarrassed by a Ward block in a 20–17 Steelers win over the Chiefs.

"I washed him all the way to the other side, just took him off the [TV] screen," Ward crowed. "I love that. They're worried about me, and at the same time here comes Jerome running the football."

"A safety has enough responsibilities without worrying about a receiver cracking on him," said Steelers safety Lethon Flowers, who added a warning for his teammate: "When they get a chance to get him coming across the middle, they're going to dig in the ground a little bit more on him than anyone else. You reap what you sow."

Selected 92nd overall in the 1998 draft, in part because he was missing an ACL, Hines Ward played with the Steelers for 14 seasons, hauling in 1,000 receptions, four Pro Bowls, two Super Bowl rings, and one Super Bowl MVP.

But they never did get Ward. The Ravens even had a bounty on Ward's head, but Ward only missed seven games in his 14-year career, all spent with the Steelers. He was MVP of Super Bowl XL and won a second ring in Super Bowl XLIII. He retired as the franchise leader with 1,000 catches for 12,083 yards. He was also a mentor.

"He showed me that I needed to knock the defender out before they knocked me out," said 2002 second-round draft pick Antwaan Randle El.

"Just a great teammate and just a hard worker," said Faneca. "I think he and I had very similar mentalities as far as work ethic and putting team first. When we stepped on the field, we never held anything back. We left it all out there."

✦ ✦ ✦

Jerome Bettis was the first piece of the puzzle that won a championship for the Steelers in 2005, and in the 1998 draft they added Alan Faneca and Hines Ward. It's not a stretch to call Bettis, Faneca, and Ward the collective heart and soul of that championship offense.

The first piece of the defensive leadership of that 2005 season was added in the fourth round of that 1998 draft when the Steelers drafted cornerback Deshea Townsend, who quarterbacked his high school team, South Panola, to the Mississippi 5-A state championship in 1993.

Townsend turned down the opportunity to play quarterback at Rice, Vanderbilt, and Memphis to play cornerback at Alabama, where he joined former South Panola teammate Dwayne Rudd. Townsend stepped into the opening-day starting lineup as a freshman, and in four years—with 40 starts against the likes of Peyton Manning, Tim Couch, and passing guru Steve Spurrier—was named All-SEC three times and intercepted seven passes. The Steelers drafted the 5'9", 180-pound Townsend to play nickel in the slot. He was a legit cover corner, but they questioned his ability to stand up against the run in their zone schemes. For that, the Steelers had drafted 6'1", 203-pounder Chad Scott first in 1997 and brought in 5'11", 193-pound veteran Dewayne Washington as a free agent in 1998. But in 1998, Scott tore an ACL, and Townsend received plenty of work.

Even though the Steelers eventually gave Scott's left cornerback job to Carnell Lake in his final season in Pittsburgh, DBs coach Tim Lewis said that Townsend had footwork skills that could match anyone else's on the team and called Townsend "a one-time guy," as in he only had to be taught something once. Those assets carried Townsend through a 13-year career that included two championship rings before he entered coaching.

Townsend was one example of how future core leaders could be found a decade ahead of a championship season, and the Steelers added two more championship pieces in the middle rounds of the 1999 draft. They selected Joey Porter out of Colorado State with the 12th pick of the third round (No. 73 overall) and Aaron Smith out of Northern Colorado with the 14th pick of the fourth round (No. 109 overall).

Porter went to Colorado State as an H-back but dropped too many passes and was moved to defensive end as a junior. He notched six sacks at his new position before erupting for 14 his senior season opposite Clark Haggans, whom the Steelers drafted in 2000.

Porter measured 6′3″, 241 pounds, and ran a 4.68-second 40 at the NFL Combine, but it was the Senior Bowl where he made his mark. "He didn't have an unusual game there," Tom Donahoe said, "but his practice tape and his one-on-one pass-rush stuff was unbelievable. That's where we got interested in him."

The Steelers thought Porter was faster on tape than his Combine time indicated, so they went to his personal workout in Fort Collins for a closer look. "He ran a 4.5 on grass," Donahoe said. "On grass that looked like it needed a baler," said college scouting coordinator Max McCartney. "It did. It looked like my backyard."

Donahoe cut the difference in Porter's time, but said "even a 4.6 is plenty fast for an outside 'backer."

With so few teams playing a 3-4 defensive alignment at the time, the Steelers were able to get such a productive and athletic player in the third round. At 241 pounds, Porter was too light to play defensive end in the NFL, but he was perfect for the Steelers' scheme.

"His quickness and his explosiveness remind you a little bit of Lloyd," Donahoe told reporters after the draft. "Now, I don't want to say he's Greg Lloyd. That's not fair to the kid. But from the movement standpoint and from the quickness standpoint, he's very similar to Greg."

The Steelers even gave Porter No. 95, Lloyd's old number. Porter exchanged it for No. 55 after the final preseason game, explaining that he wanted to forge his own identity. "Great move," Levon Kirkland said at the time. "I really didn't see Greg when he was a younger player, but I can say Joey is a little nicer than Greg. Greg just had a big chip on his shoulder the whole time, and I think that was his edge. If Joey ever gets that, you'll definitely have to watch out because he has everything else."

It didn't take long for Porter to develop that chip. After No. 3 OLB Mike Vrabel broke his forearm in the 1999 preseason finale, Porter became the first backup behind Carlos Emmons and joined the starting lineup opposite Jason Gildon in 2000. Porter remained there until he was released for cap reasons (with James Harrison knocking at the ROLB door) in 2007, and that season returned with the Dolphins to Pittsburgh for the infamous "Muck Bowl," in which Porter made eight tackles and intercepted a pass in front of Mike Tomlin and the Steelers' bench. Just as he had barked at foes throughout his Steelers career as the unquestioned leader of a championship defense, Porter howled at the Steelers all Monday night in leading the Dolphins defense throughout a close 3–0 loss.

Porter finished his 13-year NFL career with 98 sacks, 25 forced fumbles, 12 interceptions, 10 fumble recoveries, a touchdown, and a ring.

"Again, there weren't a lot of teams back then playing the 3-4 defense," said Donahoe. "We were probably lucky we got some of those guys later than where you might have to take them today. That was true with Aaron Smith, too, because Aaron was a natural-looking 3-4 defensive end. But he was a guy that we knew if we did take him we were going to have to bulk him up a little bit."

✦ ✦ ✦

Aaron Smith was born in Colorado Springs, spent some time in South Dakota, and moved back to his birthplace to become one of the greatest basketball players ever at Sierra High. But that's basketball. Smith's battles with future Big East Player of the Year Pat Garrity are part of Colorado Springs legend. Garrity gave Smith his first broken nose during one particularly physical encounter under the boards.

The football coach and Aaron's brothers talked him into playing football his junior year, and he started at defensive end and tight end. He led Sierra to the state championship game in 1992 and in 1993 Sierra got beat in the semifinals by the eventual state champion.

Aaron played at a big-school power and at 6'5" with a huge wingspan made the all-state team, but his preoccupation with basketball kept his weight down to 210 pounds. It caused him to slip through the recruiting cracks, and he ended up at Northern Colorado, a Division II school in Greeley that has the look and feel of your local community college.

Once Smith stopped playing basketball and began spending more time in the weight room, he added 40 pounds and eventually grew into a dominant defensive player. Smith led Northern Colorado to NCAA Division II national championships in 1996 and 1997. He piled up 44 career sacks, topped off by a school-record 21.5 as a senior.

The Steelers went to Greeley to scout Smith and liked what they saw. "The thing that impressed everybody with Aaron was just his toughness, his playing strength, his intensity, his work ethic," said Tom Donahoe. "He was a true team-type player. He cared more about the team than he cared about Aaron Smith. I think he maintained that his entire career."

Drafting Smith wouldn't be so easy, since the Denver Broncos were showing interest. The Broncos had called Aaron to say they were going to take him with the 61st pick. The Smith family in nearby Colorado Springs was braced for a celebration, but the Broncos instead drafted center Lennie Friedman. And then they passed on Smith twice in the third round. The Steelers took him with the 14th pick of the fourth round, and Smith began the long road to becoming a 3-4 defensive end with the Steelers.

"It was hard to adjust. Very difficult," Smith said in 2001, his second season as a starter. "It's a whole different way of playing. When you line up in a 4-3, you can attack, be aggressive, and not worry so much about double teams. Here, you see a lot of double teams, you're two-gapping a lot of times, and you've got to keep guys off your linebackers. You've got a lot more responsibilities in a 3-4."

Smith became the starter in 2000. The line at that point was still searching for an identity with newly acquired free agent Kimo von Oelhoffen playing nose tackle and Kevin Henry playing right defensive end. The right mix was found in 2001 with the drafting of nose tackle Casey Hampton in the first round. That allowed von Oelhoffen to move to his more natural position at right defensive end, as Smith, now up to a lifetime-high 325 pounds, became more comfortable and had a career-high eight sacks at left end. But it was the run defense that was becoming ornery. The Steelers went from 12th in the league against the run in 2000 to first in 2001. It became Smith's calling card as a two-time Super Bowl champion.

"You talk about work ethic with two guys that came in," Donahoe said of the Steelers' 1999 draft. "Joey Porter was a non-stop worker; Aaron Smith was a non-stop worker. Those guys were determined to be pro football players. We hit it lucky with both those guys."

It was Donahoe's last draft with the Steelers, and he left them with the nucleus of two future championship teams. Jerome Bettis, Alan Faneca, and Hines Ward were the heart of a physical offense; and Deshea Townsend, Joey Porter, and Aaron Smith were the leaders at each level of one of the great defenses to grace the AFC since the days of the Steel Curtain.

"You feel good anytime you help pick a player and help a player start on his career, whether you're there or not doesn't matter," Donahoe said. "You want the guy to do well and you want the team to do well, so you always root for those guys, whether it's Faneca or Bettis or whoever it was who helped the Steelers get there and win."

12

GRAVESTONE

THE 2000 NFL Draft featured the greatest quarterback in the history of the game, and the Steelers—drafting eighth with a new director of football operations who had monitored this young quarterback at a nearby college—passed on him.

Eight times.

"On my gravestone, it'll always say I took Tee Martin over Tom Brady," Kevin Colbert said 22 years later.

Brady grew up a Joe Montana fan in San Mateo, California, at the same high school—Junipero Serra—Lynn Swann had attended. A highly touted baseball prospect as a left-handed, power-hitting catcher, Brady opted to play football at Michigan in 1995, the same year Lloyd Carr replaced Gary Moeller as coach.

Brady expected to replace Brian Griese at QB in 1998, but a heralded in-state recruit, Drew Henson, was the local, fair-haired boy. Brady won the job in 1998 and the defending national champs finished 10–3, but Henson played in seven games and became an even bigger threat to win the job in 1999. Carr opted to platoon the two quarterbacks, with Brady playing first quarters and Henson the second quarters. Carr would choose the hot hand for the second half as Michigan got off to a 5–0 start.

In the second quarter at Michigan State, Henson threw an 81-yard touchdown pass and was chosen to play the second half. But he threw an interception deep in MSU territory late in the third quarter that turned into a Plaxico Burress TD catch and a 27–10 MSU lead, so Carr put Brady back on the field. He directed Michigan to three touchdowns in three possessions by completing 19 of 22 passes for 204 yards. Michigan only trailed by three points, but Burress recovered the onside kick and MSU ran out the clock.

Michigan lost, but Brady made his mark and started the final five games. He finished as team MVP and was invited to the NFL Combine. He measured 6'4", 211 pounds, but ran a slow 5.28-second 40 and had a puny 24½" vertical jump. He did post an extraordinarily high Wonderlic intelligence score of 33.

Colbert was the pro scouting director for the Detroit Lions, and he watched film of Michigan's 1999 games against Notre Dame, Wisconsin, and Michigan State. He even went out watch Brady practice, but returned to his office with a lackluster scouting report. Moeller, then the Lions' linebackers coach, asked Colbert for his opinion.

"He's all right," Colbert said. "He's good. He's not that great an athlete. He's got a good arm, not great."

"Listen," Moeller said, "all that guy does is win."

The comment would haunt Colbert into his retirement.

Colbert ended his 10-year run with the Lions to replace Tom Donahoe as the Steelers' director of football operations two months before the 2000 draft. Colbert did draft a quarterback, and he was a winner, too. In fact, Steelers fifth-round pick Tee Martin won a national championship.

Martin directed Tennessee to an undefeated season in 1998 and then a 10–3 record in 1999. At the Combine, he measured 6'2", 227 pounds, ran a 4.61-second 40 with a 34½" vertical jump. His Wonderlic score was 11. Colbert chose him 36 picks before New England drafted Brady.

In addition to Martin, the Steelers signed 32-year-old Kent Graham away from the New York Giants. He was 10–5 in spot starts the previous two seasons. The lone incumbent was Kordell Stewart, who, at 28, had been benched the previous season and was still learning the position under second-year offensive coordinator Kevin Gilbride.

Those factors weighed heavily in Colbert's mind as he and Bill Cowher contemplated Marshall quarterback Chad Pennington with the eighth overall pick.

"Kordell had done some very good things before we came in, and we had signed Kent Graham," Colbert said. "I remember the press conference and talking about Kordell. I said, 'Hey, I've scouted the guy. We [the Detroit Lions] played you guys in recent years, and me, doing the advance, obviously respected what he could and can still do.' So it wasn't like we were in a desperate need for a quarterback at that point."

The Steelers decided that Burress, a 6'5", 231-pounder, would better help the passing game. They added to the QB position in the fifth round with Martin.

Gilbride, the OC, muttered privately to reporters about the pick but publicly hoped the athletic Martin would bring Stewart-like playmaking skills.

"We went into that draft liking Chad a lot," Colbert said. "We spent a lot of time with him, but we just felt for the 2000 team Plaxico Burress was the better pick. Plax had a great career. But, in all honesty, we didn't go into that thinking we wanted a quarterback."

At the time, Ben Roethlisberger was coming off his first season as a high school quarterback. By the time Roethlisberger got to Pittsburgh, Brady had won two of his seven rings as a starting quarterback.

"After Tom Brady became Tom Brady in his second season," Colbert said, "I got film of him from Michigan, and we watched it again because I wanted to see for myself, and for the room, what did we miss?

"Again, we weren't alone. That was one of those things that happen here and there. Kurt Warner's another example of that. We loved Tee because Tee was a national champion. He had played very good football at a high level. There was a lot to like about Tee. But, obviously, Tee didn't have the career that Brady had."

✦ ✦ ✦

Kevin Colbert's first draft—like the drafts that ushered in the previous two powerhouse eras of Steelers football—included a left tackle. Marvel Smith was drafted in the second round and initially shored up the circus of Jamain Stephens–Chris Conrad–Anthony Brown–Shar Pourdanesh taking turns to replace Leon Searcy at right tackle. The run game improved from 10th to fourth in 2000, but one hole had become apparent: Dermontti Dawson could not recover from the hamstring injury that wrecked his 1999 season. After the 2000 season, the great center retired. He was replaced by free agent Jeff Hartings, whom Colbert had known while both were with the Lions.

The defense improved in 2000 under first-year coordinator Tim Lewis, but the run defense still ranked 12th as Kimo von Oelhoffen played out of position at nose tackle and defensive end Kevin Henry was released. The great Levon Kirkland was released, too, after a below-average 2000. So, even though the run defense had shown improvement, there were holes showing once again as the team entered the 2001 draft.

Still, the quarterbacks were ineffective. Bill Cowher had gone with a gut instinct and named Kent Graham the starter on opening day 2000. He and Kordell Stewart were in and out throughout the first half of the season before Graham was benched for good. The Steelers went 5–4 down the stretch with Stewart at quarterback to finish 9–7. Graham was released in a salary cap move and had nothing but good things to say about Stewart and the future of the Steelers in his parting interview. Colbert and Cowher were feeling the same as they approached the 2001 draft and their first season at Heinz Field. They traded down a bit to draft nose tackle Casey Hampton and traded up a bit in the second round to draft inside linebacker Kendrell Bell. But in the process of shoring up their soft middle, the Steelers passed on a quarterback who had come off a four-year starting stint at Purdue as a two-time Heisman Trophy finalist. Drew Brees was the first pick of the second round by the Chargers and went on to play 20 years at a Hall of Fame level.

"We were still of the belief that we were okay at the quarterback position," said Colbert. "We wanted to keep building around it. And, again, Casey and Kendrell were excellent players. We thought we were able to keep going with the mix at quarterback that we had. Drew Brees was a good quarterback. We all recognized it. But we didn't take a quarterback at all in that draft."

Stewart, with the help of first-year offensive coordinator Mike Mularkey and QBs coach Tom Clements, enjoyed his best season as a pro in leading the Steelers to a 13–3 record, the team's MVP award, and his only Pro Bowl berth. The Steelers—led by run-stuffer Hampton and NFL Defensive Rookie of the Year Bell—finished first in the league in defense with its No. 1–ranked run defense. In the playoffs, Stewart was mediocre in a 27–10 win over the Ravens and then poor in a 24–17 loss to Tom Brady and the Patriots in the AFC Championship Game at Heinz Field. While the Steelers' special teams were abysmal, Stewart was intercepted three times in compiling a passer rating of 45.2. Two of the interceptions occurred in the game's final three minutes.

The Steelers went into the game as 10-point favorites but never led in falling behind 21–3 on a blocked field-goal attempt that was returned for a Patriots touchdown early in the third quarter. It also didn't help the Steelers that Jerome Bettis, who had been positioned to become the first Steeler to lead the league in rushing since Bill Dudley, suffered serious hip and groin injuries in Game 11. He returned eight weeks later to play against the Patriots, but carried only nine times for eight yards. Special teams, injuries, coaching—none of it seemed to matter to a fan base that was growing increasingly intolerant of Stewart. Fabricated rumors swirled around him, and he remained reviled in Pittsburgh even after his greatest season.

Most of the issues were addressed in 2002. Kevin Spencer replaced Jay Hayes as special teams coach and James Farrior was signed as a free agent to replace departed inside linebacker Earl Holmes. The Steelers did select a quarterback high in the 2002 draft, but Indiana University star passer Antwaan Randle El would play wide receiver. Stewart was still only 30 and behind him was 31-year-old Tommy Maddox, who signed with the Steelers in June 2001, after an MVP season in the XFL. The Steelers also drafted future Super Bowl starters Kendall Simmons, Chris Hope, Larry Foote, and Brett Keisel in 2002, and signed a player after the draft who would become a Pittsburgh legend. The Steelers sent offensive assistant Mike Miller to Kent State's pro day in 2002 to scout James Harrison, a linebacker who had walked on, encountered academic difficulties, and became grossly out of shape before joining the first team and starting his final two years. In his final game for Kent State, Harrison made 12 tackles and sacked Miami (Ohio) quarterback Ben Roethlisberger on third and fourth downs in the final minutes to seal a Kent State win and its first winning season in 14 years.

That season, Harrison led the MAC with 15 sacks and won the Jack Lambert Award as Kent State's MVP. But he wasn't considered much of an NFL prospect because of his 5'11" stature and 4.8-second 40 time. His future agent, Bill Parise, while scanning film for players to represent, asked a

Kent State player, "Who is that No. 16?" When told it was Harrison, Parise called him "one of the best linebackers I've ever seen in my life."

"I spoke with NFL guys who asked about him," Kent State coach Dean Pees said in *Never Give Up*, "and the first thing they'd bring up was he was only about 5′11″. I'd tell them he's strong, really quick…no one could knock him off his feet."

Miller was sent to Kent State and told to watch him closely among the small group of Kent State prospects, because, as scout Tim Gribble told Miller, "This guy's really tough."

"The thing about James that was interesting," said Miller, "when you're at these things, inevitably every one of these kids at some point during the workout will come over and ask for their times or what they jumped, ask how they're looking— even though they've been told a hundred times, 'Don't ask. You'll find out at the end.' But James acted like this was the biggest inconvenience of his life. He was so unimpressed with the entire process. He'd get up, run his 40 and go sit down. And he would have that stare. He's just staring at you. And we'd be like, 'Okay, now we're going to do this.' Not until it was his turn would he get up. He'd come over, do it, then go sit down. Then he'd get on the bench and put up some ridiculous number, because he's so strong, and then he'd go sit down. I thought, *Wow, this guy doesn't seem very impressed with this whole thing.* So I got back and said, 'If his demeanor says anything about how tough he is, then we'd better get him.' So we brought him in as a free agent."

✦ ✦ ✦

Tommy Maddox played the second half of the 2001 finale and threw a 40-yard touchdown pass to Bobby Shaw that boosted his passer rating to 115 for the day. And in the 2002 preseason, Maddox started Game 3—the "Dress Rehearsal" of preseason games—because Kordell Stewart had suffered a concussion the previous week. Maddox threw a 29-yard touchdown pass to Antwaan Randle El, a 19-yard touchdown pass to Mark Bruener, and a 41-yard pass to Plaxico Burress to the Detroit 1 before being replaced by Charlie Batch late in the second quarter with a 21–10 lead.

Maddox finished the 2002 preseason with a red-hot passer rating of 128.1 and was in the process of establishing himself as the No. 2 ahead of Batch, whom the Steelers had brought in as a free agent. But it was unlikely that Maddox would pass Stewart, the team's MVP of the 13–3 2001 season, unless Stewart reverted to previous form and Maddox remained hot.

And that's exactly what happened. Maddox wowed everyone with his beautiful release and perfect fade passes in 2002 practices to the stellar receiving corps of Hines Ward, Burress, and exciting rookie Randle El, while Stewart struggled in early-season losses to the Patriots and Raiders.

The 0–2 start wasn't all Stewart's fault, because the running game was fading fast. Jerome Bettis was still struggling to recover from his 2001 injuries behind a 2002 offensive line that included rookie RG Kendall Simmons and fading LT Wayne Gandy. Mike Mularkey was the new offensive coordinator and couldn't mix the marriage of run-oriented QB with the exceptional receivers. Bill Cowher, in fact, called Stewart into his office during the early bye week to tell him his job was on the line. And Stewart performed poorly in the narrow win over the Browns. His fumble on third-and-goal at the 1, a blocked punt, and finally a fourth-quarter interception had the Steelers trailing the Browns 13–6 when Maddox replaced him with 4:14 remaining.

Dubbed "Tommy Gun" by Burress, Maddox completed six of seven passes on a drive that ended with a 10-yard touchdown pass to Burress that tied the game. Maddox survived an interception in overtime to march the Steelers to a game-winning field goal. He completed 11 of 13 for 122 yards in rallying the Steelers as Cowher made the move to Maddox and in effect signaled the end of the Stewart era in Pittsburgh. Even Stewart understood the move. "He brings a calmness to the game," was his apt description of Maddox's play at the time.

Maddox did endure some temporary paralysis from a concussed spinal cord in a loss at Nashville. He missed two games but came back to lead the Steelers into the playoffs, where they overcame defensive collapses to rally past the Browns. The Steelers were eliminated the following week by the Titans.

Including playoff games, Maddox directed the Steelers to an 8–4–1 record with a passer rating of 85. Stewart, in his 2001 MVP season, had a playoffs-included passer rating of 78.3. He was released February 26, 2003.

While Maddox had made a clear connection with the Steelers' exciting trio of wide receivers, the Steelers lost their identity along the way. The No. 1 rushing team in the NFL in 2001 fell to ninth in 2002. The Steelers had become a pass-happy offense. And with Gandy leaving in free agency and Simmons and Marvel Smith about to endure illness and injury throughout 2003, the offensive line was about to allow the team's identity to change completely.

◆ ◆ ◆

In his pre-Combine address to local media in 2003, Kevin Colbert listed the Steelers' off-season needs as defensive back, offensive line, tight end, and quarterback. "We need help in the passing game and on the offensive line," he said. "We could also use a playmaker in the secondary."

The Steelers got their playmaker in Dexter Jackson, the MVP of the previous Super Bowl. He played for Tampa Bay secondary coach Mike Tomlin, who received a call from Jackson while the safety was in Pittsburgh negotiating his free-agent deal with the Steelers.

"I remember talking to Dexter Jackson when he was in a bathroom," Tomlin said in *Polamalu*. "He told [the Steelers] he had to use the bathroom, and, really, he was just letting me know how the day was going, trying to glean some information in terms of decision-making."

Tomlin knew from that conversation that Jackson wasn't sold on how he could become a leader in Pittsburgh. It was his goal as he agreed with the Steelers on the parameters of a deal, but he didn't sign as the negotiators worked out the small details.

Thinking they had their new safety in hand, Colbert and Bill Cowher skipped the USC pro day where playmaking safety Troy Polamalu was working out. The Steelers' brain-trust headed instead to the University of Colorado to watch running back Chris Brown. On the way, Colbert called the office to check in, and was told by the team's lead negotiator, Omar Khan, that Jackson had a last-minute change of heart and was signing with the Arizona Cardinals.

"We had a deal with Dexter, and we didn't. It fell through," said Colbert. "Tim Lewis was at the pro day, and Troy did a great job, and it kind of started to light up at that point."

Polamalu's workout tape from USC was extraordinary. It was passed around the Steelers' offices the way the "Don Hutson tape" of John Stallworth had been almost 30 years earlier. Polamalu's pro day numbers read 5'10", 213 pounds, 4.35-second 40, 405 pounds bench, 600 squat, 353 power clean, 38.5" vertical jump, and 10'4" broad jump. The coaches were amazed at Polamalu's ability to cut at full speed and the power he brought to the ball carrier. One young coach, Mike Miller, made an appeal to trade up during the in-team mock the night before the draft and was discouraged by Cowher. "You are aware that just a little bit ago we said we wouldn't do that," Cowher told Miller, who sheepishly walked away and told Cowher, "Congratulations. We just drafted a Hall of Famer." When Miller walked into the South Side offices the next day, he learned he was getting his way, and the Steelers traded with the Chiefs that day for the right to draft Polamalu.

The Steelers certainly needed help in the secondary. The pass defense had fallen from fourth in 2001 to 20th in 2002, and those stats didn't include the 767 passing yards they allowed in two playoff games, 429 by Browns backup QB Kelly Holcomb.

The Steelers also finished 27th in third-down defense in 2002 and figured the secondary of the dime was the culprit. The Steelers went into the draft hoping to land a nickel cornerback, either Ricky Manning or Rod Babers, to help their sub-packages, but without the third-round pick they traded for Polamalu, the Steelers watched as both came off the board before their pick in the fourth round. So, they took a chance on a high-ceiling but raw converted running back out of Louisiana-Lafayette named Ivan Taylor.

"Call me Ike, please," said the gregarious Taylor. The 6′1″, 191-pounder reportedly ran in the 4.2s at his pro day. One report even had him running a 4.19. Taylor said the best time of which he was aware was a 4.24 at one point in college, and that all he really knew about his pro day was that his slowest time was 4.36. He had spent only one year at cornerback, but in Taylor and Polamalu the Steelers had just added their team's two fastest players.

"I actually attended a game Ike's senior year," Colbert said. "They played LSU and they got killed, and Ike was one corner and Peanut [Charles Tillman] was the other corner. I knew of both of them, but I really went to see Peanut. You were going to see LSU, too, but Peanut was the one that everybody was focused on because he was the player and Ike was just this size/speed prospect who was a converted runner. Ike wasn't a Combine guy. Dan [Rooney] Jr. and Gors [Mark Gorscak] watched Ike continue to develop, and that's why we brought him in for a pre-draft visit."

Taylor and Polamalu became roommates and often commiserated through difficult rookie seasons for both. The Pittsburgh media, in fact, took a critical view of the trade-up for Polamalu, who looked tiny during spring practices.

"That's because he wears those long shorts that hang below his knees," said the great scout Bill Nunn at the time.

Steelers safety Troy Polamalu in action against the Baltimore Ravens at Heinz Field on December 26, 2004. Bill Cowher called Polamalu one of the greatest players he ever coached, saying, "He changed the game with his ability to disguise, his ability to anticipate."

"If he was worried about making the roster, he'd be wearing his shorts above his knees to look taller."

Just then, undrafted free agent Erik Totten walked by in shorter shorts, and the 5'9" safety did appear to be taller than the 5'10" Polamalu.

"Like him," Nunn said with a smile.

Polamalu didn't need to worry about making the roster. And after spending his rookie season on one of the great scout-team secondaries in Steelers history—with Taylor, Deshea Townsend, and Chris Hope—Polamalu caught fire in 2004 upon the hiring of defensive coordinator Dick LeBeau. The two helped propel each other to a pair of rings and a Hall of Fame jacket apiece.

Taylor was a primary factor in the two upcoming titles, as well. He was the cornerback LeBeau used to "travel" with the opponent's best wide receiver on a weekly basis. Suffice to say the Steelers found the playmakers for the secondary they were seeking in the 2003 draft.

✦ ✦ ✦

In his least productive season with the Steelers, Jerome Bettis rushed for 666 yards in 2002. Amos Zereoue had 762 yards rushing, but it was the lowest team-leading total in 11 years. And things were about to get worse in 2003.

Kendall Simmons, the starting right guard and No. 1 draft pick in 2002, was diagnosed with diabetes two days before camp opened and reported 30 pounds lighter. And early in the season, left tackle Marvel Smith lost strength in his left hand as a result of a swollen and pinched nerve in the back of his shoulder. Now there were rotations at both tackle spots that would eventually involve All-Pro left guard Alan Faneca. Reserve Todd Fordham was injured and then, after attempting all other possible solutions, OL coach Russ Grimm brought Mathias Nkwenti off the bench, and then he got hurt. Jeff Hartings moved to guard, Chukky Okobi moved into center, Keydrick Vincent played both guard spots and tackle. Against the Broncos, Grimm used 10 different line combinations as the running game sunk to record lows and Tommy Maddox got pummeled. The new and fancy Steelers passing game had become a mess, and most of it had to do with a nonexistent running game.

"I looked around the huddle," Hines Ward said, "and Mark Bruener's not in there, Jerome Bettis's not in there. You look around, and me and Faneca are the only guys who were here when we were pounding the ball."

The Steelers finished 6–10 and last in the NFL in rushing average with 3.3 yards per carry. They were 31st in overall rushing at 93 yards per game, their first time under 100 in the modern era.

The previous low rushing average was 102 per game in 1991, but that was corrected upon the arrival of Bill Cowher, and in 1992 the Steelers averaged 135 rushing yards per game. The only offensive line/backfield change that season was the addition of left guard Duval Love, but from '91 to '92 the Steelers jumped from 17th in rushing to fourth.

Cowher hoped to do the same with a healthier line, and mindset, in 2004.

13

BEN

IF **WE ARE** to believe local legend, the title of this chapter could've been "Shawn." Or, "Greatest Steelers Draft Mistake."

And that's the legend, that Steelers coach Bill Cowher fell in love with Arkansas offensive lineman Shawn Andrews and had to be talked out of drafting him with pick No. 11 in 2004 by team chairman Dan Rooney, who was still raw from watching Chuck Noll draft Gabe Rivera instead of Dan Marino 21 years earlier.

The legend jibes with the *Pittsburgh Tribune-Review*'s end-of-draft-week story that the Steelers were looking hard at drafting Andrews, who had visited the Steelers on April 11. He talked to the media about how his medication for sinus polyps had caused his weight to balloon to 400 pounds and that his condition caused him to stay up all night and prevented him from studying well enough to pass his six-credit course load.

Andrews's weight gain and academic issues had been red flags to draft analysts, but here was the 335-pound, two-time All-American explaining how his issues had been fixed and that he was ready to road-grade his way through the NFL.

It made sense to a coach who adored physicality in his offensive football and who no doubt dreaded the prospect of waiting a year, maybe two, for a young quarterback to develop.

And, hey, the Steelers had made so many moves in the off-season that waiting two years wasn't in the plan. In the couple of months leading up to the 2004 draft, the Steelers had hired Dick LeBeau to coordinate their defense; promoted Ken Whisenhunt—a Joe Gibbs and Dan Henning disciple of pounding the rock—to offensive coordinator; hired assistants Bruce Arians, Mark Whipple, James Daniel, and Ray Horton; and promoted offensive-line coach Russ Grimm to assistant head coach. And Grimm just loved powerful road-graders who claimed to be in the best shape of their lives at 335 pounds.

Drafting Andrews made sense to a team that had brought Jerome Bettis back at a reduced salary, added 29-year-old RB Duce Staley in free agency, received word that LT Marvel Smith was fully healthy, and swallowed hard before cutting beloved veterans Mark Bruener, Amos Zereoue, Brent Alexander, Dewayne Washington, and Jason Gildon. Cowher wasn't messing around off an awful 6–10 season. He wanted to win now.

"I have a hard time when you say, 'Blow it all up,'" Cowher said when asked if he would follow the Ravens' blueprint. "I still look at Baltimore, and there are a lot of good football players who were on that Super Bowl a few years ago. So did they really blow it all up?"

No, Cowher wasn't going to blow it all up, so why would he waste the 11th pick of the draft on a developmental quarterback when he could plug Andrews into the lineup and help his running game? With that in mind, here's how the off-season's first mock draft from *SteelCityInsider* appeared in February 2004:

1. San Diego—Ben Roethlisberger
2. Oakland—Eli Manning
3. Arizona—Larry Fitzgerald
4. New England (trade with Giants)—Kellen Winslow
5. Washington—Tommie Harris
6. Detroit—Sean Taylor
7. Cleveland—Robert Gallery
8. Atlanta—Roy Williams
9. Jacksonville—Reggie Williams
10. Houston—Keneche Udezi
11. Pittsburgh—Steven Jackson

The choice of Jackson was made before the Steelers bolstered their backfield with Bettis and Staley and before Philip Rivers—proudly acclaimed by fellow alumnus Cowher a month later at the North Carolina State pro day—made a dramatic move up media boards in spite of his three-quarter sling.

Once Rivers became acknowledged as a legitimate top 10 prospect, it dawned on Kevin Colbert that Roethlisberger could fall from his perch atop draft boards and into the Steelers' laps. Colbert was incredulous and said so to those close to him.

But what about Cowher? What about Grimm? What about that withering run game? Did Tommy Maddox have anything left? And would an improved running game help him? These questions were a concern to Rooney, who was remembered—during Phil Kreidler's reread of Roethlisberger's scouting report—for standing in the back of the war room flicking his wrist near his ear, clearly saying, "Take the quarterback!"

Here's what Rooney wrote in his 2007 autobiography:

> Manning and Rivers both were picked before our turn, and so our people seemed to have focused on Shawn Andrews, a big offensive tackle from Arkansas as our likely No. 1 pick. But when our turn came, I couldn't bear the thought of passing on another great quarterback prospect the way we had passed on Dan Marino in 1983, so I steered the conversation around to Roethlisberger. After some more talk, we came to a consensus and picked Roethlisberger.

And that's what they did. Roethlisberger had been sitting impatiently in the waiting room at the NFL Draft. But he wore a black suit with a gold tie and looked as if he was fully prepared to be picked 11th.

No one knew at the time just how prepared he was.

✦ ✦ ✦

Ben Roethlisberger spent the early days of his childhood near Lima, Ohio, in a village called Elida. His father, Ken, was the star player in town who went on to become a quarterback at Georgia Tech.

Ben was busy playing soccer instead of football at the time, but that changed when his dad moved the family 35 miles north to Findlay and Ben, a fifth-grader, dropped soccer and fell in love with basketball. He also began playing baseball and football, and was a running back on his first youth football team. Then Ben took a pitchout with instructions to throw it back to the quarterback deep. Ben hit him in stride for a touchdown and it was his last play at running back. The coach moved him to quarterback and moved his son to receiver for the remainder of the season.

Another father-son relationship worked against Ben when he got to Findlay High School. The Findlay coach first left Ben on the J-V team his entire sophomore season. As a junior, he moved Ben up to play wide receiver. The coach's son played quarterback, and the coach later admitted to a local paper that, yes, he was the "nationally known knucklehead" who played his son at quarterback instead of Ben Roethlisberger.

Ben moved to quarterback his senior year and set state records by passing for 4,041 yards and 54 touchdowns in 12 games in 1999. He completed 66.2 percent of his passes, ran for seven touchdowns and threw only eight interceptions. He led Findlay to a 10–2 record and the Division I state playoffs for only the second time in school history. Findlay also won its first state playoff game but was eliminated in the second round, even though Ben threw six touchdown passes.

Roethlisberger's greatest single prep moment occurred against Napoleon, which led Findlay by four with 24 seconds left and Findlay at its own 33. Roethlisberger completed a 50-yard pass and then, with time for only one more play, had his receivers switch sides of the formation as he walked out of the huddle and scanned the defense. He knew the soft spot and hit his favored receiver for the win as time expired. It wasn't merely a revelation of athletic ability as much as it reflected Ben's natural ability to read a defense and think on his feet.

A tall and instinctive point guard as well, Roethlisberger left Findlay as the leading basketball scorer in school history with 1,095 points. He averaged 26.5 points per game as a senior. He also was a .300 hitter as the shortstop on the baseball team. Oh, and his junior football stats: 57 receptions, 757 yards, seven TDs.

Ben was voted Ohio's 1999 Division I Offensive Player of the Year, but finished second to Bam Childress—who later caught five passes in two seasons with the New England Patriots—for the state's Mr. Football award. The winner went off to Ohio State while the runner-up thought long and hard about playing his first love, basketball, before settling on Miami (Ohio) to play football.

Not to dismiss Ohio State's recruiting attempts of Roethlisberger. Then coach John Cooper did pursue him, but seemingly only after chasing other recruits. That's what the nightly 10:00 o'clock calls told Ben's father. "I'm thinking they have other phone calls they want to make first," Ken Roethlisberger told the *Toledo Blade*.

Miami coach Terry Hoeppner was the first to offer Ben a scholarship. He only needed to see the 6'5", 185-pounder play one game before showing up at the Roethlisberger home with the promise of making Ben one of the all-time MAC greats. At the time, Chad Pennington was a Heisman finalist, so Hoeppner used Pennington as the bait. Ben took an immediate liking to Hoeppner and eventually chose Miami over Ohio State and Duke. Of course, Ben knew he would have a more difficult time playing basketball at the bigger schools. That was his one hope about going to Miami. Hoeppner dashed that hope with logic.

"Do you think that's really the smart thing to do?" he asked Roethlisberger. "Look at the opportunity you have with football."

Roethlisberger redshirted in 2000 and on September 1, 2001, made his collegiate debut at No. 12 Michigan. He completed 18 of 35 passes for 193 yards with two touchdowns and three interceptions in a 31–13 loss.

Miami lost the following week to Iowa before embarking on a seven-game win streak. Josh Cribbs, James Harrison, and Kent State ended Miami's season at 7–5, but Roethlisberger was named MAC Freshman of the Year after completing 63 percent of his passes for 3,105 yards and 25 touchdowns.

Miami finished 7–5 in Roethlisberger's redshirt sophomore season but went 13–1 in his final season to finish as the Associated Press' 10th-ranked team. Miami had lost to Iowa in the opener before winning its final 13 games, including wins over Bowling Green in the MAC Championship Game and Louisville in the GMAC Bowl in Mobile, Alabama.

Roethlisberger was a three-time MVP at Miami and in his final season was named MAC MVP and third-team All-America. He was a semifinalist for the Davey O'Brien Award in 2003 after completing 69.1 percent of his passes for 4,486 yards and 37 touchdowns—all single-season school records. He ended his Miami career with 84 touchdown passes, 34 interceptions, and 10,829 yards.

Ben was asked by several local reporters whether he regretted not attending a bigger school, but Roethlisberger repeatedly answered that he loved his time at Miami. Besides, had he gone to Ohio State he might've been drafted by the Browns, who instead traded up one spot to draft Kellen Winslow Jr. with the sixth pick in 2004.

"Exactly," said Pittsburgh-born Findlay mayor Toni Iriti. "He'd have never played for the Steelers, so it all worked out."

✦ ✦ ✦

The night before the GMAC Bowl, Ben Roethlisberger told his Miami teammates this would be his last college game, and the inspired Redhawks scored touchdowns on their first five possessions against Louisville. Roethlisberger shook off defenders in his inimitable style to complete 16 of 20 passes for 291 yards and four touchdowns in the first half for a 35–7 lead. Miami went on to a 49–28 win as one official told Miami coach Terry Hoeppner there should be a re-vote for the Heisman, that Roethlisberger was the best college player he had seen that season. "How can he keep escaping like that and hitting guys in the hands with balls?" the official asked Hoeppner.

In his final five games, Roethlisberger threw 19 touchdown passes and only one interception. He headed out into the brave new world by overhauling his diet, hiring a speed and strength coach, and working out in California with Warren Moon as his quarterback coach. Roethlisberger went to the Senior Bowl, but as a junior didn't practice, only met with teams.

Philip Rivers played for Marty Schottenheimer and his staff in Mobile, and that's when Rivers got the idea that the Chargers, picking first, were enamored with him. "If not San Diego, then Pittsburgh," Rivers said. "I have a lot of respect for Coach Cowher, for what he's done in Pittsburgh. Coming from the same school, we feel like we have a tie there."

Roethlisberger and agent Leigh Steinberg went to the Super Bowl the following week for media interviews, and then it was on to the NFL Combine, where Roethlisberger threw (Rivers and Eli Manning did not), and threw poorly. He showed arm strength but not much accuracy and perhaps fell behind Rivers into third place in the draft's QB pecking order.

Roethlisberger bounced back at his March 25 pro day at Miami. He ran his 40s in the 4.76–4.81 range, and his time in the three-cone drill, used to gauge agility, was a sensational 6.81. He threw 80 passes "with very good accuracy," said legendary personnel man Gil Brandt, who added that Roethlisberger was throwing "flat-footed to receivers 60 yards away." Of course, Roethlisberger is on tape having thrown a pass 70 yards in the air for a successful Hail Mary to beat Akron in 2001.

While Packers coach Mike Sherman and Giants coach Tom Coughlin attended Ben's pro day, only one team, the

Steelers, had Roethlisberger in for a pre-draft visit. He showed up April 13 with fellow-MAC standout Jason Babin, a defensive end. The pair arrived two days after Shawn Andrews had visited. Roethlisberger talked to Pittsburgh reporters at the end of his visit and said his favorite team and player growing up were the 49ers and Joe Montana and that the only negative he had heard was that he played in the MAC.

"My response is Byron Leftwich, Chad Pennington, Randy Moss," Roethlisberger said. "I think my mobility is definitely a strength nobody knows about. I ran a good 40 at my pro day and on the field I can move even better. I think I can throw well on the run. It's something teams will have to account for and take into consideration."

He wasn't lying. As for his draft outlook, 16 anonymous scouts responded to a *Milwaukee Journal Sentinel* poll asking them to grade the quarterbacks on a scale from 1 to 4 (with 4 being the best). Manning had 60 points, followed by Roethlisberger with 47, Rivers with 31, J.P. Losman with 19, and Matt Schaub with 1.

"We kind of felt that Eli was that top guy, just because he had done some really good things at Ole Miss," Kevin Colbert said in 2022. "Philip Rivers, when he went to the Senior Bowl that year, he played for Coach Schottenheimer's staff, and you could see coming out of there that they might have a preference for him because they spent that week with him. We had all scouted Ben during the year. Phil [Kreidler] and I went to the MAC Championship, and he played great in horrible snow/rain-type conditions, and then myself, Ron Hughes, and Dan Rooney Jr. went to the bowl game in Mobile, and Ben was playing like Ben. We all said to each other, 'This guy will never make it to us.' We left with that feeling. Honestly, I couldn't tell you at that point that there were three Hall of Famers, but we knew there were three special players going to be available, and if one made it we'd be lucky to get him."

Roethlisberger wore his black-and-gold suit to the draft in New York but said later that wearing Steelers colors was merely a coincidence. "Maybe the Lord was telling me something," he said. He explained that he had other options, but ironically a family friend from Cleveland steered him to the black-and-gold attire.

Roethlisberger expected to be picked by the Giants with the fourth pick. The Giants had him rated second to Manning, who had let the Chargers know during draft week that he didn't want to play in San Diego. The Chargers were drafting first and the Giants called to express interest in a trade but nothing came of it. So under the threat of Manning not playing, the Chargers took him anyway. Manning expressed his disappointment in an ESPN interview immediately after the pick.

The Giants, meanwhile, began talking to the Browns about trading down to pick seven, where they expected to draft Roethlisberger. But the Giants learned that the Browns intended to use the fourth pick to trade up with the Chargers for Manning. This didn't sit well with the Giants so they stopped negotiating with the Browns. The Giants figured they could talk again to the Chargers about a trade, or simply take Roethlisberger fourth.

Steinberg explained the scenario to Roethlisberger, and the pair expected Ben to be picked by the Giants, who were playing a waiting game with the Chargers. The Giants finally got their call from the Chargers, who asked first about young pass-rusher Osi Umenyiora. The Giants said no—as the Falcons had in 1970 when the Steelers mentioned Claude Humphrey as a starting point for the Terry Bradshaw pick—and continued to wait.

Finally, with a few seconds remaining on the clock, the Giants gambled and selected the guy they knew the Chargers wanted, Rivers. That sparked the Chargers into making a deal that would net them three additional draft picks in the swap of quarterbacks.

When the pick of Rivers was announced, Roethlisberger forced a smile for the TV camera while Steinberg, seated next to him, appeared ill. When the Browns traded up a spot to draft tight end Kellen Winslow Jr. sixth, Steinberg shook his head in further disgust. He knew the Browns were the only team from slots 6–10 that didn't have a young, highly drafted quarterback on its roster. And the Lions (Joey Harrington), Falcons (Michael Vick), Jaguars (Byron Leftwich), and Texans (David Carr) all passed on Roethlisberger. But while the Steelers needed a young quarterback, there was also the report that the Steelers coveted Shawn Andrews.

"I guess because Mr. Rooney mentioned that in his book," Colbert explained in 2022. "Honestly, what happens once we get through all of the draft meetings, there's always myself, and it was Coach Cowher, Mr. Rooney, and Art [Rooney II]. And we sit down and go through, 'Hey, okay, this is what we're planning.' And all along Mr. Rooney would always talk about the importance of a quarterback; something we all believed but he would reinforce that. He never said, 'Well, you have to take this guy.' But he would always remind us

Ben Roethlisberger, the Steelers' first-round pick in the 2004 NFL Draft, gets introduced by Dan Rooney at a post-draft press conference on April 26, 2004. "Big Ben" would start his rookie season and for the next 17 years at QB.

that the quarterback is a very important position, and I think that's what he referenced in his book. I shouldn't say because I never read it, but specifically it wasn't a time when we sat there in that room and he said, 'Take this guy. Don't even think about the other guy.' It was nothing like that. Coming out of that meeting—and this is a few days before the draft—Coach Cowher specifically said, 'For the good of the organization, if a quarterback is available'—and we had the three, obviously—he said, 'we have to take him.' That was an unselfish move on Bill's part, because if you remember Tommy [Maddox] had done some really good things for us and he was coming off of that neck injury. We didn't know how he'd be coming back in, but we weren't desperate for a guy. Everyone talks about Shawn Andrews, and we could've used a right tackle, and that was a discussion, but it was clear coming out of there that if a quarterback was available, we were going to take him."

And they did. The Steelers selected the guy already in black and gold. Roethlisberger took the call from Bill Cowher and a wave of relief washed over his face.

"We're very, very excited about this," Kevin Colbert said in the media room that day. "We're excited about the opportunity to get a young quarterback. We said in the pre-draft stuff that we thought this was a realistic possibility. The more research that we did, the truer it became. It just came to us, and it was great. We're excited. We think this kid's potential is unlimited. I don't even think he's scratched the surface yet."

In Ben Roethlisberger, the Steelers had their guy, and they would have him for the next 18 years. They also drafted their right tackle that day, someone even bigger than Shawn Andrews. "You need a cab to get around this guy," offensive-line coach Russ Grimm said of third-rounder Max Starks, who measured 6'7", 350 pounds at the Combine.

Starks wouldn't start that season, but he became the only other starter drafted that weekend. The Steelers did sign a starter after the draft, a guy their scout, Dan Rooney Jr., had watched in a North Carolina high school game.

"After the draft, you start to call these free agents," said running backs coach Dick Hoak. "They give you a list of people to call, and this guy wasn't even on the list. You work with one of the scouts, and I worked with Dan Rooney Jr. So I came out of the draft meeting, and after about 10 minutes he comes down the hall and said, 'Hey, I got your two backs. We don't have to sign anybody else.' One was Willie Parker, and one was a fullback from Syracuse who didn't make it. I said, 'Who's Willie Parker?' And he said, 'This is a kid I watched in high school and [who] went to North Carolina and never played, but I think he should've gotten a chance.' We had just gotten Willie to fill in at training camp. Now he's a starter, and he's an excellent player and he's going to get better." Starks actually made one of the key blocks to spring Parker on his record 75-yard touchdown run in Super Bowl XL.

Roethlisberger, of course, played in that game. He broke into the Steelers starting lineup in Week 3 of his rookie season and became an instant legend. His first start was in the remnants of Hurricane Jeanne in Miami, and the Steelers won that game and their next 12 with him as their QB that season. He then quarterbacked the Steelers to a playoff win over the Jets before the Patriots stopped the unprecedented streak in the AFC Championship Game at Heinz Field.

There was disappointment that Bill Cowher had lost his third consecutive home AFC title game and fourth of his five overall, but Roethlisberger provided hope for 2005. While injuries dogged the Steelers that season, Cowher revived them at 7–5 when he cleaned the slate—aka the white board in front of his meeting room—of all past statistics, and the Steelers won their final four regular-season games to make the playoffs as a wild-card. They then won four games on the road for the Lombardi Trophy.

Roethlisberger is remembered for his abysmal passer rating of 22.6 in the 21–10 win over Seattle in Super Bowl XL, but he should also be remembered for his exquisite playoff run, particularly the AFC Championship Game in Denver when he opened with his trademark pump fake and threw a touchdown pass to a wide-open Cedrick Wilson.

It was a different Roethlisberger in the 2005 playoffs. As a rookie, he said his brain was "fried," but not this time. "I'm not as tired," he said after the Broncos win. "I saw some guys interviewing Heath [Miller], and he looked like he was ready to fall asleep. That's how I was last year. This year, I feel a lot more comfortable, a lot better. I think my play has reflected that."

Roethlisberger posted a 124.8 passer rating against the Nos. 1, 2, and 3 seeds in the AFC playoffs. In the seven games preceding the Super Bowl, Roethlisberger had a passer rating of 107.6. The term at the time to describe how Roethlisberger played in the Super Bowl was "game manager." But in getting the Steelers to Detroit, Roethlisberger truly was a gunslinger.

14

BLOODLINES & BEYOND

THE DAY AFTER the Steelers lost Super Bowl XLV to the Packers in February 2011, Kevin Colbert returned to his office on the South Side of Pittsburgh and watched the tape. His first-round draft pick the previous year, Maurkice Pouncey, surely would've handled the backup nose tackle who made the play of the game. The hit on Ben Roethlisberger caused an interception return for a touchdown and a 14–0 Packers lead. The Packers won 31–25.

Had Pouncey played, perhaps Colbert would've won his third ring; perhaps Pouncey would've won one.

The great center, drafted in the first round in 2010, was injured in his first AFC Championship Game and couldn't play in the Super Bowl. He thought he would play in another but he never did. Pouncey retired in 2021 after being named to nine Pro Bowls. It was yet another Hall of Fame–level career by a Steelers center, and Pouncey no doubt heard the echoes of a stadium chanting his name as he lay on the Heinz Field grass, injured as a rookie.

Such thoughts were flowing through Colbert's mind as he watched the next morning. But he had an important draft coming up, and it was time to put the 2010 season behind him.

Would he also be putting a dynasty behind him?

The Steelers of the aughts enjoyed a 13–3 record in 2001 that ended in the AFC Championship Game; a 15–1 season in 2004 that ended in a controversial AFC Championship Game loss to the cheating Patriots; Super Bowl wins following the 2005 and 2008 seasons; and then the previous day's Super Bowl loss in Dallas to the Packers. Colbert made his notes, checked his aging roster, and met with the media at the 2011 NFL Combine with the best of that draft's offerings: "Offensive line, particularly tackle; wide receiver; and defensive back, particularly corner, are deeper than most," he said. But what did his team need? "Take out the obvious position of quarterback," he said. "Any position is open to our potential drafting. I mean that sincerely."

Roethlisberger would quarterback the team for 11 more years, but a rebuilding process was underway. The defensive line in particular needed an upgrade. Aaron Smith was 35 and coming off his second consecutive injury-ravaged season; Brett Keisel was a Pro Bowler but about to turn 33; and Casey Hampton, coming off what position coach John Mitchell called "one of the best games Casey's played in a long, long time" against All-Pro Nick Mangold in the AFC Championship Game, was about to turn 34.

Mike Tomlin had been hired to replace Bill Cowher in 2007 and was a believer in "pedigree" in football players. So as he looked over the defensive-line prospects, how could they not study the Son of Ironhead, Cameron Heyward?

Craig "Ironhead" Heyward was a Pittsburgh legend. Owner of perhaps the greatest nickname in the town's sporting history, the elder Heyward was the town's "Bus" before Jerome Bettis even knew his favorite sport wasn't bowling.

Ironhead rushed for 1,791 yards at Pitt in 1987 and finished fifth in the voting for the Heisman Trophy. He was drafted in the first round, 24th overall, by the Saints in 1988. He played tailback at Pitt, and in the NFL he's the last fullback to have rushed for 1,000 yards. He made the Pro Bowl after that season, 1995, with Atlanta, where his son Cameron would play high school ball.

Ironhead developed bone cancer in his skull and died at the age of 39 in 2006, when Cameron had just turned 17. The young Heyward went to Ohio State to play defensive end, and the intrigued Pittsburgh media descended upon him at the 2011 NFL Combine.

He was 6'5", 288 pounds, and played defensive end and tackle for the Buckeyes. That formula meant he was a classic Steelers 3-4 end, so it all made sense for not only the Colbert-Tomlin team to take a look, but reporters, too.

"I just grew into that," Heyward said of the goatee that made him look like his late father. "I was 15 so I said, 'Why not use it?'"

Did he have anything else in common with dad?

"Using my head," he said with a smile. "I need to stop."

How would he have tackled his father?

"I would take him on full-head, and he would, too. He'd lower his head—and I'd take him down."

When Heyward made his second reference to *The* Ohio State, he was asked why he hadn't attended *The* Pitt.

"Because they're not known as *The* Pitt," he growled.

Of course, Heyward had idolized his father, and Tomlin no doubt liked the bloodlines. His first draft pick with the Steelers, Lawrence Timmons, was the son of a former Duquesne University basketball player, and many of Tomlin's ensuing pick-ups were the sons, brothers, and, in the case of latter-day linebacker Robert Spillane, grandsons of former athletic greats. So it was no surprise when the Steelers drafted Cameron Heyward with the 31st pick of the 2011 draft. The son of Ironhead was coming home.

Born in the Pittsburgh suburb of Monroeville, Heyward was hailed by Colbert as "one of those special players...not only from a football standpoint, but this kid has impeccable character, work habits, toughness, you name it. It's hard to find a hole with this guy. He is a special player. He is a special person."

"It looks like the stars aligned for us today," said Tomlin. "We feel real fortunate. I hope and I'm real positive that Cameron feels the same."

He did. Even though his father had played for five NFL teams that did not wear black and gold, and even though Cameron played prep ball in Georgia and college ball in Ohio, his favorite team was the one in his hometown.

"I have always worked hard to be a first-rounder and to be picked by the Pittsburgh Steelers," Heyward said. "It is an unbelievable opportunity, and I am really going to cherish it and I am going to work hard to show people that I deserve that spot.... To be somewhere you want to be is an unbeliev-able feeling."

As of 2022, Heyward, at 33, was still going strong. He had been named to the All-Pro team in four of his five most recent seasons, and off the field he's been that "special per-son" Colbert described on draft day. Heyward, in an organiza-tion that cherishes character, was named Pittsburgh's Walter Payton Man of the Year four times for his volunteer work in the community. In 2021, he was voted by teammates the defensive captain for a seventh consecutive season. And he's always been playful.

"He's a goofball in the locker room," said reserve Joe Long.

"Cam's like a large toddler," said Keisel. "He's like a child, an enormous child. But it's fun. That little kid that's inside of him, who he keeps hold of and still runs around with, I enjoy it as an older guy because his youthful exuberance rubs off on us."

✦ ✦ ✦

Cameron Heyward learned the Steelers Way from Aaron Smith, who learned it from Greg Lloyd, who learned it from Donnie Shell, who learned it from Joe Greene, who learned it as a teen by scaring an entire team into running out the back of its bus!

Heyward passed it along to many, including T.J. Watt, who had learned everything else from his dad and brothers while growing up in the Milwaukee suburb of Pewaukee, Wisconsin.

Steelers rookie defensive end Cameron Heyward sacks Rams quarterback
Kellen Clemens during a game on December 24, 2011, at Heinz Field.
Heyward, son of the late Craig "Ironhead" Heyward, was the 31st overall pick
of the 2011 draft and has become a perennial All-Pro.

John Watt, the first of four state shot-put champions in the home, was a firefighter in Pewaukee, and the best thing he ever taught Trent Jordan was that he had to learn to "flip the switch" on the football field. T.J. was a quarterback at the time, but he flipped the switch on the Pewaukee High field, and, through his NFL Defensive Player of the Year season of 2021, he has yet to turn it off.

Dad wasn't the only mentor for young T.J., of course. His brother J.J. was five years older and brother Derek was two years older, and they roughed it up in the backyard, especially in the annual Turkey Bowl.

T.J. never played in pads against J.J., who was off at Central Michigan and then Wisconsin playing college ball, while T.J. and Derek played together at Pewaukee High. And T.J. thought Derek was the greatest high schooler who ever played. A tailback, linebacker, kicker, punter, and return specialist, Derek rushed for 265 yards in a playoff loss, his final prep game, to finish with 1,501 rushing yards and win the AP State Player of the Year.

T.J. grew into the QB position at Pewaukee and as a senior threw for 527 yards, rushed for 554 and had five sacks to make the all-conference team and earn a scholarship to Wisconsin as a tight end, just like J.J.. And, just like J.J., T.J. eventually converted to defensive end.

That was after T.J. had surgery on both knees for a patella subluxation and missed two seasons. Upon his return, his coach, Paul Chryst, who had spent the previous three seasons as the Steelers' next-door neighbor while coaching the University of Pittsburgh, asked T.J. if he would consider switching to outside linebacker in the Badgers' 3-4 alignment. T.J. went back to his room, talked it over with his brother/roommate Derek, came back the next day, and said yes. T.J. voraciously watched YouTube clips of pass-rushers Von Miller, Lawrence Taylor, and his brother J.J., who was coming off the second of what would become three NFL Defensive Player of the Year awards.

T.J. was just a part-time player at the time, as two seniors held down the Wisconsin outside spots. J.J. did return to his old school and ran T.J. through a pass-rushing workout one time, but for the most part he wanted T.J. to find his own way at the position, which he eventually did. T.J. improved each week and by the fourth game he was put on the third-down sub-package unit as a pass-rusher—over the nose. He felt out of place but didn't back down, and eventually looked back at it as a valuable learning experience for playing the run against NFL tackles.

When an injury forced the coaches to move Jack Cichy inside late in the season, T.J. moved into the starting lineup at outside linebacker and, by the finale against Minnesota, was virtually unblockable off the edge.

T.J. wasn't just a sponge on the field. Off the field he was developing habits that continue to serve him in the NFL. T.J. monitored his sleep in order to get nine hours per night. He also became keenly aware of his caloric intake of clean foods, and in meetings became a voracious note-taker. He didn't go out on weekends. For fun, he sat in his apartment and watched football and imagined his opponent that week to be out drinking beer. T.J.'s goal every day—as taught to him by J.J.—was to improve by 1 percent.

In 2016, those 1 percents added up to NFL Draft prospect, as the Wisconsin coaching staff moved incumbent Vince

Biegel from boundary to field linebacker and more coverage, which allowed T.J. to focus on his primary asset of rushing the passer.

In the 2016 opener against LSU at Lambeau Field, T.J. showed off his old nose-tackle skills by stuffing 240-pound running back Leonard Fournette on fourth-and-1. He knew Fournette was getting the ball because Fournette, while in the huddle, kept a fixed gaze on Watt. T.J. took out the tight end, and then the pulling guard, before tripping Fournette by the ankle for the stuff.

Wisconsin went on to upset No. 5 LSU 16–14. It was a game to which Steelers coach Mike Tomlin would refer after drafting Watt almost eight months later. The game also caused general manager Kevin Colbert to send two scouts to Wisconsin for a closer look at the redshirt junior.

The Steelers got the heads-up on the underclassman from their old neighbor, Chryst. After Watt made 63 tackles (15.5 for loss) and 11.5 sacks, along with an interception return for a touchdown, Chryst texted Colbert and asked whether he should advise T.J. to come out for the NFL Draft. Colbert said yes, that Watt was a first-rounder.

But barely.

Watt was considered a second-rounder by media analysts, who knew he had tremendous bloodlines, but there were concerns about T.J.'s knees and his inexperience on defense. At the NFL Combine, T.J. impressed the medicos with his health, the coaches with his intelligence and intensity, and everyone else with numbers that were every bit as good, if not better, than his eldest brother's:

T.J. Watt—6'4", 252 pounds, 4.69-second 40, 37"
vertical jump, 10'8" broad jump, 6.79-second three-
cone, 4.13-second short-shuttle, 21 bench reps

J.J. Watt—6'5", 290, 4.91-second 40, 37" vertical
jump, 10' broad jump, 6.88-second three-cone,
4.21-second short-shuttle, 34 bench reps

T.J. wasn't as thick or as strong as J.J., but he was faster
and quicker. His agility times were, in fact, remarkable. T.J.'s
three-cone time was the best at his position at the Combine,
and his short-shuttle time was better than that of the top three
cornerbacks with the Steelers. And T.J.'s arms were over 33
inches long. Add in the potential of his frame to add weight,
his family genes, on-field enthusiasm, and Hall of Fame habits, and it was little wonder the media experts now expected
T.J. to be drafted by the two teams who not only needed
edge-rushers but were picking ahead of the Steelers. And one
of those teams, the Green Bay Packers, had to know a little
something about the Watt brothers.

The Steelers stayed the course and met with T.J. at the
Combine and again before his pro day. Tomlin, Colbert, and
OLBs coach Joey Porter dined with T.J., Biegel, and Chryst
in Madison the night before the Wisconsin pro day. Tomlin
usually finds it easy to get draft prospects to open up, but that
wasn't the case with T.J., who maintained a masculine frame
and kept his mouth shut.

"There was just a feeling that you had," said Colbert, "that
if you didn't know who his family was, if you didn't know

Steelers outside linebacker T.J. Watt, younger brother of J.J. Watt, was taken with the 30th overall pick in the 2017 draft. Seen here sacking Bengals QB Joe Burrow on November 15, 2020, Watt is a three-time All-Pro in just five seasons, and in 2021 was named Defensive Player of the Year.

who his brothers were, he certainly wasn't going to tell you. And I just think that was good for him."

"We sat down and interviewed his brother in Madison, Wisconsin, some five or so years ago, and it wasn't much difference in the personalities then," said Tomlin.

"It takes me a while to warm up to people a lot of times," said Watt in 2022. "I'm not a guy to really go out of my way to introduce myself. It's something that I want to get better at, but I like to assess the situation, kind of feel the situation out. I'm kind of doing the same thing myself, so I'm not going out there to be outlandish and be somebody I'm not. It takes me a while to warm up. In those situations, I don't want to say the wrong thing, and I know my intentions, so I don't want to open my mouth and say something I don't mean. I'd rather just stay reserved.

"But I did eat my fair share of food that night. That probably helped show that I was trying to bulk up a little bit. We had a fun time. I remember that dinner very vividly."

The next day at the workout, T.J.'s actions did his talking. He showed a workout polish beyond his years, and the Steelers figured it had to do with his older brothers. The Steelers were also impressed with T.J.'s competitiveness as a tight end when he volunteered to help the other outside linebacker, Biegel, drop in coverage. After one impressive catch, Watt winked at Chryst as if to say, "I could've done that for you, too."

The Packers were certainly impressed—with Biegel, whom they drafted in the fourth round.

Six weeks later, in a first round loaded with edge-rushers, the Browns drafted Myles Garrett first; the Eagles drafted Derek Barnett 14th; the Dolphins drafted Charles Harris 22nd; the Falcons drafted Takkarist McKinley 26th; and the Cowboys drafted Taco Charlton 28th. The Packers, up next and in need of a pass-rusher, traded down four spots with the Browns, who drafted tight end David Njoku, leaving the Steelers to draft Watt.

The Steelers finally had their roster replacement for departed 2013 first-rounder Jarvis Jones and 39-year-old James Harrison to play opposite their other young pass-rusher, Bud Dupree.

Five years, 294 tackles, 77 regular-season games, 72 sacks, 32 passes defended, 22 forced fumbles, seven fumble recoveries, four interceptions, four Pro Bowls, three first-team All-Pro selections and one Defensive Player of the Year award later, the Steelers were proved right.

✦ ✦ ✦

Kevin Colbert announced his retirement effective after the 2022 draft, and before leaving, he sat down to help with this book and answered a few questions about the latter-year Steelers drafts.

Here's the interview, minus the answers used in previous pages:

KEVIN COLBERT Q&A

Q: *Were you worried about the Packers drafting T.J. Watt?*

KC: Honestly, we never worry about what someone else might do. We just kind of let it play out, and he was someone that was hopefully going to be in the mix at some point. If we're really anxious about a player, we'll try to trade up like we did for Troy [Polamalu] and Devin [Bush]. We'll do that on occasion, but most of the time we just let it play out, and fortunately T.J. made it to us.

Q: *Mike Tomlin likes bloodlines so much. Was that part of T.J.'s grade?*

KC: I think yes, but it wasn't the reason we drafted T.J. T.J. was a very fundamentally, mechanically sound outside linebacker. Most of the time when we've had to take players for that position, they've had to learn how to play on their feet because most of them are college defensive ends. Well, T.J. wasn't. He had played that position in a 3-4 defense at Wisconsin. You could see him understanding how to play the schematic. It was very similar to ours. But his advanced use of his hands as a pass-rusher was something that stood out, and I'm sure he got a lot of that not only from the Wisconsin staff but from J.J. as well. So along those lines, he obviously benefitted from his brother's experience. But we didn't take him because his name was Watt.

Q: *The other Steelers personnel men liked to say that when your best player is your hardest worker, good things happen. You have that going forward with T.J., don't you?*

KC: Oh, yeah. It's hard to find fault with T.J. He's a great player who works extremely hard and is a team leader, albeit sometimes he'll yield to the veteran who's ahead of him. Obviously, he's been with Ben [Roethlisberger] and Cam [Heyward] his whole career. So he'll lead, but he'll do it out of respect and in a respectful way, knowing that those two were and are more experienced.

Q: *What about Cam Heyward coming out? It was close to the same spot in the first round as T.J. Did you just sit back and watch him fall?*

KC: Yeah. Cam was a very similar situation. When Cam played at Ohio State, they played a similar schematic; not quite as similar as Wisconsin's was to ours, but we envisioned Cam being able to play defensive end in our 3-4 because of his size and his abilities. He, again, was a technically sound player who played extremely hard. Obviously, his father didn't teach him defensive football techniques, but I'm sure he saw his dad play. I don't know how much he would've known or understood who his dad was, so bloodlines, yes, but again we didn't pick him because his name was Heyward, although it didn't hurt to know the bloodlines. Obviously, there's something in the genetic aspect of it. I don't know if we ever get that technical, and I don't think we ever could get that technical and truly understand it. But, coming from that background, I think it does play in their favor. They were picked because they were great players and worthy of that pick.

Q: *Let's go back to 2005. Did you determine you needed a tight end as one of the final pieces for a championship team?*

KC: Honestly, I don't think we've ever done that specifically. I say it all the time: we never use the word *need*. We understand certain positions that the guy can maybe help us more than another, and if the players are close, then we'll take that player. But we never go into it saying, 'We need this position,' and artificially enhance a player's evaluation. Heath was just a really good consistent football player.

Q: *You had no 40 time on him, right?*

KC: He was coming off a sports hernia. I always use Heath as an example. We never timed Heath Miller. He wasn't able to run a 40 because of the surgery, and we just had to trust our eyes. We just thought he was a really good player. He was. I actually attended his bowl game. His last game was against Pitt, and he had a great game right down in Charlotte. That kind of said he's the guy. We had scouted him throughout the year, but I remember that game because Dan [Colbert, Kevin's son] and I attended that.

Q: *Why did you move up for Santonio Holmes in 2006?*

KC: Going in, could we use another receiver? Might this guy make it? Those kinds of things. We were criticized because when we traded for Troy we gave up a three and a six, and when we traded up for Santonio we gave up a three and a four and moved up fewer spaces. When the criticism came, my response was that I'm kind of happy we did that because it worked. Any given season, to trade up, it varies from year to year. We all have those little charts and try to use those as guidance, but they're never a yes or no. If you want a guy, sometimes you have to do different things, and that year to trade up for Santonio we had to pay a higher price, and we did.

Q: *Was your intel that someone was going to take him?*

KC: Maybe. I can't remember who we jumped. We only went up about four spots. We just felt that to make sure because we really valued his ability as a receiver and a return guy.

Q: *Mike Tomlin came along in 2007. What was it like working with him?*

KC: It was different in that we were learning each other, much like I had to learn the Steeler Way and Coach Cowher. When Mike came in, I had to teach Mike the Steeler Way and learn about him. It was good because he brought a different perspective and we grew together along that regard, and I learned a lot in the ways he was going to approach the type of players he was looking for. Fortunately, he had stayed with the same schematics by keeping Coach [Dick] LeBeau and making B.A. [Bruce Arians] the coordinator. Mike stayed with in-house folks, so there wasn't a lot of drastic change and he was willing to learn the way we went about business, but he also gave us a lot of different ideas, too.

Q: *I realize you're very busy so I'm not going to take you through all the drafts, but does anything stand out about some of the other top picks you made in the past decade or so?*

KC: [Maurkice] Pouncey came off a great team. They had a great leader in Tim Tebow, but you could also tell Maurkice was that hub, just in his personality and then again the way the team was drawn to him throughout the pro day. It was just natural watching him in and among his teammates.

Q: *Kind of like watching him with his Steelers teammates?*

KC: Correct.

Q: *What about drafting Antonio Brown in the sixth round in 2010? Any interesting tales?*

KC: We had A.B. and Emmanuel [Sanders] rated almost equal, and we had taken Emmanuel over A.B. because Emmanuel was a senior. We had watched him in the East-West practices and game. We knew more about him. A.B. was that up-and-coming guy from the MAC who dominated. We had them rated equally, but when we took Emmanuel for those reasons I mentioned, it was like, 'Okay, we're good at receiver,' and we tried to take some other guys, and some of those guys kicked in for a little bit: Chris Scott, Crezdon [Butler], Sly [Stevenson], Jonathan Dwyer; they all played. But then when we got to that second pick in the sixth, we're like, 'Hey, this Antonio Brown's still available. We should probably take him.' He was too good to leave up there, even though we had taken a receiver.

Q: *So as you finish your career, what is the state of the team moving forward?*

KC: We never keep score. The only score we keep is what our record is. Last year we were a 9–7–1 team, so however the team comes together, that's how we judge. You know, 9–7–1 is not good enough. Anytime you don't win a Super Bowl, it's not good enough. Have we done some good things? Yeah. Two times out of the drafts we had, I can say we put together two

Super Bowl champions. Is that enough? No. It never will be. But that's the only way we measure our success. I guess we contributed. I'm proud of the fact there are six trophies, and we were able to help get two, but the organization will never rest for anything but a Super Bowl championship. If there's more down the road, great. It's a different era moving on from Ben. We've been blessed to have a Hall of Fame quarterback for 18 years. That's an unusual circumstance. The down year that we had [2003], there were three Hall of Famers available, and we were fortunate enough to get one of them. Obviously, he's been a huge part of that success.

Q: *He also hasn't allowed you to finish 4–12 like every other GM gets now and then.*

KC: Yeah, but you know what? That's okay. I think we've averaged picking around 22 or 23, and that's the challenge that you have. But some of the guys that we drafted in or after that range have turned out to be great players. Like Mike says, we never want to be in that position where we're picking at the top of the draft because it means it was a miserable season. I'll take that. I'll take the alternative all the time. Wherever you pick, you pick. Just make the most of it.

EPILOGUE:
I'M NUNN

KEVIN COLBERT *(Steelers general manager, 2000–2022)*: Bill Nunn taught us on a daily basis how to be a professional, first and foremost. I'm sure you ran across Bill in some form or fashion and you cherished every discussion with him because he could talk not only about football players, but he could talk about boxers, entertainers, baseball players, and tell you about how he rode Roberto Clemente to the airport after the 1960 World Series. He could tell you stories that were impactful life lessons.

MIKE TOMLIN *(Steelers coach, 2007–present)*: I often have good conversations with Art regarding [Nunn's] impact, particularly during that era of the '70s, but I just appreciated the mentorship that I got from him, the wisdom that I got from him, the time spent.

PHIL KREIDLER *(Steelers college scouting coordinator, 1991–present)*: He taught me virtually everything about my craft. I started in '91 as an intern, and Bill was semi-retired then, so he would come into the office almost every day. Back then there wasn't any Internet, and he had time to teach me everything he knew—and so, yeah, he taught all of our interns a whole lot over the years. We have [Doug] Whaley, Mike Butler, [Dave] Pettit, Brandon Hunt, Danny Colbert. We were all interns, and we're all Steelers scouts right now. Luke Palko, Tim Gribble, John Wojciechowski, Andy Weidl. He taught all those guys, and all those guys are still employed in the NFL. Matt Raich, Billy Davis, Lou Spanos. Nunn taught all those guys.

MARK GORSCAK (*Steelers college scout, 1995–present*): A lot of people have knowledge, but Nunn had knowledge and wisdom. I'm having a hard time giving you one specific example because it all blends in and blurs together. I know he taught me to be a good guest. He always told me to be a good guest for schools, and he's right, because you're a visitor. I bring two dozen donuts on every school visit I make. Even though now they've got so much food, a cafeteria, and they eat like kings, if you bring two dozen sliders into those schools, man, they think it's godsend.

DAN ROONEY JR. (*Steelers player personnel coordinator, 1995–present*): He was my boss when I was a young kid, as a ball boy. He would complain that I kept my room dirty and I was taking pop out of the refrigerator that I shouldn't have. I became sort of a gopher and would run and get the newspapers for him and the coaches. So I gradually worked my way up. He was always there as part of the jobs that I did. He was the camp manager. He let me sit in a few times when he would cut a player. Bill was so kind that by the time I left, I thought we were cutting a Pro Bowler. He just had a good way of dealing with people. It showed me how to treat people with respect.

BRANDON HUNT (*Steelers pro scouting coordinator, 2005–2006/2010–2021*): As part of my intern duties, I drove Mr. Nunn to training camp, and then during the season you would get to drive him home from work every day. It's an unwritten rule and everybody kind of fights over who gets to take Nunn back because A) you get the stories, and B) you get out of the office and do something different. Obviously, every time you go with Nunn, you never know what's coming out of it. It's a cool experience. So when I came back, I lived in Shady Side, and he was at his house on Center Avenue, so I drove by his house every day on the way to work. For the four years we were together, I picked him up from home every day and took him to work, and then we shared offices at work. We basically spent four years together.

ROONEY JR.: We were driving to Virginia, and I was smoking a cigar. Cellphones had just come out, and I was talking on the cell phone and basically driving with my knees. He yelled, "Pull over!" I pulled over, and he said, "As long as I'm in this car, you're not using that cellphone; you're not smoking the cigars." I said, "The only reason I'm smoking the cigars is because you keep smoking those damn cigarettes!" Moments like that were just a lot of fun.

KREIDLER: There's that book *Tuesdays with Morrie*. All the guys in town, we would all drive Nunn home because he didn't like driving at night when he got older. He would always pick different scouts to drive him home and he would always tell a great story between the South Side and his house, like a 10-minute drive. He'd talk about something during the day that reminded him of something. He loved telling stories.

BRUCE "CHILLY" MCNORTON (*Steelers college scout, 2000–present*): Brandon and all those guys, they got a chance to spend w-a-a-a-y more time with him than we did. Before we'd go on the road, we would get up here during camp and get a chance to see him and talk with him then, but those guys got a chance to be with him when he came in the office. I was able to ride with Calvin Fisher because he used to take him home sometimes, and Brandon would do that, too. We'd roll to the house, and he'd give us those stories, and, boy, he had that whiskey and he'd say, "Hey, come on in here and have a drink" (laughs).

GORSCAK: He got older and decided he wasn't going to drive, so we picked him up every day. It was started by Hunt. Hunt was a trooper. Brandon would pick him up and we would take him home. Well, once you get Nunn in the car, he was non-stop talk. He would tell you a scouting story or a life story and you would gain so much. Some you've heard many a time over about John Stallworth, taking the 16 millimeter film and all that stuff. He would tell you a story about someone famous that he met—Roberto Clemente, Muhammad Ali, jazz great George Benson—or he would tell you something about scouting, how to scout. But once you got to his house and you sat in front of his driveway, he didn't get out. He kept on a roll telling stories. So we started calling it "The Long Goodbye." I coined it, and we all said the same thing, "Man, this is a long goodbye." You sat in that driveway for probably five, 10, 15 minutes because he was on a roll telling you another story. And you couldn't stop him, because 1) they were interesting, and 2) you learned something. So we decided to make the intern pick him up and take him home because it was more beneficial for those young men to go in and learn life experiences that Nunn had, and the scouting stories, and the scouting knowledge, what you looked at.

HUNT: The things that I really appreciated most about him were the things that were non-football. Football is great, and I love it—the Steelers, right? We lived it. But I like the tales about Wendell Smith and Jackie Robinson and Clemente, that group hanging out at the Crawford Grill on the Hill District when they came to town. It was cool driving to work—we would drive through the Hill District and he would retell his stories as you drove in. He was visualizing those days all over again, and it kind of felt like a movie, where they set the stage in the chapters prior to the actual scene. As we were driving, he would be retelling stories, and you could see it come alive while we were driving through it. I was able to visualize exactly what he was saying. *Boom*, that corner. *Boom*, that corner. *Boom*, he would come here. I never took it for granted. Ever.

MCNORTON: He gave me an old history of different things, like Bethune-Cookman College. I grew up two blocks away from there, and he would talk about Jack "Cy" McClairen when he came up to play for the Steelers. He was the head football *and* head basketball coach at Bethune-Cookman. I played midget football all the way through high school with his son, Dwayne McClairen. But Cy McClairen was in Pittsburgh in the 1950s. He was a tight end out of Bethune-Cookman and made the Pro Bowl one year. He got hurt, and his career ended, but he told me he's always been dedicated to the Steelers. In fact, Coach McClairen passed away last year.

ROONEY JR.: I went to my very first pro day when I was living with my uncle down in Palm Beach, Florida. Bill was living down there for a couple of years. He lived there in the winter. We went to the University of Miami, and Cortez Kennedy was coming out. He was the big player at Miami at that point. It was really exciting to be in that aspect of it.

MCNORTON: He had all of that knowledge and he knew how to talk to people. He knew how to get people to open up. He knew how to get *players* to open up. I know the stories he told about Joe Gilliam. He went over to Joe Gilliam's house, and he's sitting in his front room waiting on him, drinking his liquor and smoking his cigarettes. Those are only the things Coach Nunn could pull off.

GORSCAK: I went to Tennessee State, and there were these old-timers out there in folding lounge chairs. I walked by, and one said, "Pittsburgh Steelers, huh? Is Nunn still alive?" I said, "Yeah." He said, "You're kidding me." They were the track coaches at Tennessee State. All of those historical Black athletes, they were in multiple sports at those schools. They all ran track, and Nunn would go see the track coaches and ask about them and get times and any type of verification of how fast they were. That's how smart Nunn was. He didn't just ask football coaches. He asked the track coaches, and those old dudes, man, at Jackson State, Tennessee State, they would all ask about Nunn, if he was alive. I thought that was really cool because he didn't just use football coaches.

KREIDLER: My first story with Nunn was when he asked me where I was from. I said Cincinnati. He said, "Ezzard Charles." I told him my grandfather went to all his fights, and Nunn told me he became real close to [Charles]. He might've been the greatest boxer, pound-for-pound, of all-time. He was a light heavyweight who boxed the heavyweights because that's where the money was. He beat Joe Louis and was the only boxer to take Rocky Marciano the full 15 rounds. Nunn would talk about any sport. He was an expert on all sports. He was good friends with Jim Brown, Muhammad Ali, Jackie Robinson, Willie Mays, a lot of the great track athletes, Olympians. He really liked track and field, basketball. He was best friends with Chuck Cooper. He was the first Black player in the NBA, and he and Nunn were close buddies. When he said, "Look for athleticism," he's seen it in so many different sports. He's been around so many great ones, he probably could tell right away.

COLBERT: From a football standpoint, Bill would always remind you of, "Let's just talk about the athleticism of this player." It's up to the coaches to take that athleticism and make him into a pro because they all don't start out as Pro Bowlers and Hall of Famers. Donnie Shell is a classic example of Bill spying raw talent as a college linebacker at South Carolina

State and saying, "Hey, Coach, I think this guy can be this type of player," which, obviously going into the Hall of Fame, he turned into. So Bill reminded us daily of the basic athletic traits that Coach Noll was looking for back then.

TOMLIN: I loved how scientific he was in terms of the evaluation of talent or pedigree and the things that he focused on in terms of the evaluation of athletes. Many of the things that he taught me, I use to this day and probably will continue to use and share with others. He was a legendary talent evaluator. His enshrinement is well deserved.

ROONEY JR.: I said to him, "What's the most important thing about scouting?" And he said, "Their feet." I thought he meant like the size of their foot. I didn't quite get it. And he said, "No, their athletic ability!" He got a little short with me because I didn't understand his lingo. But he was big on athletic ability. That was his thing. He thought that his relationship with Coach Noll was basically founded on the fact that Coach Noll wanted athletes and that he could train them into football players. That's always one of the things I try to identify if I can. Does the guy play on balance? Does he have the athletic ability to change directions? Obviously speed and those kinds of things are part of it, but it was a huge impact on me to try to identify athletic ability. If you don't have that, he didn't think you could be a great player. He knew that not everyone was going to have the same athletic skill, but that was his big speech to me, how important that was.

MCNORTON: He actually did talk about a guy's shoe size. He thought that was very important. We did our meetings and he would ask, "Do you know what size his shoe is?" We said, "What?" He said, "A guy's shoe size is very important. If he's a lineman and has big feet, then he has a good, stable base." And then if he was a wide receiver or running back and he has big feet, he said they had a lot on the ground. Those guys, they picked their feet up.

TOMLIN: He didn't like tall offensive linemen because of bend, or potential lack thereof. He always looked at how guys had weight distributed on the bottoms of their shoes. He wanted guys to have the inside instep part of their shoe to be more worn than the other parts because that was a good power source for directional change and things of that nature. Just a bunch of unique little tidbits that I could go on forever, but just tools of the trade and really examples of his expertise in that area.

MCNORTON: He stressed to me that he liked to see guys live, especially skill-position players, because you want to see their reactions, how they handle their good plays, but more importantly how do they handle bad plays? How does a quarterback handle an interception on the sideline? Is his confidence still with him? Does he lack confidence? Is he moping? Does he know what it is and take an "I'm going to get it back!" attitude? Those things. When a DB gets beat for a touchdown, how does he react? Does he react like he'll come back and be okay? Does he seem a little timid now? Is he still thinking about that last play? Same thing with receivers and drops. How does he respond to a coach coming up to him to talk about it on the sideline? What's he doing on the sideline? That type of thing. You want to see how they handle the pressure and also you see leadership-type things. When a young guy fumbles the ball, is the leader over there ridiculing him? Or is he trying to bring him up? I have to play with this guy, and I'm going to need him. Things like that.

HUNT: He taught me about evaluating players and looking at athleticism and looking at size and speed and height and all those great things, but the main thing I learned from him is professionalism, as in how to carry yourself and how to be a man and how to be a father and how to be a husband and how to be an employee. He let me know that, "Every time you're on this walk, you represent the shield, you represent the logo. People are always going to look at you as a Pittsburgh Steeler." So you have to carry yourself that way.

MCNORTON: He had a knack for knowing that not only was a guy going to be a good player, but was he a Pittsburgh Steeler–type player? That was big for him. He had to be tough. Had to. And then he had to be athletic.

KREIDLER: Nunn always talked about how he scouted Franco and never really got credit. I know [Dick] Haley scouted him, so did Art [Rooney] Jr., but Nunn really liked Franco when he scouted him. Nunn always was super proud of that draft pick. It also says something about Nunn that he was the one who went down and signed Joe Greene when the Steelers took Joe. He had some great Joe Greene stories.

GORSCAK: The stories are boundless about Nunn bringing a box of cigars, a bottle of bourbon, bottle of vodka, bottle of scotch, whatever they were drinking, to the head coach of these historical Black schools so he could gain more access. At that time, it was 16-millimeter tape. Whoever got there first, man, watched the tape. They only had two copies. I guess that's why he took the John Stallworth tape. One copy was the team's tape; one was the exchange tape. He took the exchange tape.

KREIDLER: That story of how he scouted Stallworth has changed so many times throughout the years, but Nunn told me the whole story when I was an intern, back in 1991, 30 years ago. The interesting part of the story is that Nunn went out and was at the hotel where Alabama A&M was staying the night before the game. They always played Alabama State on Thanksgiving Day. I think they still do. But Nunn told me the coaches were raving about Stallworth, and Nunn was like, "All right, you're talking so much about him. You better throw him the ball tomorrow." And they did. He had an incredible game. Nunn was so excited—back then it was 16-millimeter—that he went to get the film developed and waited there until it was done. The season was over. There weren't any 1-AA playoffs back then. But Nunn said he waited in Alabama to get the film to bring it back to show Coach Noll. That's where the whole story began about the Steelers never sharing the film.

The legend became, "Nunn stole the film," and whatever, but the season was over and he gave it to Coach Noll. Whether it got back to Alabama A&M in time for the draft in January, I don't know, but the film was only not there for a month. It wasn't uncommon for scouts to bring back film and have Mac [video coordinator Bob McCartney] copy it, or to show it to the coaches, because it was 16 millimeters. It's not like today where you can watch it on your computer the second it's put into the system. That's why the guys would go to the schools and watch the film at the schools. Back then, there was only one copy of the game in an actual canister of film. But anyway, that's my favorite Nunn story, the Stallworth story, because it has that mystery and intrigue to it. Noll watched the film on Stallworth, and he wanted to take him in the first round, and they didn't take him until the fourth. Had they taken him in the first—who knows?—maybe they never would've gotten Swann and Webster and Lambert because every pick would've been different.

HUNT: He would tell us a story, and we would go to Google and type in a name, like, "Look, Nunn. *Boom*." And he would take the articles with him. He was like an archivist. He liked to get that stuff. He would ask, "Why don't you pull up…" and the next day we would have it printed out for him, and every day he left with a stack of articles. We would say, "Poor Miss Frances." Who knows how [his wife] put it all away, piles of files printed from our office? But obviously, the journalist side of him never left. He may have been the newspaper guy who became the football guy, but he was always a newspaper guy.

KREIDLER: Nunn was always mad that the Steelers traded Frank Lewis. Nunn loved Frank Lewis, and they drafted him and he was going to be a great player, and they traded him because they had Swann and Stallworth. Back then, teams really didn't play much with three receivers on the field, so there was just no need for Frank Lewis. But Nunn was like, "There's no reason to trade a great player unless you're getting someone great in return." And that didn't happen. He just said Frank Lewis was real quiet and Stallworth and Swann were outgoing and they became buddies with Bradshaw, and so Bradshaw had a little more confidence in them. Frank was shy, and back then it was a little different, and the quarterbacks would have their favorite receivers.

GORSCAK: Kevin did a scout's field trip in the summer; all the in-town scouts. Art [II] went with us. We went down to the Clemente Museum. Had a caretaker there, the photographer, and he has all that stuff. We were reading some of his letters, this and that. He came down and met all of us, was telling us Roberto stories, and he told the story about how Roberto, after the 1960 World Series, was so mad after not winning National League MVP that year. He finished eighth in the MVP race, and he was so mad about it. He said Roberto didn't take a shower and just went straight to the airport. And Nunn was with us and he said, "Yeah, that's just about right." The caretaker looked at Nunn, this elderly guy, and he said sarcastically, "Why? Were you there?" Nunn said, "Yeah! I took him to the airport. He couldn't drive. Roberto couldn't drive. I took him to the airport." Caretaker goes,

"Wait. Who are you?" Nunn being Nunn said, "I'm Nunn." "No, no. Who are you?" "I'm Nunn!" "No. Who are you?" "I'm Bill Nunn!" I thought that was cool. That guy was so sarcastic. He apologized and then asked him a million questions about Roberto. "What else you know?" Nunn transcended a lot of public figures, and in that time period he befriended Roberto because Roberto was kind of shunned because he was Black and he was Puerto Rican. He didn't have a place during that time period.

HUNT: He was fascinated by memorabilia. It stemmed from that trip to the Clemente Museum. He was able to fill in the gaps of the historical stories from the guy who was telling them, because he lived it. But also he was looking at how people were so amazed at all the artifacts there. He was like, "I lived this stuff. Never in my day-to-day did I ever think to ask for a bat or a glove or a football or a jersey. I was just living in the moment." Off of that, he told me, "You never know how long you're going to be in this thing, but take this advice from me and don't leave without taking something with you." So I took that idea, cool, and in that particular draft Joe Greene retired. I went and took a football and asked Joe to sign it. And I had never asked Joe for anything. I treated him like a colleague, a friend, and a mentor. That was the first thing I ever asked from him, and Joe signed my ball. From there, I asked all of the great players from that '70s era, who came to see Nunn, to sign it. They would come and sit at the roundtable in my office and have conversations with Nunn. Nunn and Franco Harris would talk about football and life, and I always thought people would love to be a fly on this wall. Then I thought, *Wait a minute, I have this football.* And Nunn sparked this, so I started getting these guys to sign this football. From that, I got everybody who came and talked to Nunn. It was like an entry fee. You can talk to Nunn while I listen, and then I get an autograph. I was respectful with it. It also gave me an opportunity to introduce myself, tell them who I was, what I was doing. They got to co-sign with Nunn, and they liked that.

KREIDLER: His last year on the road was the year [Mike] Vrabel came out. Nunn scouted Vrabel in a live game. After that, he didn't go out. He scouted, but it was almost all film work. Or he would go with the interns to watch West Virginia, Pitt, the close-by schools. Vrabel split a lot of time here with Carlos Emmons opposite [Jason] Gildon, and, no, Nunn didn't fuss about it. Vrabel's now a head coach in the league, and it's a cool tie back to Nunn. Vrabel was the last guy Bill really went to bat for. Once he started doing it on film, he let the younger guys make the calls because he didn't see many of the guys live. He was more just a cross-check scout after the Vrabel draft in 1997. He was certainly active, but it wasn't a full-time job after that.

HUNT: The Bill Nunn Draft Room is right next to my office. It's the actual draft room, or what you call the "war room." One of the cool things that Kev did—and Nunn freakin' hated it—but Kev got a picture of Nunn, got it framed, and got Nunn to sign it. It's now hanging on the wall. There's also a gold plaque outside of the draft room that identifies it as the Bill Nunn Draft Room. We also have a photo from their original draft room of Nunn, Art Jr., and Dick Haley. They had two tables from Three Rivers Stadium that we still use. When Kevin came, he got them refurbished, so it still has the original cigarette holes burned on it from the '70s drafts.

ROONEY JR.: Bill and I also had a lot of fights in the scouting office over players. I'd say they were good; he'd say they weren't. He did it just to piss me off. He would end up sometimes agreeing with me, but he knew he would get me, because he was the legend, and I wanted to prove myself.

MCNORTON: We'd be looking at film when all of a sudden Coach Nunn back there would say something like, "*Tsss*. That guy. He can't play." We'd be like, "Oh-kay," and then, "Coach Nunn, I'm trying to see what you're seeing here." And then most of the time, it's a guy who doesn't pan out. He just had that instinct. It was a natural thing for him.

ROONEY JR.: There were a couple offensive linemen that I liked, and he said to me, "That guy's not worth a crap." So we went back and forth, and he started laughing and said, "Yeah, I see it the same way. I was just seeing if you would stick with your conviction."

MCNORTON: He didn't like a guy once, so I figured I could stop looking at him. But he would encourage you, "No, no, you look at him. Look at him and see what you think. I ain't always right. I didn't pick them all." He accepted that part of it. But he was a natural. We definitely miss him.

HUNT: Before draft day, we have a team draft dinner, and
Mr. Art, Kevin, Coach T, and all of our scouts get together to
break bread over at Rico's in the North Hills. It's always the
night before the draft, after we do the mock draft. Nunn officially retired from his scouting position in 1987 but Mr. Dan
[Rooney] didn't let him go. He wanted him to stay in a consul-
tant-type role because of his knowledge and wisdom. But the
funny thing is, every single year, from 1987 until he passed, at
that pre-draft dinner, Nunn retired. Every year (laughs). Every
year. Toward the end of dinner, he would stand up and start to
give a speech. It got to the point where he would start to stand
up, we would get louder. "Oh, here he goes again!" He would
tap his glass and we all knew A) at this point, Mr. Dan wasn't
going to let him leave, B) none of us were going to let him
leave, and C) he didn't really want to leave. He loved football.
He loved being around us. He loved being around the guys.
He loved being around the game. But after dinner, he always
tried to retire, and we always said, "Hey, Nunn, before you
actually retire retire, if you ever get to leave, you should write
an autobiography or let someone write your story." And he
never did. He said he never wanted to tell some of the stories
he lived, that some stories aren't for everybody, that they're not
supposed to be told, that they're supposed to be lived through.
He never wanted to put it on paper, but all of the stories that he
left with us was his version of leaving his own book. He wanted
his book and his story to be told through all of us.

MCNORTON: He went through the early times, man. He
didn't have ropes, but he put stuff down because he needed

to see a player's footwork. He vertical-jumped guys in the gym by putting chalk on their fingers and have them jump up against a wall and touch it (laughs). The innovative ways they were doing things back then, and now, look at how they do it now.

KREIDLER: I really don't think there'll be another person who got to do as much in sports as Bill Nunn. I just don't think there'll ever be anyone like that again, who gets to meet and cover so many different sports and athletes.

HUNT: There's not a lot written about him. I mean there are articles. People appreciate him. The first book was *The Color of Sundays*, but we always told him to do an autobiography, that people need to know your story before you leave.

KREIDLER: He's probably the only guy who scouted 13 Hall of Famers. Until someone tops that, he's probably the greatest scout of all time.

HUNT: The best part about him is the way he did it, the way he went about his business, the way he lived his life humbly. It's almost majestic and mysterious...not mysterious, but kind of like a scout, right? We're in the background of everything. We're not on the forefront, but we're go-getters who get things done. That's exactly who and what he was. That's...exactly how he left it. Now he's on the mountaintop in heaven, and in the Hall, and we're all here to tell the story on his behalf.

ROONEY JR.: Really, if I were to say one thing that stood out to me, it was his relationship with Coach Noll and how he was able to jibe with Coach Noll because Coach was basically saying, "Look, I can train them to be football players, but I can't train them to be athletes. Find me the athletes." That was music to Nunn's ears.

KREIDLER: Nunn was a great athlete himself. He played on the West Virginia State team that won the Black College national championship. He was a great basketball player, and his dad played football at Westinghouse (High School).

HUNT: Like Gors was talking about, "The Long Goodbye." In this microwave age, in which we're always in hurry-up-and-wait mode and everyone's in such a hurry and everything's on demand and everything's right now and I gotta go, go, go, the one thing Nunn never changed was time. He was never in a hurry. He was never in a rush. Honestly, he never wanted to leave work. So when Gors talks about "The Long Goodbye," Nunn would tell a story, and it would almost end once you make that right up Bryn Mawr, and he would begin the next story as you pull onto his street. That's what Gors is talking about. You'd think it was time to go, only because we're wired wrong and we're always in a rush. But ask any of us now if we could go back again and have some long driveway waits, we would all wait in line to go wait in the driveway to get that next story. If we all could've just slowed down and appreciated even more of what we already appreciated, there was so much more that we had there. What was on the surface was like, dang, but it showed you what you really *didn't* know, how special this man really was in Steelers history, Pittsburgh history, African American history, period. This was one of those guys, and I'm so excited that the Hall of Fame got it right in honoring this man. As Big David Baker says, he will forever be enshrined in Canton. He'll live forever. My kids and the kids behind my kids will grow up learning about Mr. Nunn.

ACKNOWLEDGMENTS

MY GRATITUDE FIRST of all goes to Jon Kendle and Brian Campbell of the Pro Football Hall of Fame. Jon supervises the museum's Archives and Manuscript Collection, and Brian worked the front lines for Jon and helped me throughout with files of research on the enshrined Steelers. They both personified professionalism and understood exactly what a research nerd such as myself needed even before I did. Thank you both so much.

To that end I would like to thank the researchers, historians, and journalists who came before me. Your spirits guided me as angels and muses throughout.

That brings me to the other book that influenced this one. I mentioned Robert Green's *The Laws of Human Nature* in the Introduction, and the second book I read to parallel this work was *The War of Art* by Steven Pressfield. If you're a creative, this is a must-read. The first half of the book dealt with blocks and resistances, and when he moved into muses and angels in the second half, I realized I wasn't the only writer who talks to spirits.

On the earthly plane, I want to thank all of those who returned calls, in particular the busy men working on their crafts during draft season, Tom Donahoe and Kevin Colbert. Thank you both for interrupting your busy schedules to answer all of my questions. And also thanks to the Steelers and Burt Lauten for arranging time for Colbert.

There are also my great friends for their help with my questions via text. They know who they are. Thank you all so much. And thanks to those who cared about my progress. I wouldn't have written so much so quickly without you.

BIBLIOGRAPHY

Blount, Roy Jr. *About Three Bricks Shy...And the Load Filled Up.* New York: Ballantine Publishing, 1989.

Conn, Charles Paul. *No Easy Game.* New York: Berkley Publishing, 1973.

Conte, Andrew. *The Color of Sundays.* Indianapolis: Blue River Press, 2015.

Donahue, Ben. *The Life and Career of Jack Lambert.* ProFootballHistory.com.

Hayes, Reggie. "Tracing Woodson's Path to Greatness," *The News-Sentinel* (Fort Wayne), August 3, 2009.

Jackson, John. Interview with Greg Lloyd. Off.Line Podcast, 2020.

Jaworski, Ron. *The Games That Changed the Game.* New York: Random House, 2010.

Lippock, Ron. *Steelers Takeaways.* Indianapolis: Blue River Press, 2016.

MacCambridge, Michael. *America's Game.* New York: Random House, 2004.

MacCambridge, Michael. *Chuck Noll: His Life's Work.* Pittsburgh: University of Pittsburgh Press, 2016.

Matthews, Missi. Interview with Lynn Swann and John Stallworth. Pittsburgh Steelers YouTube channel, 2017.

Moushey, Bill. *Never Give Up.* Glenshaw, PA: Parmoush Publishing, 2009.

Players Only: Defensive Player of the Year. Pittsburgh Steelers YouTube channel, 2022.

Pomerantz, Gary. *Their Life's Work.* New York: Simon & Schuster, 2013.

Prato, Lou. "Franco's Battle," *Blue White Illustrated*, August 21, 2012.

Radakovich, Dan and Lou Prato. *Football Nomad.* Ann Arbor, MI: Nimble Books, 2012.

Rooney, Art Jr. *Ruanaidh.* Pittsburgh: Geyer Printing Co., 2008.

Rooney, Dan. *Dan Rooney.* Cambridge, MA: Da Capo Press, 2007.

Ruck, Rob. *Rooney.* Lincoln, NE: University of Nebraska Press, 2010.

Russell, Andy. *A Steeler Odyssey.* Champaign, IL: Sports Publishing, 1998.

Rutigliano, Sam. *Pressure.* Nashville: Oliver-Nelson Books, 1988.

Savran, Stan. Interview with Franco Harris. Pittsburgh Steelers YouTube channel, 2019.

Savran, Stan. Interview with John Stallworth. Pittsburgh Steelers YouTube channel, 2020.

Savran, Stan. *Time Machine: Greg Lloyd.* Steelers Nation Radio, 2022.

Starkey, Joe. "The Heroic Story of the Steelers' First Ever Draft Pick—William Shakespeare," *Pittsburgh Post-Gazette*, April 23, 2020.

Toperoff, Sam. *Lost Sundays*. New York: Random House, 1989.

Books by Jim Wexell:
Pittsburgh Steelers: Men of Steel. Champaign, IL: Sports Publishing LLC, 2006.
Polamalu. Pittsburgh Sports Publishing, 2020.
Steeler Nation: A Pittsburgh Team, an American Phenomenon. Pittsburgh Sports Publishing, 2008.
Tales from Behind the Steel Curtain. Champaign, IL: Sports Publishing LLC, 2004.